Social Histories of Disability and Deformity

Deformed and disabled bodies have been subject to a variety of responses throughout history: being seen as omens or prodigies; divine punishment for sin; freaks and curiosities; as inducing laughter, embarrassment or compassion; and as the subjects of disciplining initiatives, institutionalisation or medical and charitable care. Essays in this collection, written by an international set of contributors, provide a scholarly social history of disability: they explore changes in understandings of deformity and disability between the sixteenth and twentieth centuries, and reveal the ways in which different societies have conceptualised the normal and the pathological.

The book provides an important contribution to the emerging field of disability history. Through a variety of case studies including: early modern birth defects, homosexuality, smallpox scarring, vaccination, orthopaedics, deaf education, eugenics, mental deficiency, and the experiences of psychologically scarred military veterans, this book provides new perspectives on the history of physical, sensory and intellectual anomaly. Examining changes over five centuries, it charts how disability was delineated from other forms of deformity and disfigurement by a clearer medical perspective. Essays shed light on the experiences of oppressed minorities often hidden from mainstream history, but also demonstrate the importance of discourses of disability and deformity as key cultural signifiers which disclose broader systems of power and authority, citizenship and exclusion.

The diverse nature of the material in this book will make it relevant to scholars interested in cultural, literary, social and political, as well as medical, history.

David M. Turner is Senior Lecturer in History at Swansea University. His most recent book is *Fashioning Adultery: Gender, Sex and Civility in England 1660–1740* (2002). **Kevin Stagg** lectures in History at Cardiff University.

Routledge studies in the social history of medicine

Edited by Joseph Melling
University of Exeter
and
Anne Borsay
University of Wales, Swansea, UK

The Society for the Social History of Medicine was founded in 1969, and exists to promote research into all aspects of the field, without regard to limitations of either time or place. In addition to this book series, the Society also organises a regular programme of conferences, and publishes an internationally-recognised journal, Social History of Medicine. The Society offers a range of benefits, including reduced-price admission to conferences and discounts on SSHM books, to its members. Individuals wishing to learn more about the Society are invited to contact the series editors through the publisher.

The Society took the decision to launch 'Studies in the Social History of Medicine', in association with Routledge, in 1989, in order to provide an outlet for some of the latest research in the field. Since that time, the series has expanded significantly under a number of series editors, and now includes both edited collections and monographs. Individuals wishing to submit proposals are invited to contact the series editors in the first instance.

1 **Nutrition in Britain**
   Science, scientists and politics in the twentieth century
   Edited by David F Smith

2 **Migrants, Minorities and Health**
   Historical and contemporary studies
   Edited by Lara Marks and Michael Worboys

3 **From Idiocy to Mental Deficiency**
   Historical perspectives on people with learning disabilities
   Edited by David Wright and Anne Digby

4 **Midwives, Society and Childbirth**
   Debates and controversies in the modern period
   Edited by Hilary Marland and Anne Marie Rafferty

5 **Illness and Healing Alternatives in Western Europe**
   Edited by Marijke Gijswit-Hofstra, Hilary Maarland and Has de Waardt

Social Histories of Disability and Deformity

Edited by David M. Turner and
Kevin Stagg

Routledge
Taylor & Francis Group

LONDON AND NEW YORK

First published 2006
by Routledge
2 Park Square, Milton Park, Abingdon, Oxon OX14 4RN

Simultaneously published in the USA and Canada
by Routledge
711 Third Avenue, New York, NY 10017

Routledge is an imprint of the Taylor & Francis Group, an informa business

First issued in paperback 2012

© 2006 David M. Turner and Kevin Stagg for selection and editorial
matter; individual contributors, their contribution

Typeset in Times by Wearset Ltd, Boldon, Tyne and Wear

British Library Cataloguing in Publication Data
A catalogue record for this book is available from the British Library

Library of Congress Cataloging in Publication Data
A catalog record for this book has been requested

ISBN13: 978-0-415-51151-3 (pbk)
ISBN13: 978-0-415-36098-2 (hbk)
ISBN13: 978-0-203-00852-9 (ebk)

Contents

Figures

Notes on contributors

Ayça Alemdaroğlu is a Ph.D. student at the University of Cambridge. She is a graduate of the Middle East Technical University (1998) and the Bilkent University (1999). She has studied social and political theory and her current research is on youth, social change and conservatism.

Anne Borsay is Professor of Healthcare and Medical Humanities in the School of Health Science at Swansea University. Trained in the social sciences, she initially researched twentieth century health and social policies before developing interests in the development of hospital medicine and the social history of disability. Her most recent publications include *Medicine and Charity in Georgian Bath: A Social History of the General Hospital, c.1739–1830* (1999) and *Disability and Social Policy in Britain since 1750: A History of Exclusion* (2005). She has also edited *Medicine in Wales, c.1800–2005: Public Service or Private Commodity?* (2003), sits on the editorial boards of *Social History of Medicine, Disability and Society*, and *Medical Humanities*, and is responsible for collections of essays in the Routledge series, 'Studies in the Social History of Medicine'.

François Buton is a full-time Researcher in Political Science at the CNRS (National Centre for Scientific Research), and the assistant director of the CURAPP, a CNRS unit in Amiens (University of Picardie, France). He has mainly published on the 'socio-history' of the State in nineteenth century France, and is currently working on science and expertise in public health policies, and on sociological approaches of voting behaviour.

Hal Gladfelder is Lecturer in English at the University of Manchester and the author of *Criminality and Narrative in Eighteenth-Century England: Beyond the Law* (2001). His most recent book is a scholarly edition of John Cleland's *Memoirs of a Coxcomb*.

David Mitchell is a faculty member of the Disability Studies programme at the University of Illinois, Chicago. To date he has edited three books on disability culture and history including *The Body and Physical Difference* (1997). He has also written two books including *Narrative Prosthesis* (2000). Recently he completed work as senior editor on the five volume set *Ency-*

clopaedia of Disability (2006). David has served as president of the Society for Disability Studies and was a founding member of both the Committee on Disability and the Disability Studies Discussion Group for the Modern Languages Association. Currently he is serving as principal organiser of the Chicago Festival of Disability Arts and Culture.

Sharon Morris trained originally as a Registered Mental Nurse. She studied History at University of Wales, Bangor, gaining a First Class Honours degree, before being awarded an AHRB grant to write an M.Phil. on 'Acts of Idiocy: Perception, Need and Responses to the 1923 Mental Deficiency Act in Local Authorities in Wales 1881–1940', which she completed in 2003. She is currently researching a Ph.D. on public welfare and voluntary sector provision for people with disabilities since 1945 at the University of Wales, Bangor.

Kristy Muir is a Research Associate with the Social Policy Research Centre at the University of New South Wales, Australia. She has a BA (Hons) degree and a doctorate in History. Her Ph.D. thesis examined the psychological effects of mental illness on war veterans and their families. She was previously an Associate Research Fellow at the University of Wollongong and taught in the School of History and Politics.

Suzanne Nunn has recently completed a Ph.D. in Film and Visual Culture at the University of Exeter; producing a thesis entitled 'Lines of Engagement: Changing Representations of the Doctor through Middle-Class Appropriation of Graphic Satire 1800–1858'. She lectures on art and media at Cornwall College and is an affiliated researcher with the Centre for Medical History at the University of Exeter.

David E. Shuttleton is a lecturer in the Department of English Literature at the University of Wales, Aberystwyth with specialist research interests in the field of medicine and literature in the eighteenth century, currently including pathography, the Scottish medical school and 'prophylactic poetry'. He co-edited and contributed to *De-centring Sexualities: Politics and Representations Beyond the Metropolis* (Routledge, 2000) and *Women and Poetry, 1660–1750* (Palgrave, 2003). Essays have appeared in *The British Journal of Eighteenth Century Studies*, *Eighteenth-Century Life* and *Women's Writing* and he recently contributed to *The Arts of Seventeenth-Century Science: Representations of the Natural World in Seventeenth-Century Culture* edited by Claire Jowitt and Diane Watt (Ashgate, 2002), and *Imagining and Framing Disease in Cultural History* edited by G. S. Rousseau *et al.* (Palgrave, 2003). In 2005 he was awarded a Leverhulme Research Fellowship in his role as a contributing editor to the forthcoming *Cambridge Edition of the Works and Correspondence of Samuel Richardson*. A forthcoming monograph is entitled *Smallpox and the Literary Imagination, from the Restoration to Regency*.

Sharon Snyder is a faculty member of the Department of Disability and Human Development at the University of Illinois, Chicago. She is the author of two books including *Cultural Locations of Disability* (2005), and editor of three collections including *Eugenics in America* (2005) and *Disability Studies: Enabling the Humanities* (2003). Most recently, she served as senior editor and illustrations editor of the five volume set, *Encyclopaedia of Disability* (2006). As founder of the independent production company, Brace Yourselves Productions, Sharon is also an award-winning documentary filmmaker whose work includes, *Self-Preservation: The Art of Riva Lehrer* (2004), *Disability Takes on the Arts* (2005), *A World Without Bodies* (2002), and *Vital Signs: Crip Culture Talks Back* (1996). Currently, she is principle investigator on the creation of a museum exhibition about Chicago disability history for the National Vietnam Veterans Art Museum.

Kevin Stagg lectures in History at Cardiff University and recently contributed a chapter on the body for Garthine Walker (ed.), *Writing Early Modern History* (Hodder Arnold, 2005). His research interests range from the body and disability in history to early modern print culture, transport and trade.

David M. Turner is Senior Lecturer in History at Swansea University. He formerly taught at the University of Glamorgan where he was director of the 'Controlling Bodies: the Regulation of Conduct 1650–2000' project. He has published widely on the social and cultural history of early modern Britain, including the monograph *Fashioning Adultery: Gender, Sex and Civility in England 1660–1740* (Cambridge University Press, 2002). His current research focuses on the idea of the 'body beautiful' in the eighteenth century and connections between disability and criminality in the seventeenth and eighteenth centuries.

Preface

This book arose out of the conference *Controlling Bodies: the Regulation of Conduct 1650–2000* held 24–26 June 2002 at the University of Glamorgan. The aim of the conference was to draw together the most recent research concerning the history of bodily regulation. Over 50 delegates attended the conference and sessions covered included bodily functions, clothing and fashioning, death and survival, disability, discipline, disease, food, institutions, moral campaigns, nations and the body politic, nature, nudity and display, policing and crime, race, regulation, religion and ritual, sex and marriage, and work. Two of the sessions held form the basis for this work. The first explored the themes of deformity and disease, and its papers make up Part One with the main focus being on early modern issues. The second (in a panel sponsored by the Wellcome Trust) covered disability and focused on nineteenth and twentieth-century topics and its presentations form the basis of Part Two. The chair for the disability panel was David T. Mitchell, who later – with Sharon Snyder – presented a film: 'A World Without Bodies' on the Nazi eugenicist programme. After the conference ended a number of participants, including David and Sharon, and the conference organisers enjoyed an evening meal in Cardiff. It was from the passion for the importance of Disability Studies and the encouragement given to the editors by David and Sharon that the inspiration for this current volume arose. The work represents a distillation of the multifaceted and fruitful discussion and debate that characterised the conference and, as editors, we hope that it acts in some small way as a tribute to all the contributors. Thus we are delighted to acknowledge the support of the Wellcome Trust, the Royal Historical Society and the School of Humanities and Social Sciences at the University of Glamorgan for their sponsorship of the conference and particularly to offer thanks to all the participants for making the proceedings such a resounding success: Ayça Alemdaroğlu, Henrice Altink, Simone Ameskamp, Delila Amir, Menachim Amir, Gerhard Ammerer, Laura Stark-Arola, Rainer Baehre, Ruth Barcan, Jennie Batchelor, Lesley Biggs, Alistair Black, Anne Borsay, Rachel Bowen, François Buton, Claire Carlin, Jonathon Conlin, David Cox, Amanda Crocker, Tom Crook, Barbara Crowther, Alison Matthew David, Julie Elb, Stefanie Ernst, Caroline Getaz, Hal Gladfelder, Sharif Gemie, Raul Ernesto Gonzalez-Pinto, Nicole Greenspan, Fiona Hackney, Sharon Howard, Chris Hudson, Anne Huebel,

Alan Hunt, Cecily Jones, Rod Jones, Jaclyn LaPlaca, Daniel Lindmark, Jennifer Susan Marotta, Dominique Memmi, David Mitchell, Isabel Moreton, Goldie Morgentaler, Sharon Morris, Kristy Muir, Chris Norris, Suzanne Nunn, Sarah Oerton, Omi, Sara Pennell, Glynn Porritt, Fiona Reid, Rachel Rich, Michael Richards, Mair Rigby, Tracy R. Rone, Jonathan Seldin, Chris Shilling, David E. Shuttleton, Henk de Smaele, Clarissa Smith, Sharon Snyder, Lynn Sorge, Lisa Tallis, Garthine Walker, Alfred St. Weiß, Ian Wiblin, Gareth Williams, Neil Wynn. The input of Andy Croll in the early stages of the project was also appreciated.

In producing this book, we are grateful to the series editors Anne Borsay and Joseph Melling for their help and encouragement and to Terry Clague at Routledge for his patience and support. We would like to thank the Wellcome Library, London for providing the images used in Chapter 4, and in particular Clive Coward for his help locating them, and the History Department at the University of Wales, Swansea for financial help with the costs of reproducing them.

David M. Turner and Kevin Stagg

Introduction

Approaching anomalous bodies[1]

David M. Turner

Deformed, disabled or otherwise anomalous bodies have been subject to a variety of interpretations and responses throughout history: as omens or prodigies, visitations of sin, freaks and curiosities, as inducing mockery, embarrassment or compassion and as the subjects of disciplining, institutionalisation or charitable provision. How different societies have conceptualised the normal and the pathological, and how these ideas have been used to uphold systems of power and authority and stigmatise deviance, have become key concerns for social historians of medicine and practitioners of body history more generally. Building on Erving Goffman's classic study *Stigma* (1963) and Michel Foucault's histories of ever more pervasive regimes of surveillance and regulation, historians have begun to uncover the myriad ways in which corporeal signs have been called upon or invented as a tool of citizenship and exclusion or to express and give credibility to social, religious and ethnic differences.[2] Relations between sin and disfigurement or physical abnormality in the early modern period have been studied by historians of religion and morality, while a good deal of research has been undertaken into perceptions of 'monstrous' births.[3] Historians of the nineteenth and twentieth centuries have focussed their attention on the development of 'disability' as a function of modernity and outlined the processes by which disabled and mentally deficient persons were subjected to institutional care and control.[4] While such studies have tended to develop in isolation from each other, the emergence of a dynamic and politically aware 'new disability history' in recent years provides a means of drawing together these disparate strands, not just shedding light on the experiences of an oppressed minority, but also exploring disability as a 'fundamental element in cultural signification', revealing the complex relationship between the biological and the social worlds.[5]

The chapters in *Social Histories of Disability and Deformity* position themselves at the centre of these historiographical developments. Through a variety of case studies, including early modern birth abnormalities, smallpox scarring, physical aberrations associated with homosexuality, orthopaedics, education of the deaf, eugenics and the experiences of psychologically damaged military veterans, this volume provides a synthesis of different approaches to the body, explores patterns of continuity and change and sets out an agenda for future research in this vibrant area of scholarship. It explores the changing ways in which exceptional bodies have been perceived from the early modern to the modern period and how cultural representations and social policies have responded to and incorporated these perceptions. Taking as their premise the notion that the relationship between the 'normal' and the 'deviant' is historically variable, the contributors consider the uses of aberrance, anomaly and disfigurement as a means of articulating broader social, political and cultural values and highlight the role of medicine in providing scientific 'legitimacy' for cultural definitions of normality, superiority and competence. In doing so, they interrogate a wide variety of source materials including medical treatises and textbooks, hospital and institutional records, popular pamphlets, novels, eulogising verses, graphic satire and political propaganda.

As Catherine J. Kudlick has argued, the questions raised by the historical study of physical stigma or disability belong not just to medical history but to humanistic scholarship as a whole, asking what it means to be human, how we can respond ethically to difference and how different societies have given value to human life.[6] Yet despite the exciting potential of this area of research, it raises a series of conceptual and methodological problems. How is disability to be defined? What is the relationship between disability, deformity and defect? How do we conceptualise change over time and how do social, cultural and medical discourses of the body relate to the lived experience of 'deformed' or 'disabled' people? The remainder of this introductory chapter highlights some of these problems and draws attention to areas of controversy in order to contextualise the chapters that follow.

At the outset it is important to address problems of definition. The relationship between deformity and disability is complex and subject to change over time. In modern usage there are no clear-cut distinctions between the two categories, although they carry different connotations.[7] Deformity is understood in aesthetic terms as the opposite of beauty, or more generally as a deviation from normal appearance. It may be accidental, man-made or occur naturally through congenital aberration.[8] While the stigma of deformity derives from the appearance of bodies, modern definitions of disability focus more on the functions of bodies and their relationship to their social and physical environment. As Steven D. Edwards has noted, disability is both a relational concept and a value-laden concept, implying a failure to match the competence and capabilities of bodies deemed 'normal'.[9] Definitions of disability, and the political issue of *whose* definitions of disability a society accepts, have been central issues in the Disability Rights movement. Such issues have a bearing not just on the academic study of disability, but on practical entitlement to state benefits, medical care and supportive technological assistance.[10] For our purposes, how a society defines disability and whom it identifies as deformed or disabled may reveal much about that society's attitudes and values concerning the body, what stigmatises it, and what it considers 'normal' in physical appearance and competence.[11] Scholars in the academic discipline of Disability Studies, established in the 1980s to give a voice to the experiences of disabled people and examine the roots of their disenfranchisement with a view to asserting their rights as citizens, have presented a critique of medicalised definitions of disability that focus on impairment and its effects on performance on the basis that they tend to personalise the 'problem' of disability and present it as a handicap that the individual needs to overcome.[12] The development of a 'social model' of disability sought to explore disability as the product of social and material forces, with an emphasis on exposing the ways that social and spatial factors serve to disable impaired individuals.[13] The social model has in turn been criticised for ignoring the differences that various disabled people face due to race, gender and other social and cultural variables and for its insistence that for inclusion in the disabled peoples' movement people must identify themselves positively as being 'disabled'.[14] An approach is required which simultaneously appreciates that disability is shaped by 'people's particular social and cultural identities and their positions', while recognising that social and medical discourses, institutional practices and spatial environments also act to shape bodies and experiences.[15]

With the development of Disability Studies, the range of bodies that may be considered 'disabled' has widened. While the concept of disability has frequently been applied to physical impairments historically associated with the 'crippled', in recent years the boundaries have widened to include sensory impairments of blindness and deafness, mental deficiency, long term psychiatric impediments and impairments associated with old age.[16] At the same time, the linguistic forms that have labelled individuals as 'handicapped', 'afflicted', 'deformed' or 'disabled' have begun to attract attention with a view to understanding their historical contingency. A 'new disability history' is taking shape which 'recognises the corporeal dimension of human experience and its consequences for daily functioning, while striving to understand the contingencies that shape, reflect, express and result from that dimension'.[17] The scholarly endeavour of revealing the centrality of disability to human experience depends on defining it broadly, in a way that encompasses functional or sensory impairment and aberrant physical appearance. The editors of a recent collection of studies of the cultural representation of disabilities argued that scholars of disability needed to attend to 'physical, sensory and mental impairments, illnesses, congenital and acquired differences thought of as disfigurements and deformities, psychological disabilities; stamina limitations, developmental differences and visible anomalies such as birth marks, scarring and the marks of ageing'. In this way, disability 'names the naturally occurring or acquired bodily variations that accrue as we move through history and across cultures'.[18]

Although this broad definition is to be welcomed, it is important to recognise that 'disability' incorporates a vast array of experiences that resist straightforward categorisation. Facial scarring, for example, may be a disability of appearance only, causing no physical difficulty but may yet have socially disabling consequences.[19] In the same way that the 'history of *the* body' has been criticised for its tendency to totalise human experience, the notion of a monolithic 'history of disability' is problematic. Disability history is comprised of a multitude of overlapping and divergent histories of physical, intellectual, psychological and sensory impairments.[20] Indeed, categorising certain impairments as 'disabilities' may itself reflect able-ist assumptions rather than the identity of those thus categorised, as the efforts of some in the Deaf movement to have 'the Deaf' defined as a linguistic community rather than a disabled minority testify.[21] What connects these disparate histories and experiences is a shared element of stigma and separation from what dominant cultural and medical discourses define as 'natural' or 'normal', leading to devaluation and socially imposed restriction.[22] Goffman's notion of stigma as a bodily or intellectual marker that serves to devalue or disqualify an individual from full social acceptance has been influential in social and cultural studies of disability. However, Goffman's theories are open to criticism for failing to explain why some attributes typecast a person and others do not.[23] By exploring the stigmatisation of different physical, intellectual and psychological impairments in their historical context, the chapters in this volume set out to provide a more complex understanding of processes of devaluation associated with human anomaly in past societies.

Between the sixteenth and the twentieth centuries, the period covered by this book, understandings of disability in Britain, America and parts of continental Europe underwent significant change. Although the details of this historical transition await fuller study, a trajectory of development is becoming apparent. In the early modern period the concept of disability was subsumed under other categories, notably deformity and monstrosity. However, it is important to note that 'monstrosity' and 'disability' were not equivalent in early modern writing. While 'monstrosity' provided a means of categorising congenital birth defects deemed to be caused variously by 'excess' or 'lack' of the 'seed' thought to be ejaculated by men and women during conception, corruption of 'seed' by sex during menstruation, or imprinted by the mother's imagination or cravings during pregnancy, not all irregular births were to be explained in this way. Sixteenth-century writers followed the Aristotelian concept that nature aimed at exact reproduction, therefore cripples or dwarfs who might resemble their parents were explicable through the principle of heredity.[24] 'Monsters' and other anomalous bodies were significant social metaphors, providing a means not just for conceptualising certain characteristics that would now be termed disability, but provided a critique of politics, religion and morals.[25] Links between sin and physical aberration were writ large in the writings of religious moralists. The condition of the mind is 'discerned in the state and behaviour of the body', observed the English puritan Thomas Tuke in 1616, while Theophilus Dorrington remarked that if one were to study the physiognomies of 'infamous sinners', and 'compar'd the Lines of their Faces with those in their consciences, we should find in them an equal Deformity'.[26] As Kevin Stagg demonstrates in his chapter in this volume, the primary concern of pamphlets detailing monstrous births was not with the embodied reality of the severely disabled children described, but with the social, religious, political or moral messages that might be drawn from such births. Monster broadsides and pamphlets, he argues, often 'reduced the body itself to a bare description, a canvas to inscribe significance'.

While the causes of monstrosity were subject to scientific and medical enquiry and explanation during this period, the notion that the corporeal and the moral mutually reinforced each other was a mainstay of early modern culture.

The term 'deformity' was used by early-modern writers to denote both ugliness and physical conditions that might cause functional impairment such as 'crooked legs, or stump feet'.[27] Types of deformity listed as qualifications for membership of the *Spectator*'s fictitious 'ugly club' in 1711 included 'a visible Quaerity' of aspect or 'peculiar cast of countenance', 'gibbosity' or 'obliquity' of figure.[28] Concepts of 'deformity' were variable and were influenced by taste, class and gender.[29] When the eighteenth-century French surgeon Nicolas Andry provided a compendium of 'deformities of children' in his classic *Orthopaedia* (translated into English in 1743), his list of bodily abnormalities included characteristics as diverse as club feet, spinal curvature, pock-marked skin, red hair, slouching posture, effeminate voices in men and deep booming voices in women. His understanding of deformity was moulded by the tastes of his genteel audience, remarking on roughness of hands that 'one is not surprised to see Labourers have such Hands, nay, in them it is no Deformity; but it is a considerable one in Persons of a superiour Rank'.[30] The stigmatisation of deformity also carried a strong racial dimension. Noting that in Guinea 'girls who would appear handsome use a great many methods to make their Lips thick', Andry remarked that in polite European society 'Thick Lips in Men are disagreeable, but in Women they are one of the greatest Deformities'.[31] While Andry has been hailed as the originator of the term 'orthopaedics' to describe a branch of surgery dedicated to the correction of physical disabilities, his wide-ranging list of 'deformities' deemed in need of repair highlights the contested and variable nature of what might be considered 'deformed' or disabling in the past.

In the early modern period, deformity carried moral stigma and could also be a source of laughter and contempt. As the crook-backed eighteenth-century English Member of Parliament William Hay noted from experience, 'Men naturally despise what appears less beautiful or useful: and their Pride is gratified, when they see such foils to their own Persons'.[32] The grotesque body proved a durable means of criticising power and authority in eighteenth-century graphic satire.[33] However, the relationship between the defects of the body and the disposition of the mind was increasingly subject to debate. While the relationship between sin and bodily marking was slow to disappear, writers began to highlight the virtues of deformity. In 1694 the popular English conduct book *The Ladies Dictionary* advised its readers that the deformed 'as well as the most Beautiful and well Proportioned, are Pictures of God's own making' albeit 'set in a plainer Frame, not so gilded and Embellished'.[34] Andry remarked that the mind often compensated for deformities of the body as, for example, 'they who are hump-backed have for the most part a great deal of wit'.[35] In England, building on the distinctions being used by providers of poor relief between the 'infirm' and 'impotent' disabled poor worthy of assistance and those 'sturdy beggars' who feigned disability out of fecklessness, enlightened writers contrasted those whose deformities were 'natural' or caused by heroic endeavour on the battlefield with 'those that deform themselves by their Irregular courses of Living'.[36] Stoically bearing the affliction of deformity was cast as a means of reaching the higher beauty of fortitude and virtue.

Between the eighteenth and the twentieth centuries, it is argued, new understandings of the body emerged whereby disability was delineated from other forms of deformity or disfigurement by a clearer medical perspective, one augmented by state concern over the health of national populations. This signified a shift from ad hoc public responses to disability to institutional regimes of training, monitoring and relocation and even (in relation to parts of continental Europe) elimination. Several related factors, representing different historiographical approaches to disability, have been proposed as causes for this transition: industrialisation and the intensification of ideas of economic rationalism associated with capitalism; the development of notions of 'normality' and 'abnormality'; and increasing medical surveillance of 'deviant' bodies. Materialist histories of disability, indebted to Marxist theories of historical development, highlight industrialisation and new modes of production as crucial factors in shifting understandings of impairment. Key to these accounts is a transition, coinciding with the shift from feudal to capitalist economies, from inclusion of disabled people within the social fabric to exclusion from the mode of production.[37] Materialist historians have argued that disabled people were included in an undifferentiated mass of the poor or relatively un-problematically integrated into a predominantly agrarian economy. The advent of industrial capitalism, in contrast, was geared to able-bodied norms which increasingly excluded the impaired from the mode of production.[38] By this token, 'disability' emerges as the product of a capitalist work ethic in the modern era where individuals were judged primarily by their economic usefulness.

Materialist histories of disability, while usefully highlighting the role of socioeconomic factors in the delineation of bodily difference, have been criticised for exaggerating the impact of industrialisation and for ignoring cultural factors. The work ethic characteristic of industrial capitalism was a feature of pre-industrial societies such as Tudor and Stuart Britain, while the dominance of factory production was not apparent until the late nineteenth century.[39] Moreover, as many materialist historians themselves recognise, the 'integration' of disabled people into the economies of medieval and early modern Europe could be accompanied by negative social stereotyping of bodily or intellectual difference.[40] Nevertheless, the intensification of economic rationality – already a feature of some early modern societies – during the nineteenth and twentieth centuries seems to have combined with other developments to change perceptions of disability. Cultural historians have drawn attention to the development of discourses of 'normality' during the nineteenth century which served to create the 'problem' of the disabled person. While the distinction between the 'natural' and the 'monstrous' was a significant way of constructing social reality in the early modern period, by the late nineteenth century, the concept of the 'natural' was becoming displaced or subsumed by the concept of normality. Lennard Davis has shown that the term 'normal' was not current in the English language before the 1840s.[41] The concept of the 'normal' shared with the earlier concept of the 'natural' the goal of establishing the universal good and right and establishing social hierarchies of inclusion and exclusion. However, the idea of the 'normal' established in the mid-nineteenth century had at its core the notion of progress. Secular, empirical and dynamic, the concept of 'normality' took as its premise the idea that one could discern in human behaviour the direction of human evolution and as such normality was implicitly defined as that which advanced progress.[42] Other shifts in terminology similarly emphasised disability as something that stood in the way to progress and economic success. Douglas C. Baynton, for example, has highlighted changes in the language used to describe deafness in nineteenth-century America from an 'affliction' that came from God and was a burden to be borne, to a 'handicap' that acted as an impediment to worldly success and as such was something that needed to be overcome.[43]

These ideas became associated in the late nineteenth and early twentieth centuries with nationalist movements and modern eugenics. Eugenics, the science of improving the human race, encompassed notions of social progress, national development and economic efficiency. Grouping together all allegedly 'undesirable' human traits that threatened the degeneration of populations, eugenicists tended to speak about criminals, the poor and people with disabilities in the same breath.[44] Eugenics influenced a number of initiatives that fundamentally changed the lives of disabled people. In its most extreme form, associated with the Nazi regime in Germany, it was used to justify the forced sterilisation or extermination of people with physical and mental impairments.[45] However, the influence of eugenics may also be seen in a variety of contexts, from the movement in parts of Europe and the United States during the later nineteenth century to 'normalise' deaf children by teaching them to communicate orally rather than by sign language, in the segregation of the mentally deficient in asylums or 'colonies' or through the development of social orthopaedics that disciplined disabled children to turn them into economically useful people – developments traced by François Buton, Sharon Morris and Anne Borsay in this volume. While there was some recognition that impairment was partially caused by environmental factors, these policies enshrined the central organising principle of the 'medical model' of disability in which social progress was believed to reside in the individual.[46]

Changes in the perception of disability were also influenced by charitable and philanthropic initiative, development of the educative and care professions, and increasing medical surveillance. The nineteenth century witnessed a raft of philanthropic initiatives aimed at providing institutional care for the disabled based on an appreciation of their separate needs. Whereas previous, somewhat ad hoc care policies, such as the old Poor Laws in England and Wales, had tried to provide for the disabled in the community, more widespread institutional care, although proceeding from 'kindness', resulted in a distancing of the crippled, the deaf and the mentally deficient from the rest of society, in the process re-inscribing the distance between 'normal' and 'abnormal' bodies.[47] The 'medicalisation' of physical impairment intensified in the aftermath of the First World War in England with increasing use of corrective surgery to remedy defects.[48] The increasing involvement of the medical professions in the discussion of physical and mental abnormalities resulted in what David Armstrong has described as 'surveillance medicine', which found its fullest expression in the development of preventative health care in which individuals were advised on patterns of behaviour most likely to improve wellbeing, placing the responsibility for illness and impairment in individuals while simultaneously bolstering the authority of the medical professions in the assessment of 'needs'.[49] Increasingly, disabled persons found themselves subject to the surveillance and disciplining gaze of professionals in education and the medical and care sciences. While the institutionalisation of disability has receded in Britain and North America in recent times, the medical and care professions still exercise considerable control over the bodies of the impaired. As Sharon Snyder and David Mitchell observe in their Afterword to this volume, disabled people still find themselves forced to obtain medical evidence of their 'condition' for access to state benefits, and consumer services such as special equipment or airline travel.

This change in perceptions of human anomaly has been described variously in terms of a shift from inclusion to exclusion, from portent to pathology, from wonder to error, from the marvellous to the deviant and from moral to medical perspectives.[50] The transition is reflective of broader developments that have been the subject of investigation since the emergence of body history in the 1970s. Theorists such as Norbert Elias, Mikhail Bakhtin and Michel Foucault have established a historical model of two bodies.[51] Although different terms have been used, Elias, Bakhtin and Foucault all describe an older bodily matrix (uncivilised, grotesque, sovereign), characterised by turbulent passions and disruptive instincts. This unruly body was viewed as extending beyond the physical form to correspond with the natural order. Thus in the early modern period, the body did not simply constitute the individual self, but was a site for cosmic intervention and divine retribution. The older body was viewed as flowing (comprised of humours and elements), disorganised and expressive. Yet over the course of the seventeenth, eighteenth and nineteenth centuries, scientific discovery, the growing professionalisation of medical practice, the development of concepts of manners and civility and a growing divide between popular and elite culture all contributed to the emergence of a new bodily paradigm, one that was reformed and subject to secular and rational control. Essentially a more 'private' body, its behaviour was increasingly restrained and conflicts internalised.[52]

The chapters in this book assist in addressing how such a shift in understandings of deformity and disability occurred, how a new medical language and practice took shape in relation to bodily difference and the institutional forms it embraced. Yet they are also united by their insistence on the contestation of meanings of deformity and disability. Mindful of recent criticisms that the theoretical paradigms upon which body history is built simply reiterate unquestioningly modernisation theories, this book shows that the interchange between different models remained highly significant.[53] While medical perspectives on disability and human anomaly became culturally dominant in the late nineteenth and early twentieth centuries, notions of a wholesale transition in which one set of ideas replaced another are open to question. Recent research on early modern monstrosity shows the importance of medical approaches to anomalous bodies in the sixteenth and seventeenth centuries that sought to explain scientifically the causes of birth defect, which co-existed with religious and moral inter-pretations.[54] The development of eugenic ideas in the late nineteenth and early twentieth centuries may have reinforced and reinvented older associations between human anomaly and deviance. Arguably the association between dis-ability and other negative traits as evidence of degeneracy in eugenic thought, together with the development of new categories of mental deficiency such as 'moral imbecility', seemed to assert afresh the relationship between deformity, disability and moral deviance, riveting it home with the stamp of scientific approval. Furthermore, concentration on 'moral' or 'medical' discourses of dis-ability itself may obscure the impact of other modes of thought on the definition and perception of disability, such as the role of the legal and philosophical thought in defining 'idiocy' and 'lunacy' in the medieval and early modern periods.[55] Rather than showing one model simply replacing another, some con-tributors to this volume emphasise the co-existence of a variety of bodily dis-courses at a particular historical moment.

The first part of this book examines the social, cultural and political context in which deformed and disabled bodies were understood between the sixteenth and the early nineteenth centuries. Contributors examine the moral and political meanings ascribed to monstrosity and other somatic markers of anomaly. How, and in what contexts, was deformity stigmatised? To what extent did medical knowledge impact upon and change perceptions of deformity and disfigure-ment? In the chapter that opens this section, Kevin Stagg re-examines sixteenth-and seventeenth-century accounts of monstrous births to explore the interaction of the corporeal and the symbolic in early modern English culture and society. Stagg's chapter raises a key analytical problem faced by historians of early modern anomalous bodies. While monster literature shows the omnipresence of deformity and disability as social metaphors in early modern culture and society, their use as a 'master metaphor' for social ills serves to suppress the personal and social implications of disability. Stagg explores the processes by which this took place, showing the narrative strategies that were adopted to equate bodily deformity with sin. While the plight of these severely disabled infants disap-peared from view under the weight of metaphorical signification, Stagg never-theless shows how the 'monsters'' bodies themselves might play a role in their own interpretation, since configurations of deformity were important in deter-mining the messages derived from them.

Although the literature of monstrous births was 'the *locus classicus* of early modern accounts of the normal and the pathological', the broad association between physical deformity and moral character at this time necessitates that the study of physical defect be undertaken in a broader context that takes into account other cultural and political meanings of disfigurement.[56] David E. Shuttleton's chapter looks at the depiction of smallpox scarring – a commonplace form of physical disfigurement in the seventeenth and eighteenth centuries – in the literary culture of the Stuart Restoration. Smallpox, which replaced plague as the most terrifying malady in the later seventeenth century, and was considered a doubly cruel disease in that if it did not kill its victims, was likely to leave them disfigured or physically impaired. Relating the 'semiotics' of smallpox to power structures, Shuttleton shows how the stigma attached to smallpox revealed itself at moments of political transition. The chapter uses literary and medical texts to show the ways in which the imagery of smallpox scarring entered political debate, serving as a means of generating sympathy for the Stuart regime through images of beauty cruelly disfigured, and (for the opposition) a way of signifying corruption and retribution.

Deformity had long associations with sexual deviancy in early modern thought. Monstrous births, physical abnormality and mental deficiency were commonly seen as divine punishment for incest, bestiality and adultery in village communities in the seventeenth and eighteenth centuries and beyond.[57] Focussing on representations of male and female homosexuality, Hal Gladfelder's chapter seeks to deepen our understanding of the relationship between deformity and deviance in the early modern period, but also draws attention to its instability. Comparing the representation of the bodies of homosexuals in the literary and medical writing of the eighteenth-century novelist John Cleland, best known for his pornographic *Memoirs of a Woman of Pleasure* (1749), and the theories of nineteenth-century sexologists, Gladfelder suggests that although the stigmatisation of moral deviance through bodily deformity was a feature of eighteenth-century writing, it may actually have intensified in later modernity. In contending that deviance was congenital and could by clinically diagnosed from external symptoms, Victorian sexologists such as Henry Havelock-Ellis modified older notions of deformity as a sign of deviance or punishment for sin, by seeking medical proof that deviance was rooted in bodily 'deformity'.

Taking the analysis forward to the turn of the nineteenth century, Suzanne Nunn demonstrates the persistent cultural force of images of the grotesque body by examining satirical engravings covering the topic of smallpox vaccination. Exploring images as 'part of a set of communicative practices that made shared anxieties about the body and medicine meaningful in a unique and vibrant way', Nunn analyses satires produced in the debates that surrounded Edward Jenner's discovery in 1798 of a vaccination for smallpox by injecting its victims with cowpox, which depicted vaccinated smallpox victims as starting to develop animal characteristics. Nunn shows the use of the grotesquely deformed body in graphic satire as a means of questioning medical progress and authority, in the process showing the atavistic aspect of representations of deformed, monstrous and disabled bodies. Building on perceptions of the deformed or disabled body as being antithetical to progress and modernity, such images provided a powerful means to express concerns about vaccination and a critique of scientific advancement.

Chapters in the second part of this collection re-examine the cultural, medical and institutional factors that delineated disability in the nineteenth and twentieth centuries, discuss shifting approaches to the 'problem' of disability in the modern era, and compare policies towards, and perceptions of, physical and mental impairment. Anne Borsay's chapter examines how orthopaedic medicine was applied to the disciplining of disabled children in Britain between 1800 and the outbreak of the Second World War. She traces the development of physical impairment as a personal pathology in the practice of social orthopaedics in which disabled children were subjected to the disciplining rigour of the orthopaedic hospital with the ultimate aim of not just correcting their impairments, but also turning them into economically independent adults. The 'normalisation' of disabled children was a policy taken up by educators and civil servants as well as medical professionals. Initiatives to 'normalise' deafness by teaching the deaf to speak had been debated since the seventeenth century, yet it was not until the nineteenth century that these initiatives received much interest from the state and within debates about education. Douglas C. Baynton has shown how efforts to replace sign language with oral methods in nineteenth-century American deaf education reflected anxieties about progress and degeneracy.[58] François Buton's chapter in this volume traces similar developments which, in the early French Third Republic (1880s), led to the banning of French sign language and to the mandatory use of oral methods in schools for deaf mute children. Debates about the introduction of this policy revealed not only varieties of opinion about the perception and 'treatment' of deaf children, but also broader trends such as the bureaucratisation and secularisation of educational policy towards the disabled which ultimately resulted in a diminishing role for the deaf in their own education.

Notions of social progress, national development and economic efficiency came together in the late nineteenth and early twentieth centuries in the modern eugenics movement. Ayça Alemdaroğlu in her chapter traces the origins of eugenics in Social Darwinism, and explores its impact in the context of Turkey's emergence in the 1920s and 1930s as a nation state. In the process, she highlights the way in which corporeal discourses, in particular the devaluation of disabled or 'degenerate' bodies, played an important role in modern nationalist movements and defining the relationship between the state and the individual. The case of eugenics, she demonstrates, shows the ways in which political power was combined with medical discourse in the early twentieth century, providing a rationale for inclusion and exclusion.

Perhaps the most notorious aspect of eugenic thought was its support for sterilisation – and in some cases elimination – of those deemed defective. Although this sterilisation programme was most assiduously followed in Nazi Germany, the question of sterilisation was debated in other countries during the early twentieth century.[59] Sharon Morris's chapter examines the impact of these ideas in early twentieth-century Britain in the context of the 1913 Mental Deficiency Act and the inter-war debate on the sterilisation of the mentally deficient. These debates brought together in a particularly vivid manner ethical and medical discourses on disability, and provide an insight into the interaction of these different perspectives on the control of disabled bodies. Creating 'colonies' for the segregation of the mentally ill from the gene pool, the 1913 Act is viewed as the most overtly eugenic legislation of the period in Britain. Using records from England and Wales, her chapter reveals a vigorous public discussion about whether the more able mentally deficient or 'moral imbeciles' should be prevented from procreating, and traces the source of demands to control the reproduction of the mentally deficient.

As Morris notes at the end of her chapter, although eugenics were a product of their time, and were commonly associated with the oppressive policies of inter-war regimes, eugenic ideas persist to the present through practices such as antenatal screening and 'the relentless repair of those who are born less than perfect'. More generally, eugenics, by associating disability with socially unde-sirable qualities such as alcoholism and criminality, have created a legacy that people with disabilities are still struggling to overcome.[60] The effects of dis-abling mental illness are felt particularly hard by military veterans whose train-ing instilled notions of self-control. In her chapter, Kristy Muir provides a sensitive analysis of ways in which mentally ill Australian veterans of the Second World War and Indonesian Confrontation (1963–1966) struggle to cope with this hidden disability. In examining the effects of mental illness within the context of military training and the model of disciplined masculinity it engen-dered, Muir shows how this disabling condition was experienced as stigma. Also, by foregrounding individual experiences of mental illness, accessed through the oral testimonies of veterans themselves, Muir shifts attention away from social, political and institutional efforts to control disabled people to ways in which the disabled themselves have sought to regain control of their lives. In doing so, she provides an alternative perspective on the issues of stigma and dis-ciplining that are central to this volume.

By foregrounding the personal experiences of veterans disabled by Post-Traumatic Stress Disorder, Kristy Muir moves towards what Sharon Snyder and David Mitchell refer to in their Afterword as the perspective of disability as 'an enunciated subject position'. In spite of the contribution made by Disability Studies, both to the liberation of disabled people from oppressive regulatory and institutional discourses and for exposing to criticism the medical, cultural and environmental factors that construct certain bodies as 'anomalous', the challenge of exploring the impact of medical and cultural discourses of deformity and dis-ability on the experiences of individuals themselves – and assessing how class, race, gender, sexuality and other factors have further shaped these experiences – remains. As Snyder and Mitchell have argued elsewhere, while the presence of anomalous bodies in many historical and cultural contexts has been recognised, scholarly analyses have tended to reduce these bodies to metaphors for other cat-egories of difference such as race, class, gender and sexuality. As such, bodily distortions are reduced to the merely metaphorical, while the physicality of these bodies disappears from view. In this way the disabled body 'serves as the raw material out of which other socially disempowered communities make themselves visible'.[61] Disability Studies, by forcing scholarship to confront the embodiment of difference, challenges academia to address its own aporias as well as addressing those of medicine, institutions and social practice. Integrating experiences of the body's physicality into historical analyses of disability and deformity is a priority for future research. Exploring oral testimonies as Muir does in her chapter, may provide one way forward. Searching for disabled people in past societies outside the walls of institutions or away from the surveillance of poor relief officials, doctors or care professionals is also necessary.[62] So too, as Snyder and Mitchell emphasise here, must universities become more accommodating environments for disabled scholars. Practical issues such as enabling access to archives are only just being addressed. Historians also need to attend more closely to attend to regional and national variations, to explore the perceptions and experience of disability and bodily anomaly in non-Western cultures.

Douglas C. Baynton has remarked that 'disability is everywhere in history, once you begin looking for it, but conspicuously absent from the histories we write'.[63] The essays in this volume contribute to a burgeoning area of scholarship that seeks to examine the meanings and experiences of physical, sensory and intellectual difference in past societies and they showcase the variety of approaches to these subjects currently being undertaken by scholars in this field. Their aim is not to provide a comprehensive history of deformity and disability, but to suggest some of the issues involved in writing such a history, and, by drawing attention to the rich diversity of themes such a history might encompass, act as a catalyst for future research. While it is recognised that social histories of deformity and disability are only partially realised through the history of representations and social policy and need to engage more fully with the more problematic topic of experience, a fuller understanding of the meanings attached to impairment, defect and anomaly in the past is important in showing that attitudes are not fixed. Exposing stigma to rigorous historical analysis in this way provides a means by which it may ultimately be overcome.

Notes

1 I am grateful to Kevin Stagg and Carys Turner for their comments on earlier versions of this chapter.
2 Erving Goffman, *Stigma: Notes on the Management of Spoiled Identity*, [1963], Harmondsworth: Penguin, 1968; Michel Foucault, *The Birth of the Clinic: An Archaeology of Medical Perception*, [1963], trans. A. M. Sheridan Smith, New York: Vintage Books, 1975; Foucault, *Discipline and Punish: The Birth of the Prison* [1975], trans. Alan Sheridan, Harmondsworth: Penguin, 1977. For discussions of the influence of these writers see Chris Shilling, *The Body and Social Theory*, London: Sage Books, 1993 and Rosemarie Garland-Thomson, *Extraordinary Bodies: Figuring Physical Disability in American Culture and Literature*, New York: Columbia University Press, 1997, ch. 2. See also Colin Jones and Roy Porter (eds), *Reassessing Foucault: Power, Medicine and the Body*, London and New York: Routledge, 1994; Mark S. R. Jenner, 'Body, Image, Text in Early Modern Europe', *Social History of Medicine*, 12:1, 1999, 143–54.

3 For example: Alexandra Walsham, *Providence in Early Modern England*, Oxford: Oxford University Press, 2001; Katherine Park and Lorraine Daston, 'Unnatural Conceptions: the Study of Monsters in Sixteenth- and Seventeenth-Century France and England', *Past and Present*, 92, 1981, 20–55; Marie-Helene Huet, *Monstrous Imagination*, Cambridge: Harvard University Press, 1993; Dennis Todd, *Imagining Monsters: Miscreations of the Self in Eighteenth-Century England*, Chicago: University of Chicago Press, 1995; Mary E. Fissell, *Vernacular Bodies: The Politics of Reproduction in Early Modern England*, Oxford: Oxford University Press, 2004. This literature is discussed further in Chapter 1.

4 For the scope of recent work see the essays in David Wright and Anne Digby (eds), *From Idiocy to Mental Deficiency: Historical Perspectives on People with Learning Disabilities*, London and New York: Routledge, 1996; David A. Gerber (ed.), *Disabled Veterans in History*, Ann Arbor: University of Michigan Press, 2000; and Paul K. Longmore and Lauri Umansky (eds), *The New Disability History: American Perspectives*, New York and London: New York University Press, 2001. See also Catherine J. Kudlick, 'Disability History: Why We Need Another "Other"', *American Historical Review*, 108:3, 2003, 763–93.

5 Douglas C. Baynton, 'Disability and the Justification of Inequality in American History', in Longmore and Umanksy (eds), *New Disability History*, p. 52; Kudlick, 'Disability History', 793.

6 Ibid., 764.

7 For a sensitive discussion of the overlap between deformity and disability see Robert Garland, *The Eye of the Beholder: Deformity and Disability in the Graeco-Roman World*, London: Duckworth, 1995, pp. 5–6.

8 For a discussion of differences between 'deformity', 'defect' and 'disability', see Helen Deutsch and Felicity Nussbaum, 'Introduction', in Helen Deutsch and Felicity Nussbaum (eds), *"Defects": Engendering the Modern Body*, Ann Arbor: University of Michigan Press, 2000, pp. 1–28, especially pp. 2–3.

9 Steven D. Edwards, *Disability: Definitions, Value and Identity*, Oxford and Seattle: Radcliffe Publishing, 2005, p. 7.

10 Michael Oliver, *The Politics of Disablement*, London: Macmillan, 1990, ch. 1; Susan Wendell, *The Rejected Body: Feminist Philosophical Reflections on Disability*, New York and London: Routledge, 1996, ch. 1; Deborah Marks, *Disability: Controversial Debates and Psychosocial Perspectives*, London and New York: Routledge, 1999; Edwards, *Disability: Definitions, Value and Identity*, Part 1.

11 Wendell, *Rejected Body*, p. 32.

12 Oliver, *Politics of Disablement*; Marks, *Disability: Controversial Debates and Psychosocial Perspectives*, ch. 4.

13 Carol Thomas, 'Disability Theory: Key Ideas, Issues and Thinkers', in Colin Barnes, Mike Oliver and Len Barton (eds), *Disability Studies Today*, Cambridge: Polity Press, 2002, pp. 38–57.

14 Marks, *Disability: Controversial Debates and Psychosocial Perspectives*, pp. 87–8.

15 Ibid., pp. 89, 94.

16 Anne Borsay, *Disability and Social Policy in Britain since 1750*, London: Palgrave, 2005, p. 8. On the disabilities of old age see Margaret Pelling and Richard M. Smith (eds), *Life, Death and the Elderly: Historical Perspectives*, London and New York: Routledge, 1991.

17 Paul K. Longmore and Lauri Umansky, 'Introduction: Disability History: From the Margins to the Mainstream', in Longmore and Umansky (eds), *New Disability History*, p. 20.

18 Sharon L. Snyder, Brenda Jo Bruggemann and Rosemarie Garland-Thomson, 'Introduction: Integrating Disability into Teaching and Scholarship', in Sharon L. Snyder, Brenda Jo Bruggemann and Rosemarie Garland-Thomson (eds), *Disability Studies: Enabling the Humanities*, New York: The Modern Language Association of America, 2002, pp. 1, 2.

19 Garland, *Eye of the Beholder*, p. 6.
20 For these criticisms of body history see Mary E. Fissell, 'Gender and Generation: Representing Reproduction in Early Modern England', *Gender and History*, 7:3, 1995, 433; Jenner, 'Body, Image, Text', 153–4. There are, of course, considerable differences of experience *within* categories of disability as well as *between* them. For a sensitive analysis of varieties of deaf experience in early modern England see Emily Cockayne, 'Experiences of the Deaf in Early Modern England', *Historical Journal*, 46:3, 2003, 493–510.
21 Kudlick, 'Disability History', p. 782.
22 Longmore and Umansky, 'Introduction', p. 4.
23 Wendell, *Rejected Body*, pp. 57–9.
24 Alan W. Bates, 'Good, Common, Regular and Orderly: Early Modern Classifications of Monstrous Births', *Social History of Medicine*, 18:2, August 2005, 155.
25 Kudlick, 'Disability History', p. 765.
26 Thomas Tuke, *A Treatise Against Painting and Tincturing of Men and Women*, London: Edward Marchant, 1616, p. 17; Theophilus Dorrington, *The Excellent Woman Described by Her True Characters and their Opposites*, London: Joseph Watts, 1692, p. 182.
27 N. H., *The Ladies Dictionary*, London: John Dunton, 1694, p. 162.
28 *The Spectator*, ed. Donald F. Bond, 5 vols., Oxford: Oxford University Press, 1965, I, p. 75 (no. 17, 20 March 1711).
29 Deutsch and Nussbaum, 'Introduction'; Felicity A. Nussbaum, *The Limits of the Human: Fictions of Anomaly, Race and Gender in the Long Eighteenth Century*, Cambridge: Cambridge University Press, 2003.
30 Nicolas Andry, *Orthopaedia: Or, the Art of Correcting and Preventing Deformities in Children*, 2 vols., London: A. Millar, 1743, I, p. 157.
31 Ibid., II, p. 107.
32 William Hay, *Deformity: An Essay*, London: R. and J. Dodsley, 1752, p. 34. Laughter is discussed in Paul Semonin, 'Monsters in the Marketplace: The Exhibition of Human Oddities in Early Modern England', in Rosemarie Garland-Thomson (ed.), *Freakery: Cultural Spectacles of the Extraordinary Body*, New York and London: New York University Press, 1996, pp. 69–81.
33 Roy Porter, *Bodies Politic: Disease, Death and Doctors in Britain 1650–1900*, London: Reaktion Books, 2001, ch. 2; Diana Donald, *The Age of Caricature: Satirical Prints in the Reign of George III*, New Haven and London: Yale University Press, 1996.
34 N. H., *Ladies Dictionary*, p. 163.
35 Andry, *Orthopaedia*, II, p. 172
36 N. H., *Ladies Dictionary*, p. 103.
37 The classic statement of this development is provided by Vic Finkelstein, *Attitudes and Disabled People: Issues for Discussion*, New York: World Rehabilitation Fund, 1980, pp. 8–11. See also Deborah Stone, *The Disabled State*, London: Macmillan, 1984; Oliver, *Politics of Disablement*.
38 Brendan Gleeson, *Geographies of Disability*, London and New York: Routledge, 1999, ch. 5.
39 Borsay, *Disability and Social Policy*, pp. 11–14 provides a useful summary of these debates.
40 For example, Gleeson, *Geographies of Disability*, p. 98.
41 Lennard Davis, *Enforcing Normalcy: Disability, Deafness and the Body*, London and New York: Verso, 1995, p. 24 and ch. 2 *passim*.
42 Baynton, 'Disability and the Justification of Inequality', pp. 35–6.
43 Douglas C. Baynton, *Forbidden Signs: American Culture and the Campaign against Sign Language*, Chicago and London: University of Chicago Press, 1996, p. 102.
44 Davis, *Enforcing Normalcy*, p. 37.

45 The development of modern eugenics and its national variations is discussed in Chapter 7.

46 Longmore and Umansky, 'Introduction', p. 22.

47 Borsay, *Disability and Social Policy* examines the development of social policy in Britain. See also Davis, *Enforcing Normalcy*, p. 3.

48 Anne Borsay, 'History, Power, and Identity', in Barnes, Oliver and Barton (eds), *Disability Studies Today*, p. 111.

49 David Armstrong, *Political Anatomy of the Body: Medical Knowledge in Britain in the Twentieth Century*, Cambridge: Cambridge University Press, 1983.

50 Garland-Thomson, *Extraordinary Bodies*, p. 58. See also Rosemarie Garland-Thomson, 'Introduction: From Wonder to Error – A Genealogy of Freak Discourse in Modernity', in Garland-Thomson (ed.), *Freakery*, p. 3; Davis, *Enforcing Normalcy*, p. 3.

51 Norbert Elias, *The Civilising Process*, [1939] trans. Edmund Jephcott, 2 vols., Oxford: Blackwell, 1978, 1982; Mikhail Bakhtin, *Rabelais and His World*, [1965] trans. Helene Iswolsky, Cambridge and London: MIT Press, 1968; Foucault, *Discipline and Punish*.

52 This model of change over time and its influence on historical writing is discussed in Kevin Stagg, 'The Body', in Garthine Walker (ed.), *Writing Early Modern History*, London: Hodder Arnold, 2005, pp. 205–26.

53 Ibid., pp. 207–9; Jenner, 'Body, Image, Text', p. 154.

54 Bates, 'Good, Common, Regular and Orderly'.

55 Jonathan Andrews, 'Begging the Question of Idiocy: the Definition and Socio-Cultural Meaning of Idiocy in Early Modern Britain: Part 1', *History of Psychiatry*, 9, 1998, 65–95.

56 Jenner, 'Body, Image, Text', p. 153.

57 For example, Robert Hole, 'Incest, Consanguinity and a Monstrous Birth in Rural England, January 1600', *Social History*, 25:2, 2000, 183–99.

58 Baynton, *Forbidden Signs*. Educational developments in Europe and America are also discussed in R. A. R. Edwards, '"Speech Has an Extraordinary Humanising Power": Horace Mann and the Problem of Nineteenth-Century American Deaf Education', in Longmore and Umansky (eds), *New Disability History*, pp. 58–82.

59 Anne Digby, 'Contexts and Perspectives', in Wright and Digby (eds), *From Idiocy to Mental Deficiency*, pp. 13–14.

60 Davis, *Enforcing Normalcy*, p. 35.

61 David T. Mitchell and Sharon Snyder, 'Introduction: Disability Studies and the Double Bind of Representation', in David T. Mitchell and Sharon L. Snyder (eds), *The Body and Physical Difference: Discourses of Disability*, Ann Arbor: University of Michigan Press, 1997, p. 6.

62 Elizabeth Bredberg, 'Writing Disability History: Problems, Perspectives and Sources', *Disability and Society*, 14:2, March 1999, 189–201.

63 Baynton, 'Disability and the Justification of Inequality', p. 52.

Part I

Disability and deformity

The medical and moral world of monstrosity

1 Representing physical difference

The materiality of the monstrous

Kevin Stagg

The seventeenth century physician John Bulwer published four works that explored the body including *Philocophus; or the Deafe and Dumbe Mans Friend* (1648) and *Anthropometamorphosis: man transfor'd* (1650).[1] With the former work, Bulwer became 'probably the first British person to write emphatically about deafness and sign language in any depth', a feat that established him as a founding father of British sign language.[2] With the latter he presented a survey of ethnic monstrosity based on bodily modification and adornment. *Anthropometamorphosis*, a 'strange grab bag of ethnographic shudders', offered a sustained critique of cultural artifice equating fashion and foreignness with the monstrous body.[3] Whilst the xenophobia and misogyny evident in the 1650 work were common currency for the period, to modern sensibilities it fits uneasily with an enlightened and progressive concern for the deaf. This incongruity is reflected in academic studies relating to Bulwer and in turn highlights the uneasy juxtaposition of contemporary academic discourses regarding the body. The work and interests of Bulwer would suggest that academic studies of disability and of monstrosity potentially have something in common, that their respective interests could be expected to coincide and overlap. In actuality a divergence is apparent that reflects the discipline of body history. In relation to Bulwer, studies have been divided between those focusing on deafness and the rhetoric of gestures and those exploring the proto-anthropology of *Anthropometamorphosis*.[4] As Graham Richards observes in the *Oxford Dictionary of National Biography*, the 'overall unity' of Bulwer's work has been largely overlooked.[5]

Such partial appreciation of Bulwer thus can be extended to make a more general point about the academic approach to the subject of physical difference. Academic studies relating to monsters have appeared with great frequency over the past decade. The same period has also witnessed the growing prominence of disability studies. There seem to be obvious connections between the disciplines in that both tend to focus on the body and issues of physical difference. Equally both monster studies and disability studies have tended to draw on representations of the body in their exploration of their topics at the expense of embodiment. Such an emphasis is in part related to available sources, but the neglect of lived experience in relation to the history of body has meant that the disabled body has invariably been analysed as an 'alien condition', an 'absolute state of otherness' in relation to the normative body.[6] Where the discourses of disability and monstrosity diverge is in their intent. Disability studies seek, through an interdisciplinary approach, to 'think about disability not as an isolated, individual medical pathology but instead as a key defining social category on a par with race, class, and gender'.[7] Works dealing with monstrosity on the other hand tend to evade the specific social context of physical difference, preferring to examine the subject in relation to such topics as providential literature, secularisation, the imagination, changing ideas of maternity and reproduction, and religion amongst others. The monstrous thus stands for error, abnormality and the 'other' or becomes a vehicle for conveying historical shifts from (say) religious to scientific perspectives.[8] Robert Garland's *Eye of the Beholder*, which incorporates analysis of ancient portents, omens and rituals of pollution with a sensitive appreciation of the treatment of the disabled, stands out as a work effectively synthesising disability studies with the monstrous.[9]

David T. Mitchell has set out a more developed critique regarding disability and representation. As disability has tended throughout history to be perceived as a problem in need of a solution, it has resulted in not only a range of state interventions and policies but also made it a 'primary object of literary representation'.[10] Literary representations have a rarely acknowledged dependency upon disability. Unlike other marginalised identities (gender, sexuality, race and ethnicity), disability is omnipresent throughout literature creating a conundrum whereby disability's social invisibility is accompanied by its cultural profusion. In their concept of 'narrative prosthesis' Sharon Snyder and David T. Mitchell propose that narratives need anomaly; they are structurally dependent upon deviant or extraordinary elements to propel the narrative, and these elements draw upon an underlying archetype and historical association with a physically different body. Through their notion of the 'materiality of the metaphor' Snyder and Mitchell draw attention to the degree to which disability is also called upon as a 'master metaphor for social ills'. Such metaphors lend bodily abnormalities a greater metaphysical significance. The personal, social and political implications of disability are constantly elided whilst the physically different body is incessantly invoked. Thus, discourses of monstrosity invariably reflect on issues of gender, sexuality, race and ethnicity but the disability or deformity that underpins the original category of monstrosity is overlooked. Where works exploring issues of gender, sexuality and race have highlighted the problem posed by invisibility, of being excluded from discourse, for disability the opposite is true. Disability is represented everywhere but its specific social significance is invisible. As Mitchell argues, 'the social navigation of stigma or the physical demands of a disability are slighted in favour of gesturing toward a symbolic register of commentary on the conditions of the universe'.[11]

To test this hypothesis I wish to explore a body of early modern works which invoke such metaphorical richness in relation to physical abnormality, in the form of the monster and, more specifically the 'monstrous birth'. A monstrous birth was the usual early modern term for congenital malformations; the term 'monstrous birth', although imprecise effectively meant anything out of the ordinary such as conjoined twins. Tales of monstrous births made up part of a genre of providential news printed in broadsides and pamphlets. Stories of bewildering and horrific births were a popular form of news in England and Wales over the course of the sixteenth and seventeenth centuries. They combined sensational detail of malformed bodies and horrified and distressed families with dire warnings of the need for all to repent. Such monsters were seen as signs of the last days, and, like the celestial comet prodigies, heralds of the apocalypse or at least of political and social upheaval. Monstrous births joined other notable signs of divine disfavour including extraordinary fish, beached whales, unusual animals, unexpected weather and celestial phenomena. Thus under the banner of providential signs a varied range of phenomena could be drawn upon:

> plague, pestilence, warre, famine, scarcity, dearth, new sicknesses and diseases, Comets, blazing stares, flashing lights, shooting and streamings in the ayre, monsters of man and beast &c.[12]

Thus within the portent tradition, monstrous births were viewed as just one of a number of unusual occurrences that were deemed significant in determining divine intentions.

Although there is no simple correspondence between the overlapping discourses of disability and monstrosity, physical difference lies at their core. Overall, the monster birth ballads and pamphlets offer a useful support for Mitchell's argument regarding the 'the materiality of the metaphor' as these are works that are centrally about birth abnormalities but their content tends to focus on matters of sinful conduct, on concern over maternity, or they act as satirical comments on religious and political issues. In this sense early modern tales of extraordinary births disqualify the represented child 'from possessing a shared social identity'.[13] Between 1550 and 1700 in England, some 70 ballads and a similar number of pamphlets along with a number of book-length collections utilised monstrous births as prodigies. These monster works tended to follow a format that combined a written description of the prodigy (often augmented with an illustration) with a reflection on its significance.

Early modern attitudes to disability and deformity reveal three main themes: improvement and repair; artifice; and providence. This range of responses is clearly expressed in the writings of the sixteenth-century French surgeon Ambroise Paré whose complete works were translated into English by Thomas Johnson and published in 1634. The 23rd book of Paré's collected works, 'Of the Meanes and Manner to Repaire or Supply the Naturall or accidentall defects or wants in mans body', sets out examples of surgical procedures to treat wounds including the loss of eyes, teeth, parts of the nose, tongue; to treat defects afflicting the face and ears, hunchbacks, fingers and thumbs, legs and feet. The 25th book, 'Of Monsters and Prodigies', offers an account of the causes of monstrous births (invoking both natural and supernatural sources) and includes a chapter ('Of the Cozenages and crafty Trickes of Beggars') to the counterfeits of beggars describing the use of a hanged man's arm to claim alms; using a sponge to imitate an ulcer, with examples of those mimicking leprosy, deafness, St. Vitus' dance and scabies. In Paré's work medical advice for the deformed and maimed jostles alongside accounts of monstrous births derived from demonic and bestial intercourse and a harsh judgement of the social practices of beggars.[14] According to Paré, physical difference could result from divine wrath for sinful conduct; it could also, following Aristotle and Hippocrates, be related to the superfluity, deficiency or misplacement of the male seed; to the active shaping faculties of the conceiving woman's imagination or to the influence of the stars. However defects and blemishes could be healed, so that nature's deficiency could in many cases be overcome and superseded. William Turner's 1697 encyclopaedic work on providential wonders lists examples of the blind, deaf and other defects 'improved by Art and Industry'. Unlike Paré, Turner does not offer examples of surgical repair, but of the benefits of the arts:

> Where Nature is defective, there the Assistance of Art is required: Nothing makes us more Ingenious than Necessity: Rather than Men shall suffer all the Inconveniences consequent upon a Total Eclipse of any of their Senses, especially that of Sight, and the comfortable use of the Sun, they will set their Brains upon the rack, and use the greatest intention of Thought, to procure a Compensation.[15]

Turner describes human prodigies overcoming handicap by displaying extraordinary abilities to read, learn and perform actions. A woman from Basle is noted for 'Spinning Artificially with her Feet, Sweeping the House, and performing all other the Offices of a good Houswife', whilst a British woman 'born with Arms and Legs, distorted in so strange and unusual a manner' was able to thread a needle, tie a knot and write with her tongue.[16]

The most prominent themes in relation to the disabled evident in popular representations associated disability with fraud. This is evident in the 1614 pamphlet, *Deeds against Nature, and monsters by kinde*, which describes the trial of John Arthur, a London cripple, for murder. Arthur's case was set alongside that of a case dealing with infanticide. The sinful and corrupt nature of Arthur is evident from his physical form:

> An unperfect wretch wanting the right shape and limbes of a man though in forme and visage like unto one of us, this decreped creature ... lived and maintain'd himselfe with the charitie and devotions of almes-giving people, and by his lame and limblesse usage purchased more kinde favours then many others of his base fraternitie.[17]

The fact that the 'wretch' appears 'like unto us' allies disability with deception suggesting that it operates as a hidden treachery. John Arthur is described as 'continually abusing the gifts of charitie, and wasting away the same with drunkennes', and along with his ilk ('such begging vagabonds and disordred liners') viewed as being 'instruments of the divell'.[18] The popular ballad about the 'stout Criple of Cornwall' made similar accusations linking fraud and disability.[19]

This association of disability with deceit in the accounts of beggars and cripples was also evident in accusations about the status of freaks displayed at such places as Bartholemew Fair.[20] Establishing the veracity of the reported monstrous birth was also the constant concern of ballad and pamphlet writers.

In ballads and pamphlets, abnormal or monstrous births were usually regarded as omens, signs of trouble ahead which came as admonishments from God for the sinful conduct of his flock. Such popular monster works covered more than human disability. Firstly, animal abnormalities were popular as exemplified by the most famous sixteenth-century monster broadsides – Martin Luther's Monk-calf and Philip Melancthon's Pope-ass, translated and published in London in 1579. Pigs and cows were the most usual animals featured and their inclusion suggests that it was the unusual nature of birth that was significant in monster works, rather than the human dimension. Another popular theme concerned prophesying children as featured in works such as Cornelius Pet's *An Example of Gods judgement . . . upon two children* (1582) and Sampson Jones, *Vox Infantis or The Propheticall Child* (1649).[21] The 1678 *Strange and Wonderful News from Bull-and-Mouth Street* similarly, but less sensationally, describes the words uttered by an infant, which, in being described as a 'lusty Man Child' demonstrates that a prodigious nature and physical monstrosity did not always correspond.[22] Other works incorporated details such as murders, drawing monstrous births into a broader genre of sensational literature. Anthony Munday's 1580 *A View of sundry examples* offered up a hotch-potch of gory snippets of news covering blasphemy, suicides, servants killing masters, infanticide and earthquakes. Thus monstrosity was a concept applied to a range of phenomena unusual and striking enough to signify a transgression against divine law.

The monster works tended to focus on particular deformities, mainly conjoined twins, though some works described older living monstrosities. Two pamphlets described horned women. The 1588 *A Myraculous, and monstrous, but yet most true, and certayne discourse, of a woman* described Margaret Griffith whose frontal horn grew late in her life. Suspected by some gossips of 'light behaviour', the accusation was that having given her husband the horn (i.e. been unfaithful to him) the deformity manifested on her forehead as a rebuke. Here deformity is regarded as a personal punishment but one with an obvious message to others. With the 1676 pamphlet, *A Brief Narrative of a Strange and Wonderful Old Woman that hath a Pair of Horns* the horns are described as having a natural cause – from wearing a straight hat, and it is noted that the horn causes pain when the weather changes. Some concern is expressed that the horn might be a fake. Thus, within 90 years, there is a change in tone from divine punishment for sinful actions to natural cause or possible artifice.[23]

Although births made just one sort of prodigy, they were more useful for writers than celestial prodigies such as meteor showers, comets or phantasms seen within the clouds as they highlighted sinful outcomes within the household. Birth was a rite of social significance and for it to go awry pointed to a disruption of the local order, of potential shame and stigmatisation for the parents. Thus the significance of the monster child partly lay in its social context, but also in the figurative utility of the body. The bolt of lightning and the deformed child could both serve as signs of God's wrath, but the body of the child acted as a more fruitful symbol, as the specific nature of the child's condition could be analysed.

Teratoscopy, or prognostication from the bodies of deformed foetuses and infants (human and animal), was a divinatory art of Babylonian lineage. The Babylonian tradition probably passed from the Hittites to the Etruscans and from them to the Romans. Julius Obsequens collected the Roman portents into one work *The Book of Prodigies*, in the fourth century AD. It was this work that connected the Roman tradition of portents with that of the early modern Reformation. Translated by Conrad Lycosthenes in 1552, its contents were utilised in Lycosthenes' own work on prodigies five years later: *Prodigiorum ac Ostentorum Chronicon*. Lycosthenes' 1557 work was translated, adapted and updated for an English readership by the Anglican clergyman, Stephen Batman, and published in 1581 as *The Doome Warning All Men to the Iudgemente*. The early modern monstrous portent was a humanist and reformation revival of a classical form pursued for religious and political ends. In early modern portents, the classical concern with ephemeral discord in the body politic was combined with a biblical emphasis on the monster as a herald of the apocalypse, the impending catastrophe of the latter days. This suffusion of the biblical and pagan took place within a new vibrant print culture drawing together the moral imperatives of the reformation with the thirst for news for the ephemeral and the commercial imperatives of print. In England, indigenous monster broadsides first appeared in the 1550s (the first continental translation had been prepared in 1531) with the 1560s a particularly prolific decade; monster pamphlets followed from the 1580s.

In many respects early modern monster broadsides followed a template established by the Babylonian omen series. The comprehensive Babylonian system provided details of the cause and effect of every possible variation of birth anomaly. Each omen had an introductory and concluding part, a protasis which established the nature of the prodigy and an apodosis that divulged the outcome and diagnosis.[24] The protasis would establish the origin of the monstrosity – whether it was human or animal – and then describe the body parts, usually running in sequence from the head to the toes. The apodosis would distinguish between public and private omens, those having significance for the whole country and those with a bearing merely on the family involved. Most public apodoses would offer a standardised, formulaic response, though a few would establish connections with specific historical events. In many respects a similar structure is evident in early modern popular works. The actual interplay between the corporeal (as related in the protasis) and the symbolic (the apodosis) reveals a range of responses that develops Mitchell's concept of the 'materiality of the metaphor'. While Mitchell pointed to the neglect of the physical demands of disability, the monster broadsides and pamphlets often reduced the body itself to a bare description, a canvas on which to inscribe significance. However, in other cases the clear link between bodily deformation and moral implication is described.

William Fulwood's *The shape of ii monsters* (1562) opens with a description of the birth of a piglet belonging to a Charing Cross joiner, Mark Finkle. The protasis establishes that the animal 'had a head muche lyke unto a dolphins head, with the left eare standing up forked', and continues to elaborate the specific details concerning the form and likeness of the limbs. The apodosis is subtitled as 'An Admonition unto the Reader', and determines that 'we have great cause in deede,/ Our sinnes for to confesse, / And eke to call to God with speede, / The same for to redresse'. The portent is non-specific though, operating more as a general warning against sinful conduct, but not engaging with specific manifestations of the deformity. The distinction between these two narrative elements is heightened by spatial and textual separation. The protasis is set out in prose beneath the illustration, whilst the apodosis is in verse and at the foot of the page. In *The True reporte of the forme and shape of a monstrous childe* (1562) and *Nature's Wonder?* (1664) the spatial arrangement of the protasis and apodosis are reversed. The meaning of the prodigy is still in verse, followed by a prose description of the child's physical debilities. The 1664 ballad carries a more detailed title which acts as a protasis précis, offering an abstract briefly outlining the key details. With *The True description of two monsterous children* (1566), a brief protasis is set out beneath the black-letter titles. The verse apodosis, below the illustration of George and Margery Stevens' conjoined twins, covers half of the single page. With *The Forme and shape of a Monstrous Child* (1568) the broadside is spatially arranged in three sections: an illustration of the child (with front and rear views) set in a decorated frame and containing proverbial rhymes ('In Gods power all flesh stands, / As the clay as in the potters hands'). Under the illustration the prose protasis describes a male child with a 'Lizardes mouth, terrible to beholde' amongst other deformities and relates the circumstances and occasion of the birth, along with the names of three witnesses. Making up the final section of the broadside, the apodosis, titled 'A warnyng to England', is carefully set out in three columns.[25]

This ballad establishes a clear linkage between the warning in the apodosis and the infant's bodily deformations. The tripartite construction of the broadside suggests a distinction was being made between the versified moral, which might be sung by the minstrel or balladeer, and the prose news. The evidence (the illustration) of the latest manifestation of divine displeasure (the news) and its spiritual significance (the moral) form a cohesive whole. This structure is utilised most frequently, with the kind of minor variations already described, in the works published in the 1560s and 1570s. Later ballads tended to eschew such a formal format but maintained the dichotomy within the text of describing the physical circumstances and relaying the providential truths the child's appearance embodied.

The majority of the ballads and pamphlets used monsters as emblems of social disorder and danger. They generally offered sweeping denunciations of collective sinfulness though a few targeted more specific categories of transgression, such as the vanity of pride (particularly in relation to female fashions) or heretical and sectarian religious practice (Catholicism, Ranters, Familists and Anabaptists were all attacked). The most usual approach adopted by writers of monster portent literature was to focus on a particular birth event, to compare the latter to other historical examples, and to draw general conclusions of relevance to the wider community. Invariably in such works the parents of the monstrous child would be described as righteous and honest folk. The personal stigma would be evaded to deflect more widely onto the broader congregation of sinners. However, with some accounts more personal peccadilloes would be stressed. An unmarried mother of a monstrous child, Margaret Mere was noted for having 'played the naughty packe'. The child of Anthony Smith and his wife had been conceived outside marriage, so Nature wreaked 'her spyte on parentes sinne'. Monstrous offspring were borne by a Popish gentlewoman who cursed Parliament to the wife of Philip Miller, a persecutor of nonconformists and to a woman whose child had been fathered by a renegade priest.[26] John Mellys addresses the distinction between private and public warnings in describing the conjoined twins born in Swanbourne, Buckinghamshire in 1566, noting that such a birth was usually seen as denoting sinful conduct on the behalf of the parents:

> But some proude boasting Pharisie
> The parents wyll detect,
> And iudge with heapes of uglie vice
> Their lives to be infect.

Mellys emphasises not only the collective dimension of such warnings, but lessens the culpability of the parents:

> No, no: but lessons for us all,
> Which dayly doe offend;
> Yea, more, perhaps, than hath the friends
> Whom God this birth did lend.[27]

The warnings in some monster works made more specific recommendations as with the cleric John Locke's exhortation to accept that there is 'one Lord, one faith, and one baptisme' in a pamphlet which attacked the beliefs of sectaries who regarded the use of the sign of the cross in baptism as a relic of Roman Catholicism. A ballad concerning a monstrous child born at Southampton in 1602 attacked male fashion:

> Alonge his necke and shoulders hung black lockes of curled hayre
> Much lyke the locks that many men upon their heads do weare-
> Which sight is growne soe odious, as good men yt detest,
> Because it makes a man to seeme as yf he were a beast.

The bestial presentation of the child – monkey-faced and with feline ears – stood as a warning against indulgence in sinful conduct, the remedy for which was speedy repentance.[28] One author recommended the reading of the work of reformist authors Philip Stubbes, William Hergest and Stephen Batman to assist the amendment and reform of sinful lives.[29] For other authors the monster story did not so much provide a remedy as proof of an argument, as with the 1599 monster whose prophecies contradicted the Anabaptist assertion that newborn infants were not in possession of the Holy Ghost.[30]

Within monster texts narrative strategies were adopted to clearly equate bodily deformity with sin. In accounting for the significance of deformity, writers usually turned to the parable of the blind man in John's gospel. The blindness here was deemed by Jesus not to be a matter of personal sin but rather of God's decision. However, monster works often drew direct links between the nature of the deformity and sinfulness. The figurative approach, as espoused by early sixteenth-century continental authors such as Philip Melancthon and Martin Luther, whereby every fold of skin and bodily aberration was subjected to precise exegesis, was usually reserved for satirical monster works published in England.[31] Much as official censorship from the 1550s till the 1640s modified the political thrust of English monster works as compared to their continental versions, the symbolic association between deformity and sin was likewise more modestly expressed. The author of a 1562 broadside states that deformed shapes reflect and so 'declare' 'what sinnes beset the secrete minde', but qualifies this with by saying that it is not always the case that deformity links 'fraughted minde with vice'.[32] Sometimes a loose link was established between corporeal form and significance as with John Barker's 1564 broadside *The true description of a monsterous chylde, borne in the city of Antwarpe.* Having set out a description of the monster alongside a woodcut illustration, Barker notes:

> For whence the shape of Gods image: of man is tourned soo,
> It is a warning in this age: and token of great woo.[33]

In some works the symbolic affinity between the protasis and apodosis was clearly established. Christian Jermin was born in 1565 with fleshy skin growing around her neck and shoulders, which the author describes as 'if it were with many ruffes set one after another … like as many womens gownes be'. The deformation made an explicit link to the excessive pride of women as demonstrated by their fondness for fine clothes: 'Our pride this childe doth bere, / Our rages and ruffes, that are so lewd'. In describing, this 'ruffeling world, in ruffes al rolde, / Dooth God detest and hate', the author draws a punning link between 'ruffling' as a description of disorder and irregularity and the starched linen neckwear of fashionable attire. A newborn child's lack of fingers in Maidstone, Kent in 1568 '(d)oth well set forth the idel plight, / Which we in these daies chuse', while:

> The leg so clyming to the head,
> What meaneth it but this –
> That some do seeke not to be lead,
> But for to leade amis.

The child's disfigured bestial 'gaspyng mouth' stood as a warning against blasphemy with its 'filthy talke, and poysoned speech'.[34] Such associations could also be interpreted not as a likeness but as a reproach. John Mellys drew attention to conjoined twins facing and embracing each other as a divine sign that upbraided people for their 'false discemblyng sinnes'. These words echo those of an anonymous ballad published a year before (which Mellys may have written or just borrowed some of the content) regarding conjoined twins born at Herne, in Kent who appeared – and were so illustrated – to be embracing each other. The posture was seen as a rebuke to 'false dyssemblynge and Judas condycyons and countenaunces', and as an exhortation to 'sincere amytie and true frendshyp, voyde of all counterfeytinge'. Thus the twins represented both the duplicity of betrayal and the ideal of true friendship.[35]

The civil war polemicist, John Vicars, in his 1643 work, *Prodigies and Apparitions*, makes pointed historical connections between the birth of monstrous children and events, by metaphorically associating deformities and their significance. Thus historical and associative ideas link the protasis and apodosis of the work. The birth of a two-headed child born in Old Bridewell in October 1633 is directly related to national conflict. The dual heads are seen as revealing God's 'hastening judgements and wrath' on the divisions between King and Parliament and Papists and Protestants. A stump of a head growing from the child's body represents the 'miserable and monstrous stump of an arme in lamentably torne and mangled Ireland'. The relationship between the body and the body politic is spelled out in the description of the child:

> Two distinct heads it had, and like two hearts,
> Two arms, whence grew a stump. In other parts
> Like other children. What may this portend?
> Sure monstrous plagues doe monstrous sinnes attend.
> The sinnes of Heads, in government abus'd,
> The sinnes of hearts, opinions false infus'd,
> And broacht abroad to raise up foes and factions,
> And Armes and Armies to confound with fractions,
> Dis-joynted states (like stump-like Ireland)
> Whiles brothers thus 'gainst brothers lift their hands.
> This (surely) God seemes hereby to foretell,
> That having plagues must hideous Sinnes expell.[36]

Whilst the conjoined twins born at Herne invited reflection upon the nature of betrayal and friendship, those of Old Bridewell forewarned of civil discord.

Thomas Bedford's observation of conjoined twins born at Stonehouse, Plymouth, in 1635 leads him to a number of religious reflections:

> The twins you see are males; brothers had they been born alive. To love as brethren is the duty of Christians ... To love is to have one soul in two bodies ... These two were one body; Christians are one spirit, though several bodies and souls, yet one and the same spirit diffused into all to enliven and quicken all ... .To these twins (had they quarrelled), a man might have said, 'You are one body': to Christians a man may well say. 'You are one spirit, why do you wrong one to another'?[37]

David Mitchell's critique of the materiality of the metaphor notes the degree to which the symbolic is emphasised at the expense of the corporeal; the body becomes a base for operations for making metaphysical statements. What perhaps can also be acknowledged is the degree to which the nature of the bodily anomaly itself shapes the metaphorical appropriation. Judging by the illustrations and descriptions offered, the Herne and Stonehouse monsters were *thoracopagus* twins, the most common form of conjoined twins in being joined at the chest. The Bridewell monsters were *parapagus* (or *diprosopus*) twins, a very rare form involving the union of the lower half of the body. The appearance is of a single child with two heads rather than, as with thoracopagus, of twins inextricably united. The thoracopagus body was more likely to draw out reflections on fraternity and important bonds, whilst the parapagus body presented an image of a single body divided. To this extent, the corporeal shaped the metaphor. Writers were of course able to adopt those bodies that suited their specific purpose though the evidence from English monster ballads and pamphlets is that the majority of authors made little explicit link between the nature of the physical form and its moral significance. This may reflect the lack of imagination on behalf of the hack writers who turned in such works, or the desire not to alarm censors by developing a sustained critique, but it also points to the degree of resistance and the challenge that the anomalous body posed.

The ballad, *The Lamenting Lady* (1620) offers another example where monster narratives were shaped by particular physiological circumstances. A female begging with her twins is refused charity and she curses the householder who consequently gives birth to 365 children. This preposterous but popular medieval tale may have had some biological basis as a distorted description of a hydatidiform mole containing hundreds of cysts.[38]

Rosemarie Garland-Thomson has argued that literature turns disabled characters into freaks, as representation 'exaggerates an already highlighted physical difference'.[39] Like disabled characters in novels, monster births are little more than ciphers on which to hang moral comment, political or religious critique or sensational news. However, many of the ballads and pamphlets just offered description without the 'gloss'. The relationship between body and significance depended on the form that monster works took. Generally styled as examples of cheap print providential news, these works could also appear as biographies.

The biographical format looked at lives (either good or bad) involving such elements as historical narrative (Robert, Duke of Normandy), living monstrosities (Margaret Griffith, Tannakin Skinker), exemplary material (Mary Adams, the Ranters 'monster') and satire (Judge Jeffreys).[40] Whilst the biographies of the virtuous operated as exemplars; those of the 'monstrous' served – like all portent material – as warnings. Historical biography looked to birth omens to establish the veracity of later behaviour traits. The monstrous nature of Robert, Duke of Normandy (like that in a later work concerning Louis XIV) was established whilst he was a newborn baby. Robert not only possessed early teeth but he put them to good use in demonstrating his bestial nature:

> This infant in his swathing clowtes gave certain testimonie his future outrages, for being born beyond the custome of nature with all his teeth . . . was inchanted, for in stead of drawing nutriment from his nurse, hee bit off her nipples, and being kissed in the cradle by the Ladie of Sancerres, hee bit off her nose: in his foode he was ravenous; in his fashions & behaviour rigorous.[41]

On the other hand, the seventeenth-century prophetess, Mother Shipton, was described as being physically deformed at birth, 'the strange and unparrallel'd Phisiognomy of the Child, which was so misshapen that it is altogether impossible to express it fully in words'. Her likeness to a witch drawn out by her possessing a 'nose of an incredible and unproportionable length, having in it many crooks and turnings, adorned with many strange Pimples of divers colours'.[42] The relationship between character and physical appearance was a theme frequently deployed in early modern literature. Thus, the trope of a monstrous birth operated as a warning about the evil potential of the person. This was a device rarely applied in more newsy providential reports of ordinary children, who had usually died shortly after birth or were being displayed to public view; rather such births heralded a broader engagement with public sinfulness or occasionally parental indiscretion. They gave credence to sinful sexual conduct or matters of vanity, carelessness in expression and dubious affiliations. Biographical works however, used birth complications to determine the character flaws of later life, or described a monster birth as a sign of evil intent.

A monster by reputation generally expressed a consistent character trait. Classic monsters of this type would include Nero, Richard III, Guy Fawkes and Titus Oates. Invariably underpinning unnatural behaviour, as was noted with Robert, Duke of Normandy and Mother Shipton, was some physical blemish, emphasising a link between disordered conduct and bodily deformity. In such cases, the corporeal and the moral mutually reinforced each other. Richard III, whom Shakespeare described as that 'lump of foul deformity', was born abnormally, having spent two years in the womb. He emerged feet first and already had grown teeth and shoulder-length hair.[43] Sir Thomas More's description of Richard, influencing Shakespeare as it did, was central to the monsterising of Richard:

[he was] little of stature, ill fetured of limmes, croke backed, his left shoulder much higher than his right, hard favoured of visage, and suche as is in states called Warlyke, in other menne otherwise. He was malicious, wrathful, envious, and from afore his birth, ever forwarde . . . hee came into the worlde with the feete forwarde.[44]

Being born with teeth was regarded as an ill omen, one that foretold a violent death. The fact that such essential details were attributed to the person by biographers after the actual death on the battlefield does little to diminish their impact. Christina Hole argues that being born with teeth was a sign that the child would grow up to become a murderer. Such beliefs were likely to be accumulative, developing their meaning over the course of time, so an association with Richard III may assist in shaping and developing the initial associations and attributed meanings. It was Shakespeare who turned the detail of Richard possessing one shoulder higher than the other into him taking the form of a hunchback.[45] The association of the birth scene with evil was also invoked. Margaret, Duchess of Burgundy (Edward IV's sister) was described as the midwife to Perkin Warbeck:

to deliver her wombe of this monstrous birth of *Peter Warbeck*, whom she taught the cunning and audacious impudency of personating *Richard* Duke of *Yorke* murthered with his brother in the Tower by *Richard* the third some eight yeare before.[46]

Aside from these biographical works, the concerns of most monster ballad and pamphlet writers focused on establishing the veracity of their account and of rendering an emotional response from their readers, the surprise of the strange news in combination with the horrific nature of the scene. Thus, the birth of a physically different child served as an opportunity to proclaim the truthfulness of the wretched and disgusting state of sin.

Establishing the veracity of the work became a central stratagem of monster birth works publications. In early sixteenth-century continental works, the prevailing tendency was for emblematic works, often highly stylized with recognisable elements such as papal hats or lion's heads. The portentous significance of the monster could be more easily decoded from the symbolic clues. Attention to some degree of anatomical accuracy would preclude repetition. In contrast, the majority of monster illustrations in English-language broadsides and pamphlets make some attempt at verisimilitude. The monster portrayed was usually the monster described. Credibility became a vital ingredient in the identity of popular monster literature with efforts made by many writers to establish with some accuracy the date of the birth, the names of the parents involved, along with such crucial detail as father's occupation, verbatim accounts of the circumstances of the birthing room and the mother's condition, along with close attention being paid to a description of the infant, who had visited the birth room and the state of the child's health. The narrative style of the works frequently sought to place the reader in the role of witness to the proceedings.

The problem of credibility became more acute after the abandonment of official press censorship. Monster and other wonder works became entangled in factional dispute, and there was a stronger need to establish proof.[47] From the 1660s accounts of monster births were frequently presented to the Royal Society. Such accounts used similar truth effects as those utilised by cheap print writers – detailed description and personal details – but also made use of anatomical illustration and a more specialised language of medical terminology. The visual dimension served to heighten the narrative testimony in broadsides and pamphlets. A good example of a realistic presentation is evident in the earliest English broadside – of conjoined twins born at Middleton Stoney, near Bicester, Oxfordshire in 1552. This work, printed by the technically proficient John Day, offers a realistic depiction of the front and back views of the infants. As well as establishing the work's purpose the opening preface also frequently addressed of the truthfulness of the piece. John Vicars openly acknowledges that the reader may be either 'benevolent or malevolent' and does not doubt that his work will 'meet eyes of enmity and hearts of rancour, as it shall of Amicability and Christian candour', but professes his 'care and diligence' in establishing the truth of all that is written within.[48] Edward Gresham's preface to the reader in the 1606 pamphlet *Strange fearful & true news* takes great efforts to reassure the time and trouble taken to prepare an accurate translation from the Dutch original, in order to avoid giving credence to anything of a 'false or frivolous import'.[49] The author of the 1676 pamphlet about Mrs Davies, the horned woman, encourages readers to go and see the living monstrosity to 'satisfie thy Curiosity' but also so that they can 'tell the World whether this following Narration be truth or Invention'.[50]

The problem of verification is thus one that continually haunts printed accounts. However, suspicion about the accuracy of reports of monsters occurred without printed works. The corpses of deformed infants were occasionally disinterred to satisfy local curiosity or suspicion. The vicar and midwife of Kirkham, Lancashire arranged for the grave of a headless child to be opened in 1645.[51] A similar act occurred in Allington in the same county in 1613.

> the report whereof not giving full satisfaction to some people that were incredulous of it, unless they might be made also eye witnesses of such an unheard of accident: the grave was opened againe wherein it had been buryed, and the body layde to the view of a great number of beholders: which were at the least five hundredth, that not onely beare a bare report, but can also give true Testimony of this occurrent to their much wonder, and admiration.[52]

The accusation of fraud in relation to the monster drew on scepticism about providential stories and the wiles of monster-mongers in fairs. The social condition of the child is skirted in favour of anxiety about authorial or fairground fabrication. The monster becomes a site for a debate about truthful reportage.

As well as concerning themselves with bringing accurate news, broadside and pamphlet works sought to convey a degree of surprise, a sense of wonder at the unique nature of the phenomenon. The sensational descriptive style they used was designed to create an immediate interest and expectation. Familiarity with the genre conditioned purchasers as to the type of material to expect. Peter Lake has, in a similar vein, noted the use of gory details in murder pamphlets. Descriptions of 'bizarre, bloody and grotesque killings' were utilised to satisfy a popular interest in sex and violence.[53] Similarly in monster works, the extensive details of an infant's deformities may, on the one hand, have been an attempt to establish the truthfulness of the report, as well as pandering to sensationalism in gratuitously lingering on the unusual arrangements of limbs or the bestial like-nesses that the child's body had taken on. Reports of monstrous births invariably described a personal reaction or invited the reader to imagine how they might respond if confronted by such a sight. Encouraging empathy with the parents was a useful stylistic device that emphasised the horrific nature of the monstros-ity. Monster and murder pamphlets both offered a 'frisson of horror laced with disapproval' invariably within a domestic setting.[54] The inclusion of such hor-rific elements was sanctioned by their operation as aspects of providence. The divine warning legitimised the sensational excess. When a monster with a colt's head, long ears and 'little stumps of horns' was born to a woman from West Grinstead in August 1661, the horror of the creature lay not just in the descrip-tion of its bestial features but also in the reactions to it. 'The Midwife was so affrighted at this birth that she fell ill immediately, and was not recovered in some weeks after'.[55] When the Ranter Mary Adams gave birth to what was described as 'the most ugliest ill-shapen *Monster* that ever eyes beheld', the reactions of the women in the birthing room was followed by a description of the child:

> they buried it with speed, for it was so loathsome to behold, that the womens hearts trembled to look upon it; for it had neither hands nor feet, but claws like a Toad in the place where the hands should have been, and that every part was odious to behold.[56]

The 1617 pamphlet, *A Wonder Worth the Reading*, set out a detailed portrayal of the drama of the birthing room, which invoked not only the alarming description of the child but also the actions and reactions of the attendant women and the family. The time and place are initially established with details of the child's deformities:

> In Kent-streete there dwelleth one, whose name is John Ladyman whose wife (upon the 21. of August 1617) after long travel was delivered of a female child with a halfe forehead, without any scull, having a faire propor-tioned body from the brest downward: the said child had its mouth & eyes miraculiously placed in the sayd halfe forhead neere upon the breast, upon the said halfe fore-head lay a peece of flesh of two fingers thicke round-about, the flesh being wonderfully curled like Gentlewomens attire: being of a very blew coullour like a turcke Cocke, the eyes being very bigg staring and very firy red.[57]

The sight of the monster, which touches upon a familiar concern of the moralistic works of sumptuary transgression, affects those assisting with the delivery:

> which greatly terrified the midwife and all that were present, the child being dead, the midwife labored to close the staring eies but could not, they presently fell all to prayer desiring God to take from them this so sodayne astonishment and feare, the midwife after prayer arising, and so the rest of the women, beholding agayne the Child, they saw the eares of it fastened to the halfe forehead, not being like to Christians eares, but stood pricking up, behind each eare, was two little bones standing up overgrowne with flesh, and having very long heare. In this hideous and fearefull forme was this child brought forth alive, to the great astonishment of the beholders, and grievous lamentation of the parents.[58]

The provision of details of personal reactions at the scene of the birth heightens not only the sense of truthful observation but also the appropriate emotional response. In such a pamphlet, sensation worked to prepare the ground for the moral message. The monster's shocking appearance reinforces the interpretation of the omen. *A Wonder Worth the Reading* focuses clearly on the misuse of the Sabbath and particularly on those who treated sermons and church attendance as if they were sports or theatre. In the spirit of moral reform, the author explicitly attacks dancing and the playing of stool-ball.[59]

Illustrations in broadsides and pamphlets occasionally offered some social context within which to appreciate the consequences of monstrous births. A 1609 pamphlet portraying three monstrous offspring beneath a woodcut of a house ablaze is more typical. The mother of the children had her house destroyed by lightning as a simple equation between monstrous births, sin and divine punishment. However, the 1642 *A Strange and Lamentable accident* has a front cover showing the birth of a 'headless' (acephalic) child. The child is set upon the bed where the mother is attended by three other women. A similar birth-room scene is shown in *The Wonder of Wonders*, whilst *The Lamenting Lady* shows the doorstep encounter of the poor beggar woman with her babies and the Lady who later suffers as a result of her lack of charity. Such pictorial elements were probably incorporated to encourage the illiterate and semi-literate readership in that they offered a brief exposition of the main context of the work.[60] It is only with the 1642 pamphlet that a social context is established. However crudely, the child was thus humanised. A reader can establish a sense of the horror facing the mother and the attending gossips from giving birth to a severely deformed child. Because the body of the child is drawn to scale, it is the circumstances which become monstrous. The majority of monster illustrations treated the child as a mere spectacle or relic.[61]

An overview of sixteenth and seventeenth-century English popular works on monstrous births supports the Mitchell and Snyder thesis that the physically different are treated as cultural symbols for other topics. Much as monsters, like other prodigies, were regarded as signs of divine providence, physical difference is generally handled as representational and in so doing its personal and social reality is avoided. In the early modern period the birth of a physically anomalous child was regarded as a sign of impending disaster. For much of the period this took the form of a threatening message from God, a sign of the punishment to follow if reform in personal conduct was not undertaken. From the 1660s the emphasis shifted with the increasing popularity of the role of the maternal imagination as a cause of monstrous births. Thus the monster became a signifier of the mother, of her passions and the circumstances surrounding her pregnancy. The ideology of maternal impressions emphasised discipline and deportment, susceptibility and vulnerability and the danger of women exceeding their natural bounds. The imagination made reproduction and its errors a human concern, as the monstrous child now reflected the maternal environment over the bitter judgement of a wrathful God. In both cases the child operated as the sign of disorder, a symbol of divine or maternal power: the former to be deterred by repentance and reform, the latter by closer scrutiny and control of female desire. The symbolic importance of the physically different body was uppermost, though there were examples (as with different physical forms of conjoining) where the body could itself resist and define the nature of the representation particularly where the symbolic meaning relied on specific physiological details. Above all, the monstrous body served as a site of horror and fascination, a passive spectacle of difference.

Notes

1 J. B., *Philocophus, or, The deafe and dumbe mans friend exhibiting the philosophicall verity of that subtile art*, London: Humphrey Moseley, 1648; J. B., *Anthropometamorphosis, man transform'd, or, The artificial changeling historically presented in the mad and cruel gallantry*, London: J. Hardesty, 1650.

2 Jennifer L. Nelson, 'Bulwer's Speaking Hands: Deafness and Rhetoric', in Sharon L. Snyder, Brenda Jo Brueggemann and Rosemarie Garland-Thomson (eds), *Disability Studies: Enabling the Humanities*, New York: Modern Language Association of America, 2002, p. 221.

3 Mary Baine Campbell, '*Anthropometamorphosis*: John Bulwer's Monsters of Cosmetology and the Science of Culture', in Jeffrey Jerome Cohen (ed.), *Monster Theory: Reading Culture*, Minneapolis: University of Minnesota Press, 1996, p. 205.

4 For deafness see: Kristiaan Dekesel, 'John Bulwer: The Founding Father of BSL Research', *Signpost*, Spring 1993, 36–43; Stephen Greenblatt, 'Toward a Universal Language of Motion: Reflections on a Seventeenth-Century Muscle Man', *Literature in North Queensland*, 21:2, Oct., 1994, 56–62; James R. Knowlson, 'The Idea of Gesture as a Universal Language in the XVII and XVIIIth centuries', *Journal of the History of Ideas*, 26:4, Oct.–Dec., 1965, 495–508; Jeffrey Wollock, 'John Bulwer's (1601–1656) Place in the History of the Deaf', *Historiographia Linguistica: International Journal for the History of the Language Sciences/Revue Internationale pour l'Histoire*, 23:1–2, 1996, 1–46. For monstrosity see: William E. Burns, 'The King's Two Monstrous Bodies: John Bulwer and the English Revolution', in Peter G. Platt (ed.), *Wonders, Marvels, and Monsters in Early Modern Culture*, Newark: University of Delaware Press, 1999, pp. 187–202.

5 Graham Richards, 'Bulwer, John (*bap.* 1606, *d.* 1656)', *Oxford Dictionary of National Biography*, Oxford University Press, 2004. Online. Available at: www.oxforddnb.com/view/article/3934 (accessed 4 September 2005).

6 Sharon L. Snyder, Brenda Jo Brueggemann and Rosemarie Garland-Thomson, 'Introduction: Integrating Disability into Teaching and Scholarship', in Snyder, Brueggemann and Garland-Thomson (eds) *Disability Studies*, p. 2; Kevin Stagg, 'The Body', in Garthine Walker (ed.), *Writing Early Modern History*, London: Hodder Arnold, 2005, pp. 206–7.

7 Catherine J. Kudlick, 'Disability History: Why We Need Another "Other"', *American Historical Review*, 108:3, June 2003, 764.

8 On providence see: Alexandra Walsham, *Providence in Early Modern England*, Oxford: Oxford University Press, 2001, ch. 4; William E. Burns, *An Age of Wonders: Prodigies, Politics and Providence in England, 1657–1727*, Manchester: Manchester University Press, 2002; on secularisation: Katharine Park and Lorraine Daston, 'Unnatural Conceptions: The Study of Monsters in Sixteenth- and Seventeenth-Century France and England', *Past and Present* 92 (1981), 20–54; on science and medicine: Zakiya Hanafi, *The Monster in the Machine. Magic, Medicine, and the Marvelous in the Time of the Scientific Revolution*, Durham: Duke University Press, 2000; Nina Lykke and Rosi Braidotti (eds), *Between Monsters, Goddesses, and Cyborgs: Feminist Confrontations with Science, Medicine, and Cyberspace*, London: Zed Books, 1996; on imagination: Marie-Helene Huet, *Monstrous Imagination*, Cambridge, MA: Harvard University Press, 1993; Dennis Todd, *Imagining Monsters: Miscreations of the Self in Eighteenth-century England*, Chicago: University of Chicago Press, 1995; on maternity and reproduction: Clara Pinto-Correia, *The Ovary of Eve. Egg and Sperm and Preformation*, Chicago: University of Chicago Press, 1997; Mary E. Fissell, *Vernacular Bodies. The Politics of Reproduction in Early Modern England*, Oxford: Oxford University Press, 2004; on religion: Timothy K. Beal, *Religion and its Monsters*, New York: Routledge, 2002.

9 Robert Garland, *Eye of the Beholder. Deformity and Disability in the Graeco-Roman World*, London: Duckworth, 1995.

10 David T. Mitchell, 'Narrative Prosthesis and the Materiality of Metaphor', in Snyder, Brueggemann and Garland-Thomson (eds), *Disability Studies*, p. 15.

11 Ibid., p. 25. These ideas are developed further in David T. Mitchell and Sharon L. Snyder, *Narrative Prosthesis: Disability and the Dependencies of Discourse*, Ann Arbor: University of Michigan Press, 2000.

12 I. L., *A Most Straunge and True discourse*, London: Richard Jones, 1600, sig. A5. See also, Anon., *A Wonder Worth the Reading*, London: William Jones, 1617, sigs. A2–3, for a similar list.

13 Mitchell, 'Narrative Prosthesis', p. 23.

14 Ambrose Paré, *The Workes of that Famous Chirurgion Ambrose Parey,* London: Thomas Cotes and R. Young, 1634, pp. 869–84 (23rd Book); 961–1026 (25th Book). See pp. 992–7 for treatment of beggars.

15 William Turner, *A Compleat History of the Most Remarkable Providences*, London: John Dunton, 1697, Part 3, Ch. 2, p. 2 [p. 324].

16 Ibid., Part 3, Ch. 2, p. 6 [p. 326].

17 Anon., *Deeds against Nature, and monsters by kinde*, London: E. Winter, 1614, sig. A2r.

18 Ibid., sig. A3v.

19 Anon., *A New Ballad, intituled, the stout Criple of Cornwall*, London: Thomas Symcock, 1629.

20 See Paul Semonin, 'Monsters in the Marketplace: The Exhibition of Human Oddities in Early Modern England', in Rosemarie Garland-Thomson (ed.), *Freakery: Cultural Spectacles of the Extraordinary Body*, New York: New York University Press, 1996, pp. 69–81.

21 Cornelius Pet, *An Example of Gods judgement shew[n] upon two children*, London: William Bartlett, 1582; Sampson Jones, *Vox Infantis or The Propheticall Child,* London: S.N., 1649.

22 Anon., *Strange and Wonderful News from Bull-and-Mouth Street*, London: D.M., 1678.
23 Anon., *A Myraculous, and monstrous, but yet most true, and certayne discourse, of a woman*, London: Edward White, 1588; Anon., *A Brief Narrative of a Strange and Wonderful Old Woman that hath a Pair of Horns*, London: T.J., 1676.
24 Erle Leichty, *The Omen Series Summa Izbu*, New York: J. J. Augustin, 1968, pp. 2–3.
25 William Fulwood, *The shape of ii monsters*, London: Thomas Colwell, 1562; Anon., *The True Reporte of the forme and shape of a monstrous childe*, London: Thomas Marsh, 1562; Anon., *Natures wonder? Or, [An ac]count how the wife of one John Waterman an ostler … was delivered of a strange monster*, London: E. Andrews, 1664; Anon., *The True Description of two monsterous children*, London: Owen Rogers, 1566; Anon., *The Forme and Shape of a Monstrous Child*, London: John Awdelay, 1568.
26 Anon., *The Forme and Shape of a Monstrous child, borne at Maydstone in Kent, the .xxiiij. of October*, London: John Awdelay, 1568; Anon., *The True Reporte of the Forme and Shape of a Monstrous Childe, borne at Muche Horkesleye*, London: Thomas Marsh, 1562; Anon, *A Declaration, of a Strange and Wonderfull Monster*, London: Jane Coe, 1646; Anon., *Mirabilis annus secundus, or, The second year of prodigies*, London: S.N. 1662, pp. 49, 61.
27 John Mellys, *The True Description of Two Monsterous Children*, London: William Lewes, 1566.
28 Andrew Clark (ed.), *The Shirburn Ballads 1585–1616*, Oxford: Clarendon Press, 1907, pp. 295–6.
29 I. R., *A Most Straunge and True Discourse*, London: Richard Jones, 1600, pp. 9, 11.
30 Anon., *A Strange and Miraculous Accident*, London: J. Wolfe, 1599, sig. A4r.
31 John Brooke, *Of Two Wonderful popish monsters*, London: Thomas East, 1579; Mark Thornton Burnett, *Constructing 'Monsters' in Shakespearean Drama and Early Modern Culture*, Basingstoke: Palgrave Macmillan, 2002, p. 31.
32 *True Reporte of the Forme and Shape of a Monstrous Childe* (1562).
33 John Barker, *The True Description of a Monsterous Chylde*, London: William Griffith, 1564.
34 *The Forme and Shape of a Monstrous Child* (1568).
35 Anon., *The True Description of two Monsterous children borne at Herne in Kent*, London: Thomas Colwell for Owen Rogers, 1565.
36 John Vicars, *Prodigies and Apparitions, or, Englands warning piece*, London: Tho. Bates and Ralphe Markland, 1643, pp. 20–3.
37 Thomas Bedford, *A True and Certaine relation of a strange-birth*, Plymouth: William Russell, 1635, p. 20.
38 See Jan Bondeson, *The Two-Headed Boy and Other Medical Marvels*, Ithaca and London: Cornell University Press, 2000, p. 84. The tale is discussed at length pp. 64–94.
39 Rosemarie Garland-Thomson, *Extraordinary Bodies: Figuring Physical Disability in American Culture and Literature*, New York: Columbia University Press, 1997, p. 11.
40 Thomas Lodge, *The Famous, True and Historicall life of Robert second Duke of Normandy*. London: Nicholas Ling and Iohn Busbie, 1591; Anon., *A Myraculous, and monstrous, but yet most true, and certayne discourse, of a woman* (1588); Anon., *A Certain relation of the hog-faced gentlewoman*, London: F. Grove, 1640; Anon., *The Ranters monster: being a true relation of one Mary Adams* London: George Horton, 1652; Anon., *O Rara show, a rara shight! a strange monster*, London: R. Janeway, 1689.
41 Lodge, *Famous, True and Historical Life*, pp. 4–5.
42 Anon., *The Life and Death of Mother Shipton*, London: B. Harris, 1677, p. 10.
43 William Shakespeare, *Richard III*, Harmondsworth: Penguin, 1988, p. 41 (Act 1, Sc.2, l.57); James Gairdner, *History of the Life and Reign of Richard III*, Cambridge: Cambridge University Press, 1898, p. 3.

44 *The Complete Works of St. Thomas More*, (ed.) Richard S. Sylvester, 2 vols., London: Yale University Press, 1963, I, 7.

45 Christina Hole, 'Notes on Some Folk Survivals in English Domestic Life', *Folklore*, 68:3, (1952), 411–19, at p. 413; Alison Hanham, *Richard III and His Early Historians 1483–1535*, Oxford: Clarendon Press, 1975, pp. 165 n.3, 191.

46 Thomas Gainsford, *The True and Wonderfull history of Perkin Warbeck, proclaiming himselfe Richard the fourth*, London: Nathaniel Butter, 1618, p. 2.

47 Walsham, *Providence*, p. 220.

48 John Vicars, *A Looking-Glasse for Malignants*, London: John Rothwell, 1643, sigs A2r, B1v.

49 Ed. Gresham, *Strange fearful & true news*, London: G. Vincent and W. Blackwall, 1606, sig. A3r.

50 Anon., *A Brief Narrative*, London: T.J., 1676, p. 4.

51 Anon., *A Declaration of a Strange and Wonderfull Monster*, London: Jane Coe, 1646, p. 7.

52 Anon., *Strange Newes of a prodigious Monster*, London: S.M., 1613, sig. B2r.

53 Peter Lake, 'Deeds against Nature: Cheap Print, Protestantism and Murder in Early Seventeenth-Century England', in Kevin Sharpe and Peter Lake (eds), *Culture and Politics in Early Stuart England*, Basingstoke: Macmillan, 1994, pp. 257–83 at p. 259.

54 Ibid., p. 262.

55 Anon., *Mirabilis Annus Secundus*, London: S.N., 1661, p. 43.

56 Anon., *The Ranters Monster*, London: George Horton, 1652, p. 3.

57 *A Wonder Worth the Reading* (1617), sig. A3r-A4v.

58 Ibid., sig. A4v.

59 Ibid., sig. Br.

60 Anon., *A true relation of the birth of three monsters in the city of Namen in Flanders*, London: Richard Bonion, 1609; John Locke, *A strange and lamentable accident that happened lately at Mears-Ashby*, London: Richard Harper and Thomas Wine, 1642; Hyder Edward Rollins, *The Pack of Autolycus*, Cambridge, Mass.: Harvard University Press, 1927, p. 187; W. G. Day (ed.), *The Pepys Ballads, Vol.1*, Cambridge: D. S. Brewer, 1987, p. 44.

61 Philip M. Soergel, 'The afterlives of monstrous infants in Reformation Germany', in Bruce Gordon and Peter Marshall (eds), *The Place of the Dead. Death and Remembrance in late Medieval and Early Modern Europe*, Cambridge: Cambridge University Press, 2000, pp. 288–309 at p. 300.

2 'When a disease it selfe doth Cromwel it'

The rhetoric of smallpox at the Restoration

David E. Shuttleton

By the close of the seventeenth century smallpox had rapidly overtaken bubonic plague, leprosy, and syphilis as the most common pathogenic cause of premature death.[1] Epidemiologists have offered various reasons for an apparent increase in the disease's vigour, ranging from the effects of increased urbanisation and foreign trade to the possible emergence of a more virulent viral strain. Although smallpox had already been responsible for causing the wholesale destruction of non-immune native populations in the Americas, in the British context what had hitherto been largely considered a relatively minor contagious disease of childhood certainly became endemic and occasionally epidemic, posing a major threat to the entire adult population.[2] As detailed below, two royal deaths immediately after the Restoration brought smallpox to the centre of the English cultural stage, prompting fresh debate amongst the medical faculty over the nature of the disease and the best method of treatment.[3] This chapter is primarily concerned with the intensification of moral and political meanings being attached to this characteristically sudden, disfiguring disease at this particular historical juncture. As this implies, my focus is primarily upon discourse, in that I examine related rhetorical constructions of the disease across a range of generically diverse texts – elegiac public poems, private memoirs and a medical treatise – to consider how contemporary conceptions of the disease were framed within prevailing cultural assumptions to serve specific, politicised interests.[4]

In the only sustained discussion of the rhetoric of smallpox in seventeenth-century imaginative literature Raymond A. Anselment distinguishes between the cultural meanings commonly attributed to smallpox and those attached to other early-modern diseases. While elegists in particular drew attention to smallpox's 'double cruelty' in disfiguring as well as killing its victims and talked of its fierceness, foulness, and envious nature yet, Anselment argues, theirs 'is not the metaphoric meaning Susan Sontag finds in dreaded disease; they did not fashion figurative embodiments of evil in which the ills of society are "projected onto a disease" and "the disease (so enriched with meaning) is projected onto the world" '. In contrast to 'the vision of the plague' presented by early-modern poems, in those addressing smallpox Anselment finds that it 'seems no divine punishment for some unspecified sin or national transgression'.[5] He is no doubt broadly correct to suggest that smallpox did not accumulate the *same* moral and political meanings that Margaret Healy, another literary scholar, has since shown were typically projected onto plague-ridden or syphilitic bodies in imaginative and political writings of the sixteenth and seventeenth centuries.[6] But in what follows I do challenge Anselment's somewhat over-sweeping assertion that smallpox was significantly less vulnerable to being loaded with punitive social meanings than syphilis, the bubonic plague and leprosy or indeed, if we look forward to the nineteenth century, tuberculosis or cancer as described by Sontag herself in her groundbreaking study *Illness as Metaphor* to which Anselment himself refers.

When writing *Illness as Metaphor* in the 1970s Sontag's sincere, compassionate desire had been to demystify disease from what she presented as the oppressive clutches of metaphor: 'I want to describe, not what it is really like to emigrate to the kingdom of the ill and live there, but the punitive or sentimental fantasises concocted about that situation'. Her subject she declared was not 'real geography' but stereotypes of national character', nor 'physical illness itself but the uses of illness as figure or metaphor'. Sontag was to insist that 'the most truthful way of regarding illness – and the healthiest way of being ill – is one most purified of, most resistant to, metaphoric thinking'.[7]

Since these declarations were first made, several commentators have argued that Sontag's project of liberation might have been be misguided or even futile. For example, the medical sociologist Howard Brody in his important study *Stories of Sickness* championing the patient's perspective on their own disease, urges us not to 'dismiss the importance of metaphor as a way that real people grapple with the experience of sickness'.[8] While assenting to Sontag's warning that nothing 'is more punitive than to give disease a meaning – that meaning being invariably a moralistic one', Brody nevertheless observes that 'it is precisely by giving meaning to illness that one succeeds in alleviating suffering'.[9]

Echoing Brody, but with a more specific concern for the particular tasks faced by cultural historians of disease, Roy Porter and G. S. Rousseau assert in the conclusion to their study *Gout: the Patrician Malady* that 'the witness of history weighs heavily against' Sontag's position that 'disease should be a scientific category not a cultural and moral sign or stigma'. They observe that 'people and cultures have always given a meaning to disease' in part 'because disease categories have helped to articulate the experience of the body itself, and hence the project of the individual person'. As such it is perhaps inevitable that 'over the long haul' there is valuable human 'meaning to the metaphors, images, and representations of disease'.[10] While readily upholding Porter and Rousseau's suggestion that Sontag's stance was 'perhaps guilty of swallowing the propaganda of scientism', it would emphasise that in accepting that the representation of disease cannot be drained of metaphorical meanings, we should not succumb to a solipsistic post-structuralism which, by reducing disease down to mere trope, runs the risk of grossly insulting our ancestors by seeming to deny the felt reality of their embodied sufferings. What surely matters, as Porter and Rousseau emphasise, is to ask in whose hands 'the power over the semiotics of sickness lies'.[11]

In what follows I read across the poetic and medical literature of smallpox generated at the Restoration to suggest that neither is any the less laced with metaphor, nor marked by evidence of political interest. In particular I focus upon royalist voices, because it was the sudden deaths from smallpox of the restored king's younger brother and sister within months of their respective returns from exile that alerted the nation to the changed nature of what had hitherto traditionally been discussed as a relatively minor disease of childhood barely distinguishable from measles.

The first of these royal deaths was that of Charles II's younger brother, Henry, Duke of Gloucester at the age of 21 in September 1660, a mere four months after he had accompanied the king out of exile to attended the May coronation.[12] In so far as the succumbing of the royal prince to smallpox suggested Stuart weakness rather than a sign of newly restored strength, pro-monarchist poets were immediately faced with the task of papering-over a faultline smallpox appeared to have opened up in their own ideology of royal infalibility; not least in the light of Stuart claims for the monarch's own quasi-divine power to heal disease. This challenge was in part to be negotiated through appeals for pity for those who have suffered the ravages of civil war and protracted exile and partly through a related stigmatising medico-religious discourse which attributed the sudden somatic eruption of smallpox to a corrupt 'air' of ingratitude and sin on the part of a nation still contaminated with the spirit of rebellion.

Some of these strategies of deflected, stigmatising blame can be seen in the elegiac tribute to the Duke of Gloucester by the Royalist poet Katherine Philips. Typically Philips contrives to justify the prince's death in terms of an act of divine retribution designed to teach a sinful, ungrateful post-Restoration nation a lesson in humility:

> Great Gloucester's dead, and yet in this we must
> Confesse that angry heaven is wise and just.
> We have so long and yet so ill endur'd
> The Woes which our offences had procur'd,
> That this new shock would all our strength destroy,
> Had we not knowne an interval of joy.
> And yet perhaps this stroke had been excus'd
> If we this interval had not abus'd.
> But our ingratitude and discontent
> Deserv'd to know our mercies are but lent;
> And those complaints heaven in this rigid fate
> Doth first chastise and then legitimate.
> By this it our divisions doth reprove,
> And makes us joine in griefe, if not in love.[13]

With an implicit reminder of the fate of the disobedient Israelites, Philips exploits the notion that the threat of disease is ultimately under the control of an all-wise creator to insist that Gloucester's death stands as a providential lesson to his erring subjects who have not shown enough gratitude for the blessings bestowed upon them through the Stuart restoration. Philips maintains that grief over this royal death will bring about a national unity that his erring, ungrateful subjects failed to achieve when he was alive.

Similar sentiments were to be expressed by Martin Lluelyn in his 'Elegie on the Death of the Most Illustrious Prince, Duke of Glocester [sic]' (1660), but in this instance the role of elegist is complicated by that fact that Lluelyn (1616–1682), a pro-Royalist Oxford wit and army captain who had been obliged to join Charles I in exile, was himself one of the court physicians who had actually administered to Prince Henry.[14] Lluelyn published his poetic tribute in the face of court rumours, as recorded by Pepys, that Prince Henry had died 'by the great negligence of the doctors'.[15] Lluelyn's lines 'All shipwrecks horrid are; but yet none more,/Then that, which for its witnesse takes the shore', probably alludes to the widely known fact that at one stage in his illness Henry seemed to rally and had been declared out of danger by his physicians only to begin haemorrhaging and die on the tenth day after onset.[16] Seen in context, Lluelyn's entire elegy can be read as an attempt to counter any charges of personal incompetence on the part of the poet in his role as a royal physician. In so doing Lluelyn's elegy resembles that of Philips in placing moral blame for Henry's disease at the feet of his unworthy subjects.

Lluelyn's tributary verses open with the poet-physician anticipating the public scenes of mourning at Gloucester's state funeral and assuming the grief-stricken voice of a loyal populace who, like 'Indians wise that die with those they love' (a reference to the custom of suttee) 'would beg Tenement in your Tombe' by seeking to throw themselves into the grave of a prince who had been buried 'first in Exile' then 'in Dust'. It is a scene of national atonement: 'And no lesse penance can these Nations shrive,/Which make Thee dead so long, while yet alive'.[17] Lluelyn points up the irony that Gloucester – who managed to survive the rebellion, the assassination of his father and a cruel exile – returns to England only to die:

> Affronts, plots, scandals, false friends, cold Allyes,
> Exiles, wants, tempests, battails, rebels, spies,
> Restraints, temptations, strange aires: in all these
> Was there no Feaver, no maligne Disease?
> The Royal Line (England this brand must weare.)
> Suffer abroad, but perish only here.
> So to the sun the Phoenix doth repair,
> Through each distemper'd region of the Aire.
> Through swarms of Deaths, she there victorious flies,
> But in her cruel Nest she burnes, and dies.[18]

Pursuing these poetic tropes of restoration and betrayal Lluleyn observes how 'Twas savage beyond fate; for others lie,/Dead off Disease, you of Recovery'.

Arguing that young Gloucester's death was a well-earned release from an unbearable burden of exile, he suggests that smallpox has completed what the cowardly Oliver Cromwell had only contemplated:

> Thy sufferings Inventary rose so high,
> There scarce was other left Thee, but to die.
> And this was that in all his rage and storme,
> Though Cromwel wisht, he trembled to performe.
> When pawzing here after Thy slaughter'd Sire,
> He seem'd to fear this was to murder High'r.
> And bathing his black soule ith' sacred flood,
> He durst gorge Royal, but not tender blood.
> Where then shall Innocence in safety sit?
> When a disease it selfe doth Cromwel it.[19]

Lluelyn shifts the blame for the Henry's death onto his political enemies through the metaphorical implication that the prince was double-crossed by a treacherous disease which, working as Cromwell's posthumous agent of assassination was able to achieve what even the usurper and regicide himself never dared. If Gloucester had died back in the dark days of the commonwealth when life itself was 'lesse lovely' than death and when 'the kind graves did but receive our Care,/And the survivers only wretched were', then, so Lluleyn argues, 'Our greedy Interests might tempted be,/To call Thy vertues back, but hardly Thee'. But for him to die now at the time of restoration when 'Vines drop wine from every trunk,/To chear their owners, not make Rapine drunk', when sequestered goods have been returned, when 'Crimes make persons guilty, and not Lands', when the houses of cavalier widows are not occupied by hungry troops, when the spoiling of churches 'is sacriledge, not zeale', and when his 'just Brothers equal Government' has brought peace and order, it is as if the prince's very senses had been 'satiated' by 'so rich an odour'. In other words, Henry was simply overcome by sheer joy at his brother's restoration.

Such pro-Stuart rhetoric needs to be read in the context of other, critical and oppositional voices, summarised by the retrospective comments of the Whig memoirist Bishop Gilbert Burnet when he observed of the death of Prince Henry, that 'the mirth and entertainments of that time raised his blood so high, that he took the small-pox; of which he died.'[20] In contrast to Lluelyn's poetic diagnosis rooted in a lingering atmosphere of rebellion, Burnet attributes Henry's succumbing to smallpox to a sanguine plethora brought on by his over-indulgence in the luxurious excesses of the Stuart court.[21]

Viewed in retrospect the death of Prince Henry had profound dynastic and political consequences. Had he survived as an acceptable Protestant heir to Charles II, then the Exclusion Crisis and other sectarian plots which marked the reign of the Catholic James VII (II) and culminated in the Revolution of 1688–1689, might have never occurred. Certainly the politically loaded temptation to suggest a moralistic association between smallpox and Stuart luxury was strengthened when Princess Mary of Orange also died of smallpox on Christmas Day 1660, a mere three months after she had first landed from the Hague to join the English Court.[22] Princess Mary, daughter of Charles I, had already been deeply affected by smallpox when, back in 1650, it had killed her husband William II of Orange at the age of 24. As evident in their poetic eulogies, for loyal monarchists Mary's death served to intensify their own sense that small-pox was a belated, rebellious assault upon the House of Stuart and as such a sign of national sin. Henry Bold, for example, in his verses 'On the Death of Mary Princess Dowager of Aurange' (1664), refers back to the loss of Gloucester to ask rhetorically if 'more Royal Blood be Spilt/To make atonement for the Sub-jects Guilt?/Thus the Lamb suffers, while the Fox still thrives,/Heaven's King-dome's near! 'tis time t'amend our lives'.[23] While in Thomas Shipman's 'Beauty's Enemy, Upon the Death of M. Princess of Orange, by the Small pox, 1660', in an overt allusion to the compulsory appropriation of Royalist property during the Interregnum, the disfiguring action of smallpox are equated with the criminal activities of Parliamentarians who acted out of mere 'spite' as 'Seques-trators, on the Eminent'.[24]

In making such analogies Cavalier poets were able to draw upon a pre-Restoration elegiac tradition in which the disfiguring power of smallpox had already been compared to the insults of Parliamentarian usurpers and regicides.[25] A notable example was the memorial volume *Lachrymae Musarum: The Tears of the Muses ... .upon the Death of the most hopefull, Henry Lord Hastings* (1649), dedicated to Henry, Lord Hastings, the last and only surviving son of the Sixth Earl of Huntingdon when he died of smallpox at the age of 19 on 24 June 1649. Though largely known for containing John Dryden's first printed poem, 'Upon the Death of Lord Hastings', the volume as a whole has been read as a coded production in which Royalist grief over the regicide of Charles I is being partially displaced onto Hastings.[26] In so doing, the poets sought to employ typically contrived literary conceits designed to make forced poetic comparisons between pock-marks and flowers or 'constellations' of jewels or stars to rescue the disfigured body of their beautiful schoolfriend from the insult of defilement (prompting Samuel Johnson in his 'Life of Dryden', to later remark somewhat glibly how 'Lord Hastings died of smallpox; and his poet has made of his pustules first rose-buds, and then gems; at last exalts them into stars.').[27]

The subsequent loss of two of the restored king's siblings to such a gruesome disease prompted a continuation of this tradition as loyal poets charged smallpox with being an affront to the beautiful body of English aristocratic manhood. Thus in 1664, Katherine Philips opens her verses 'On the Death of my Lord Rich, Only Son to the Earle of Warwick who dy'd of the Small Pox' (1664), by asking:

> Have not so many precious lives of late
> Suffis'd to encrease the mournfull purple Flood,
> As well as Noble, she drank the Royal Blood;

That not content against us to engage
Our own wild fury, and Usurpers rage;
By Sickness now, when all that Storm is past,
She strives to hew our hero's down as fast.[28]

Philips's angry charge that smallpox is an agent working for the enemies of the Stuarts takes on added poignancy when it is noted that she herself was to die of smallpox within a few weeks of publishing this poem. While Abraham Cowley's famous elegy on Phillip's own death set a precedent for several generations of poets wishing to defend the chasteness of female poets, an increasingly femi-nised trope of smallpox as 'Beauty's Enemy' – to quote the title of Shipman's elegy to Princess Mary – was already established by the 1660s. In a formulation typical of poems on female disfigurement, Shipman suggests that the disease only blemished Mary's body, not the eternal soul:

This fatal Mask, that thus beclouds her Eyes,
Is no Deformity, but a disguise.
'Tis but an Angel's Veil she now has on;
For veil'd they are, when they approach the Throne.[29]

Shipman's flattering equation between earthly and heavenly courts requires no further explanation, but it should be noted that his choice of metaphor reflects the early-modern social ritual of smallpox victims, including members of the Stuart court, donning masks in public. Ben Jonson, for example, told William Drummond of Hawthornden that Sir Philip Sidney's mother 'after she had ye litle pox never shew her self in Court yrafter bot Masked'.[30]

The pro-Royalist elegiac tradition is enough to illustrate the extent to which smallpox was far from being resistant to moralising metaphors and politicised rhetorical appropriation, but contemporary medical tracts on smallpox could be no less polemical. Tobias Whitaker's 1661 treatise *An Elenchus of Opinions Concerning the Cure of the Small Pox Together with Problematicall Questions Concerning the Cure of the French Pest*, is particularly notable as evidence of how medical theory was politically inflected.[31] As the title-page declares, Whitaker, who had earlier found notoriety with a treatise promoting wine as an elixir of long-life, had been made 'physician in ordinary to his majesty and House-hold' at the time of the Restoration (an office he had first been offered by the exiled monarch in 1649).[32] Publication of *An Elenchus* was specifically prompted by the death of Prince Henry which, as other contempor-ary medical tracts reveal, had brought ignominy on the medical profession.[33] Royalist assumptions linking the control of the body personal with the right gov-ernance of the body politic are active at several levels in Whitaker's treatise, but for the sake of discussion we can distinguish three distinct elements in his bla-tantly propagandistic framing of the disease; after considering Whitaker's strat-egies of self-fashioning in presenting himself as patriotic physician, I shall examine the ideological implications behind his preferred theoretical model of smallpox before finally examining the broader professional political climate shaping his markedly nationalistic arguments in favour of a particular curative regimen.

In a prefatory 'Epistle to the Reader' Whitaker discusses his responsibilities as a physician towards achieving the management of smallpox by patriotically offering his account of the disease as a 'studious' attempt to 'salute my Nation with an acceptable present'. Signing himself as 'faithful friend and country-man', Whitaker intimately aligns himself and his medical endeavours with the fate of Charles II: 'It is not as yet a complete year since my Landing with His Majesty in England, and in this short time have observed as strange a difference in this subject of my present discourse, as in the variety of opinions and disposi-tions of this Nation, with whom I have discoursed'.[34] As part of his patriotic pos-turing Whitaker emphasises his own heroic self-sacrifice, having 'snatcht many houres from my sleep and other employments' and being 'in daily Expectation of the infirmities of Old Age' to produce his account: 'I do put my self upon action for the generall [sic] good of my Country so long as I have time amongst the Living, till I shall passe away and be seen no more. It is well known I have been buryed in Exile from my own Country the major part of three Lives, and by the same providence am raised and restored again'.[35] With typical immodesty, in identifying with the fate of his king, Whitaker invokes a quasi-messianic image of his own resurrection from the grave of political exile and assured by his reli-gious convictions that 'I must enter into the terrestrial womb of my Mother before this Corruption shall put on Incorruption', he offers his short testamen-tary tract as 'my Will'.[36] In particular he presents his role as physician in terms of the need to exert control over potentially unruly bodies, claiming that 'out of my own experience and quotidian practise, I have...presented this short direc-tion of Government in this disease'.[37] Whitaker's usage of such analogies implies more than just a figurative link between disease as evidence of both per-sonal somatic imbalance and national or political disruption: from the outset, when he attributes the increased virulence of smallpox to something in the 'present constitution of the ayre' his pointed choice of language suggests that he equates this apparent physical alteration with the changed sociopolitical climate of the nation to which he has recently returned from enforced exile. Whitaker's use of these politicised needs to be read in the context of contemporary pre-viral theories of the nature of smallpox.

Seventeenth-century popular opinion, supported by traditional medical theory recognised that smallpox was a communicable infection, though neither had any knowledge of the *variola* virus nor the actual mechanics of infection. Whether or not it killed its victims, smallpox had such a visible, disfiguring impact upon the body of the sufferer that it was perhaps inevitable that in a Christian culture such gruesome symptoms invited interpretation as evidence of the innate corrup-tion of Man's fallen nature. As many elegists complained, the pock-ridden, oozing, bloated body of the smallpox victim suggested a horrid anticipation of the putrefaction of the grave. Lluelyn typically reflects on how:

Most feavers Limbecks though with these they burn,
They leave the featur'd carcasse to the Urne,
But thine was borne of that offensive race,
Arm'd to destroy, she first strove to deface.[38]

And mourning the Princess of Orange, Shipman writes of a disease whose effects are 'So loathsome ... the Soul would hardly, own/The Body, at the Resurrection!'.[39] Partly as a reflection of such instinctive reactions and in part as a way of explaining why not all persons caught smallpox in a particular family or infected area, contemporary medical opinion tended to cover all possible contingencies by positing both external and internal notions of how the disease originates; effectively holding to both of the two distinct, historical concepts of epidemic disease usefully labelled by medical historian Charles Rosenberg as respectively the 'configuration' and 'contamination' models.[40]

Early-modern contamination models of smallpox posited that it was communicated either through direct contact with victims, their foul bedding or clothing, or by breathing in the particle-filled infected air of sick chambers.[41] Infectious particles theory was often aligned with more general conceptions of contagious environmental conditions such as those Whitaker, amongst many, terms 'pestilential constitutions' of the air (sometimes called 'miasmas'), which might infect a particular geographical district as result of local climactic or terrestrial conditions. In contrast, an internal configuration model posited that smallpox represents the eruption of a dormant so-called *seminaria* or *seed* that is originally implanted in the victim's blood as a corrupt residue of the stagnated menstrual blood of the mother during gestation. The disease was subsequently triggered by certain external, environmental conditions such as bad air, but also by fear, particularly at the sight of another smallpox victim at the height of their disfigurement. Evidence for the wearing of masks by seventeenth-century smallpox victims, including members of the Stuart court, should therefore not be read as a merely a matter of vanity or good manners, but rather as a medically theorised prophylactic measure designed to avoid spreading the disease by causing fright. Pregnant women in particular were considered particularly vulnerable, with the added risk of them imprinting of smallpox onto the unborn child through the sheer force of their disturbed imaginations. These closely linked ideas have common roots in an ancient discourse linking the purportedly aberrant, unregulated feminine body with monstrousness that can be traced back at least as far as Aristotle.[42] As I have discussed more fully elsewhere, the popular belief that smallpox could be triggered by fear, and the dependent medical theory of smallpox as an innate seed continued to fill an explanatory conceptual gap with respect to the observable phenomena long after the introduction of inoculation in the 1720s.[43]

Returning to Whitaker's *Elenchus*, we find him asserting that although he does not know 'from what present constitution of the ayre this childish disease hath received such Pestilential Tinctures' yet since 'the Small Pox, was Antiently and generally in the common place of *Petit* and *Puerile* diseases, and the Cure of no moment', then he is sure that a disease that easily treated for hundreds of years before medical practice was 'so Exquisite' cannot be incurable 'in this age'.[44] In a survey of established authorities he does cite the maternal seed mode, but he has little time for what, in a telling neologism, betraying the common etymological roots of both 'menses' and 'monstrous', he calls the theory of 'menstruosity'.[45] And while he attributes the actual eruptive symptoms of smallpox to 'the corrupt disposition of the humorable masse internal', Whitaker asserts that it is clearly caused 'by the malignity of the air, conjunct with vitious humours':

> because the Vehicle of universal infection is the ambient air, which apprehendeth suddenly all matters subject and disposed to receive contagion. Moreover, when the Small Pox are universally spreading, they frequently usher in the grand Pest, upon a stronger infection of the air: and that it is a malignity especially of the air, hath been frequently proved by the creatures of the air, which have fallen dead to the earth, and killed by the poyson of the air. Again if this disease were conveyed in the principles of Nature, from maternal bloud, which is administred to the production of all animals, then there were an universal reception of this disease, not onely in humane nature, but also in all animals whose production is *ex semine & sanguine*. But this disease is apprehended by no subject matter indisposed to receive the impression of such venemosity, as is of this nature; nor is all mankind capable of such reception.[46]

Whitaker was not alone amongst contemporary physicians in rejecting the notion of maternal seeds, but it is surely telling that a physician-in-ordinary to the Stuarts should favour an external contamination model of smallpox infection over traditional theories which rooted the disease in inherited corruption. Whitaker's ideological motives in preferring environmental causes become fully transparent in the ensuing passage where we observe that in discussing contagion: 'The contagion that infected rebellious Spirits, is known to come, and be received from the malicious breath of some venene [i.e. poisonous] Natures; and hath been permanent for many yeares, and conveyed to severall parts of this region (not extinct at this day)'.[47] Read in the wider context of Whitaker's rhetorical strategy, the phrase 'malicious breath' clearly works as a metonym for the rebellious speech of anti-Royalist political usurpers.

For Whitaker smallpox is symptomatic of the polluted climate to which the Stuart court has returned; a lingering enemy that could be routed by a well-armed, loyal physician like himself. That physician's role is to shield against both internal and external assault: the 'various Affects which besiege the body of man, and are continually storming or laying battery to it; such as Luxury and intemperance in dyet and exercise; also the distemper of the ayre and popular infection, with many other causes, some Celestial influence without us, others from various firmentations [*sic*] within us'.[48] As Brody has observed, militaristic metaphors are a commonplace of the rhetoric of illness and disease in any age, but Whitaker's account of how to manage the smallpox is particularly replete with such tropes.[49] For example, he compares the work of a physician treating smallpox to that of an army commander who should avoid any sort of interference that might disrupt or impede what contemporary physicians widely recognised as a natural physiological process of eruption, fever crisis and expulsion:

> Nature hath at this time set her self in a Batalia posture, to encounter the enemy *vi & armis;* and if upon the charge it shall make discovery of assistance, it will retard the present encounter, which addeth courage to the enemy, and giveth him greater choice of ground, but if any of these auxiliaries should put Nature into disorder by conjunction with it, the enemy will not neglect the opportunity of conquest; and on this argument a Simile may be not a perfect demonstration, because diseases are as mutineers against natural government; & Nature, when it is it self and without disturbance, will give no entertainment to a resisting, rebellious and heterogeneall quality, to incorporate it self into the most noble parts; but upon disorder and disturbance than false appetites break in, and open the gates to all heterogeality, to the ruine of the whole government; therefore when Nature is harmoniously set, the course is to preserve it so.[50]

In this self-conscious, extended simile Whitaker draws out a blatant analogy between bodily and social disorder in which 'Nature' is equated with a normative balance of power which, by implication, is inherently royalist, while a suddenly eruptive disease like smallpox represents an act of mutiny against such 'natural government'. Given his desire to deflect attention away from possible charges that smallpox is a sign of Stuart luxury, it is perhaps deliberate that Whitaker's 'false appetites' are of themselves the result of 'disorder and disturbance'.

Certainly Whitaker's wider discussion of conflicting medical opinion over the nature of smallpox and the best regimen to adopt in successfully managing the disease was overtly shaped by his political and professional affiliations. At the opening of his account Whitaker insists that smallpox is an organic disease ('that it is a disfiguration is manifest to commonsense'), while denouncing those who consider it a 'disposition praeternatural'.[51] Such fanciful ideas are symptomatic of the parlous state of English intellectual life as it has developed during the Interregnum, for allowing that there 'will never be wanting as many varieties of Opinions, as distinctions in complexions' there has never been 'so many separatists in Arts and Sciences, as in this present age; nor any region so insane and ill-principled at present, as this Region of England hath lately been; our Universities for more than two Ages rather an Amsterdam of Opinators, then the learned schools of well-grounded Philosophers'.[52] By drawing upon the environmental concerns of a Hippocratic tradition which suggested that the healthiest place for the individual to reside was their native terrain, Whitaker presents medical management as fully commensurate with political management, arguing that native English-trained physicians are best able to recommend regimens appropriate to the national environment and temperamental constitution. Small-pox, he argues, is 'in this Land or Nation of English' most safely cured by 'regular Government and little medicine':

> we must not rashly reject the Antient, National and successful Government of our own Nation, ridiculously to perish by the mode of another as much unknown to us, as we to them in Education, Humour, and Intellect; as is manifest a difference in all, as is the originall of colours: and very Nation doth build upon their own basis, and their own observations and experience, both natural and moral, which are the rule of their Government and Commerce with strangers, which rule is natural to them.[53]

Amidst warnings against medical over-reaching, Whitaker's discussion of best practice rapidly develops into a rant regarding the abandonment of religious and medical orthodoxy during the Interregnum and the current reluctance of the English to recognise their native educational and medical superiority:

> I have lived a long time amongst divers Nations ... and (without National indulgence) could not apprehend any excellency unmatchable in England, especially before these latter Rebellious Ages, which was the discouragement of all Artists, and suppression of Arts and Sciences; and in policy formented by all neighburing Nations for the universal advance of their profit, and reputation of their Nation: and by their Industry and our own rebellious spirits, the Gallantry, Honour, Education and Antient renown of our own Country hath been sepulted in oblivion. And now those Sects and Sadduces, that would not entertain faith of a resurrection, are now forced with grief and shame to confesse it, and without doubt shall daily see this corruption to put on incorruption, and our Nation return to their former principles, more purified by this fiery tryall, and to re-erect the Antient Memory and the monuments of all the Antient Professors of Arts, and Sciences so odious to the spawn of this last Age, some of which were then thankfull they had forgot the Lords Prayer; and others that had turned all the Schools of Antient Philosophy into furnaces and luxurious houses for sweating intemperate persons; and these are the off-spring of Phaeton driving on their fiery Chariot, till they have crackt their skulls with their own sublimation of spirits, for ayre rarefied must find vent or force.[54]

Responding in particular to accounts of purported recoveries from smallpox after the adoption of non-traditional Galenist methods of treatment, Whitaker launches into a tirade against those who would abandon 'reasonable axioms which are eternal & of undeniable validity' in favour of 'the phanatick ebulitions of an ill-principled brain'.[55] He challenges all medical innovators to publish the solid ground for their practice 'for the glory of the Nation to wherein they were educated or born' or otherwise 'acquiesce in the Doctrine and practise of the most learned, antient, and modern professors of healing'. In particular they should not, like Van Helmont, 'blaspheme all University and School-educated and methodicall proceedings, contradicting all principles in Doctrine and practise, putting out all light, and leaving the world to grope in darkness'.[56]

Whitaker's professional target was the English followers of the Flemish-born chemist and anti-Galenist medical theorist Joan Baptista Van Helmont (1579–1644), whose works promoting natural magic and chemical cures had been influentially translated into English in 1649 and 1651. His attack forms part of a contemporary controversy in which the Helmontians had challenged the prerogatives of the College of Physicians of which Whitaker was himself a member. As first outlined in two studies by P. M. Ratasani this controversy, with professional roots in a long-established demarcation dispute between the Royal College and the Guild of Apothecaries, had gained a very distinct and politicised momentum under Cromwell when the anti-Aristotelian, mystical medical ideas of Van Helmont (and Paracelsus) had circulated more freely after the lapsing of government control over the press and consequently found favour amongst adherents of the anti-rationalist sectaries.[57] Early in his *Elenchus* Whitaker complains that 'My self hath been so many years dead in exile, that in this my resurrection I neither find the same places nor faces as I left them; as if the restless spirit of that mad Vanhelmont hath set up his rest in the spawn of this late production'.[58] Immediately after the Restoration the Helmontians launched a bid to oust both traditional Galenists and iatro-mechanist corpuscularians from the College of Physicians and the Universities, and even petitioned for their own college. Whitaker's account of the correct means of treating smallpox clearly formed part of this rear-guard action on the part of a newly-restored conservative members of the now 'Royal' College of Physicians and their defence of professional territory against these anti-academic onslaughts of the Helmontians. More broadly, every aspect of his treatise, from his diagnostic emphasis upon contagious 'breath' to his demands for institutional reform is concerned with deflecting attention away from the potential charges of Stuart corruption prompted by the death of Prince Henry, towards the need to bring the unruly bodies of a rebellious nation under good 'Government'.

In conclusion, it has been shown how, at this crucial moment in the recognition of smallpox as newly epidemic, poets and physicians alike – some writers, like Lluelyn, were both – framed the disease to serve their own, predominantly Royalist interests. Although soon to be overshadowed by the Great Plague of 1666, the perceived increase in smallpox immediately after the Restoration was interpreted within the context of recent political rebellion and buttressed by pointedly inflected punitive notions of divine providence and accusations of faltering national faith. But while smallpox was to continue to take its toll on the Stuarts, eventually contributing to their downfall, it is noticeable that even by the time of Queen Mary's death from smallpox in 1694 the rhetoric attached to the disease had markedly changed. Although some of the many elegies mourning Mary's premature passing continued to employ rhetoric equating a royal death with the wages of national sin, there is a much greater shift towards the more direct condemnation of the cruelty of a disease that has disfigured the beautiful face of a pious queen and loyal consort.[59] Indeed throughout the ensuing century it is to be the politics of gender rather than that of dynasties or parties which shapes the dominant representations of smallpox for, as Isobel Grundy has remarked 'eighteenth-century smallpox discourse was gendered: referring to men, it spoke of the danger to life; referring to women, of the danger to beauty'.[60] For young, marriageable upper-class Georgian women being scarred by smallpox was popularly equated with the threat of social death.[61] Although the adoption of the Turkish practice of inoculation ('variolation') amongst English aristocratic circles in the 1720s was surrounded by medical and theological controversy this was rarely, if ever, cast in crudely political terms other than – through a remarkable act of imperialist legerdemain – as evidence of imperial British medical progress. Encouraged by Lady Mary Wortley Montagu's leading part in its introduction and by her celebrity status as a courtier whose own beauty had been marred by the disease, this was invariably couched within a gendered, chivalrous discourse in terms of 'Beauty's Triumph'.[62] As addressed in Suzanne Nunn's chapter of this present volume, it was only when Edward Jenner sought to promote his smallpox vaccine derived from cowpox during the heightened political climate of the 1790s and the reactionary war against Napoleon, that we find smallpox once more accruing such blatantly politicised rhetorical force that it had once done in the months immediately following the 1660 Restoration.

Notes

1 The standard histories are Charles Creighton *A History of Epidemics in Britain*, 2 vols. [1891, 1894] reprinted London: Frank Cass and Co., 1963; C. W. Dixon, *Smallpox*, London: J and A Churchill, 1962; Donald R. Hopkins, *Princes and Peasants, Smallpox in History*, Chicago and London: University of Chicago Press, 1983 [reprinted as *The Greatest Killer: Smallpox in History*, 2002], and J. R. Smith, *The Speckled Monster: Smallpox in England, 1670–1970, with particular reference to Essex,* Chelmsford: Essex Record Office, 1987.
2   For colonialist contexts see 'Smallpox in the New World and in the Old: From Holocaust to Eradication, 1518 to 1977', in Sheldon Watts, *Epidemics in History: Disease, Power and Imperialism*, New Haven and London: Yale University Press, 1997, pp. 84–114.
3 Hopkins, *Greatest Killer*, pp. 32–41 and especially Genevieve Miller, *The Adoption of Inoculation for Smallpox in England and France*, Philadelphia: University of Pennsylvania Press, 1957, pp. 26–44.
4   I borrow the concept of 'framing' from 'Framing Disease: Illness, Society and History' in Charles E. Rosenberg, *Explaining Epidemics and Other Studies in the History of Medicine*, Cambridge: Cambridge University Press, 1992, pp. 305–18.
5 Raymond A. Anselment, *The Realms of Apollo: Literature and Healing in Seventeenth-Century England*, Newark and London: University of Delaware and Associated University Presses, 1995, p. 196. Anselment quotes from Susan Sontag, *Illness as Metaphor*, New York: Farrar, Straus and Giroux, 1978, pp. 58, 73.
6 Margaret Healy, *Fictions of Disease in Early Modern England: Bodies, Plague and Politics*, London: Palgrave-Macmillan, 2001.
7 Susan Sontag, *Illness as Metaphor* [1977], *Aids and its Metaphors* [1988], London: Penguin, 1991, p. 3.

8 Howard Brody, *Stories of Sickness*, New York: Oxford University Press, [1987] revised second edition, 2003, p. 82. For Brody to 'give disease a meaning' is not something we can choose to do or not do; we are inevitably involved in the business of attributing meaning to illness whenever we tell stories about sick people or even if we engage merely in medical diagnosis.

9 Ibid. p. 83. Brody allows that cancer and tuberculosis are seen as highly individualistic compared with plague or even syphilis, so they allow for the victim to ask 'Why me?'. By seeming to carefully select their victims TB and cancer encourage a punitive search for a psychological type: 'Metaphors that blame the victim serve only as a primitive, social denial mechanism; they allow us the tenuous luxury of convincing ourselves that we are "different" from the sick person and hence need not worry about falling ill or dying' (Ibid., p. 84).

10 Roy Porter and G. S. Rousseau, *Gout: the Patrician Malady*, New Haven and London: Yale University Press, 1998, p. 285.

11 Ibid.

12 For Prince Henry's death and a chart mapping the many subsequent deaths from the disease amongst members of the House of Stuart see Hopkins, *Greatest Killer*, pp. 37–41.

13 Katherine Philips, 'On the Death of the Duke of Gloucester' in *The Collected Works of Katherine Philips*, Patrick Thomas (ed.), 2 vols, Stump Cross: Stump Cross Books, 1990, I, 76.

14 For details of Lluelyn's career as poet, dramatist and physician see Charles Clay Doyle, 'Lluelyn Martin (1616–1682)' in H. G. C. Matthew and Brian Harrison (eds) *Oxford Dictionary of National Biography*, 60 vols, Oxford: Oxford University Press, 2004), XXXIV, 173–4.

15 As quoted in Bishop Gilbert Burnet, *History of My Own Time*, Osmund Airy (ed.), 2 vols, Oxford: Clarendon Press, 1897, I, 299, footnote.

16 Hopkins, *Greatest Killer*, p. 37.

17 Martin Lluelyn, *Elegy on the Death of the Most Illustrious Prince, Duke of Glocester*, Oxford: Richard Davis, 1660, p. 3.

18 Ibid., pp. 3–4.

19 Ibid., pp. 4–5.

20 Burnet, *History*, I, 299.

21 Physicians and social commentators were to attribute the new ferocity of smallpox with modern luxury well into the Hanoverian period. See Miller, *Adoption*, pp. 30–5.

22 Mary of Orange actually landed three days after her brother Henry's funeral.

23 'On the Death of Mary Princess Dowager of Aurange' in Henry Bold, *Poems Lyrique Macaronique Heroique*, London: Henry Brome [*et al.*], 1664, p. 235.

24 As discussed in Anselment, *Realms*, p. 208.

25 The contributors to *Lachrymae Musarum* were working within an established poetic mode, the 'formal aristocratic elegy' which takes poetic cues from the circumstances of death. Thus Marchmont Needham's contribution talks of how 'envious Pimples too dig graves apace,/To bury all the Glories of his face'. Dryden's own attempt to spin metaphors and similes of the physical symptoms of smallpox – fever, reddened skin and disfiguring pustules – was far more complex, but for many critics, no more artistically successful.

26 For evidence of royalist family loyalties and subtexts see H. T. Swedenberg Jr. 'More Tears for Lord Hastings', *Huntingdon Library Quarterly*, 16, 1952–1953, 43–51; Michael Gearin-Tosh, 'Marvell's "Upon the Death of Lord Hastings" ', *Essays and Studies*, XXXIV, 1981, pp. 105–22; and Ruth Wallerstein, *Studies in Seventeenth-Century Poetic*, Madison: University of Wisconsin Press, 1950, pp. 115–22.

27 As quoted in Anselment, *Realms*, pp. 206–7.

28 *Collected Works of Katherine Philips*, I, 206. Lord Rich died just a few weeks short of his 21st birthday.

29 Thomas Shipman, *Carolina, or Loyal Poems*, London: Samuel Heyrick and William Crook, 1683, pp. 78–9.

30 Ben Jonson, *Discoveries 1641, Conversations with William Drummond of Hawthornden 1619*, facsimile edition, Edinburgh: Edinburgh University Press, 1966, p. 15.

31 Tobias Whitaker, *An Elenchus of Opinions Concerning the Cure of the Small Pox Together with Problematicall Questions Concerning the Cure of the French Pest*, London: Nath. Brook, 1661, (reprinted 1671). An 'Elenchus' means a refutation, or sophism.

32 Whitaker's *Tree of Humane Life, or the Bloud of the Grape, proving the possibilitie of maintaining Humane Life from Infancy to Extreame Old Age, without any Sicknesse, by the Use of Wine* (1638) was often reprinted and translated.

33 For example, 'Mr N.N.', the respondent cited by the anonymous author of *Hactenus Inaudita: or, Animadversions Upon the new found way of Curing the Small Pox*, London: John Martin and James Allestry, 1663, remarks that he knows ' not by what fate, Physitians of late have more lost their credit in these diseases then ever: witness the severe judgement of the world in the cases of the Duke of *Gloucester* and the *Princess Royal*; so that now they stick not to say, with your *Agrippa*, that at least in these a Physitian is more dangerous then the malady'(p. 65).

34 Whitaker, *Elenchus*, [sig. A4, verso–recto].

35 Ibid.

36 Ibid.

37 Ibid., p. 59.

38 Lleulyn, *Elegy*, p. 5.

39 As cited in Anselment, *Realms*, p. 197.

40 Rosenberg, *Explaining Epidemics*, p. 295.

41 Theories are detailed in Miller, *Adoption of Inoculation for Smallpox*, pp. 241–66.

42 See G. S. Rousseau, 'Pineapples, Pregnancy, Pica, and Peregrine Pickle' in G. S. Rousseau and P.-G. Boucé (eds) *Tobias Smollett: Bicentennial Essays Presented to Lewis M. Knapp*, Oxford: Oxford University Press, 1971, pp. 79–109; P.-G. Boucé, 'Imagination, Pregnant Women, and Monsters, in Eighteenth-century England and France', in G. S. Rousseau and R. Porter (eds) *Sexual Underworlds of the Enlightenment*, Manchester: Manchester University Press, 1987, pp. 86–100; and Dennis Todd, *Imagining Monsters: Miscreations of the Self in Eighteenth-Century England*, Chicago and London: University of Chicago Press, 1995.

43 David E. Shuttleton, 'A Culture of Disfigurement; Imagining Smallpox in the Long Eighteenth Century' in George Sebastian Rousseau with Miranda Gill, David Haycock and Mate Herwig (eds) *Framing and Imagining Disease in Cultural History*, London: Palgrave-Macmillan, 2003, pp. 68–80. I also discuss fear in 'Contagion By Conceit: Imagining Smallpox into the Age of Inoculation' in Claire Carlin (ed.) *Imagining Contagion in Early-Modern Christian Culture* (London: Palgrave-Macmillan, 2005).

44 Whitaker, *Elenchus*, [sig. A3 recto].

45 Ibid., pp. 10–11, where Whitaker refutes those 'Physitians that affirm the Small Pox to proceed from maternal menstruosity'.

46 Ibid., pp. 11–12.

47 Ibid., [sig. A2, verso].

48 Ibid., p. 1.

49 Brody, *Stories of Sickness*, p. 90.

50 Whitaker, *Elenchus*, pp. 24–5.

51 Ibid., pp. 4–5.

52 Ibid.

53 Ibid., pp. 65–6.

54 Ibid., pp. 73–4.

55 Ibid., p. 74.

56 Ibid., p. 31.
57 P. M. Rattansi, 'Paracelcus and the Puritan Revolution' and 'The Helmontian-Galenist Controversy in Restoration England' in *Ambix: The Journal of the Society for the Study of Alchemy,* II:1, February 1963, 24–32; and XII:1, February 1964, pp. 1–23.
58 Whitaker, *Elenchus*, p. 4.
59 Anselment, *Realms*, p. 199.
60 I discuss gender and smallpox disfigurement more fully in 'A Culture of Disfigurement', pp. 68–80.
61 See Jill Campbell, 'Lady Mary Wortley Montagu and the "Glass Revers'd" of Female Old Age', in Helen Deutsch and Felicity Nussbaum (eds) *"Defects": Engendering the Modern Body*, Ann Arbor: University of Michigan Press, 2000, pp. 213–51 and Felicity Nussbaum, *The Limits of the Human: Fictions of Anomaly, Race, and Gender in the Long Eighteenth Century*, Cambridge: Cambridge University Press, 2003, pp. 109–32.
62 The key revisionist study is Isobel Grundy, 'Medical Advance and Female Fame: Inoculation and its After-Effects', *Lumen* XIII, 1994, 13–42.

3   Plague spots

Hal Gladfelder

To his enduring shame and disgust, the eighteenth-century writer John Cleland was known during his lifetime for only one of the many books he produced over an authorial career of more than 40 years: the scandalous 1749 *Memoirs of a Woman of Pleasure*, more familiarly known today by the name of its first-person narrator, Fanny Hill. In that work's first edition, Cleland provided his readers with something no other pornographer or novelist of his day had the nerve (or the desire) to write, an explicit and soon-to-be-excised description of sex between men; and in doing so he was taking a considerable risk, as he would have been aware. In 1726, when Cleland, a Londoner, was 16 years old, three men convicted of 'the heinous and detestable Sin of Sodomy' were hanged after a highly publicised series of trials at the Old Bailey.[1] No author, of course, would have been subject to hanging for the mere act of writing about sodomy, but it was very likely this passage that led to Cleland's arrest for obscene libel later in 1749, and the pillorying to which conviction would have led was dangerous enough.[2]

Later in life, Cleland was apparently dogged by rumours of being a sodomite himself, though such rumours may simply be attributable to the scandal of this very scene from the *Memoirs*.[3] If so, the author had reason to wince at the irony, for of all the licentious scenes Fanny takes part in or observes in the course of her narrative, this is the only one for which she reserves the language of criminal denunciation. After she is thwarted in her aim to turn the two young men in to the police – her 'full design to do their deserts instant justice' – she tells her friend and advisor, Mrs Cole, what she has seen, and Mrs Cole fills Fanny in on the true nature of sodomites. 'Whatever effect this infamous passion had in other ages, and other countries', she declares, 'it seem'd a peculiar blessing on our air and climate, that there was a plague-spot visibly imprinted on all that are tainted with it'.[4] Perversity, runs the argument, is written on the body; infamous passion leaves a visible imprint.

The belief that deviance produces a bodily signature, some deformation of the frame or plague spot defacing the skin, appears, at first, atavistic: a throwback to an earlier discourse of (sexual and bodily) monstrosity. The plague spots Mrs Cole points to, seen in this light, are a supernatural or divine visitation, a providential marker of guilt. Yet far from disappearing with the emergence of scientific rationality and the enlightenment, such beliefs continued to figure in both professional and popular medical discourses through the later nineteenth century – and beyond, as responses to the AIDS pandemic have often flagrantly shown.[5] Indeed the prevalence of this discourse of bodily deformity and monstrosity in late nineteenth-century scientific discussions of same-sex sexuality by Richard von Krafft-Ebing and Henry Havelock Ellis (among many others) suggests that the discourse in question was less a throwback than a product of scientific rationalism itself. For references to monstrous or corrupted bodies do not play a significant part in eighteenth-century accounts of sodomy or sodomites; these focus, instead, on criminal acts and public enactments of deviant identity. The broad trajectory of theories of same-sex sexuality from the early eighteenth to the later nineteenth century is from sodomy conceived as a kind of *disability*, an incapacity or failure to perform a sexual role in accordance with prescribed gender norms, to homosexuality or inversion conceived as a clinically identifiable set of physiological and psychological *deformations*, visible stigmata.

I do not mean, in setting out this contrarian claim, to go against the larger argument that deviant or exceptional bodies are differently understood over time, in light of a shift from moralistic to medical modes of explanation and judgement. Instead, I want to foreground some of the paradoxes and tensions within that historical shift, which is also a shift in the locations of discourse. One of the aims of the late nineteenth-century sexologists – laudable in intention if problematic in effect – was to relocate the discussion of same-sex desire from the criminal spaces of courtroom and prison to the scientific spaces of laboratory and consulting room. Instead of moral condemnation and the infliction of suffering – whether pillory or prison or gallows – the new science would provide an etiology, a diagnosis, and, most desirably, a cure. But while scientific accounts were undoubtedly more tolerant, and more sympathetic to the presumed suffering of the sexually afflicted, than the accounts that emerged from eighteenth-century sodomy trials and anti-molly campaigns, the belief that deviance is rooted in an organic disorder meant that the person under scientific examination was organically flawed, congenitally malformed. The study of such persons thus became a branch of teratology, the science of monsters.

No eighteenth-century text, except for Cleland's, manifests a comparable interest in the sodomite's body. In no other text is the male transgressor examined for visible signs of inward or congenital perversity. As the work of Valerie Traub and others has made clear, the situation was quite different in cases of what I will here, anachronistically, call lesbian transgression: the early modern tribade was, like the nineteenth-century invert, above all an organic anomaly, and a figure of fascination precisely because of her anatomical superfluity. I want to return later to the reasons for this difference in the uses to which female and male bodies were put in eighteenth-century accounts of same-sex desire; for the purposes of this introduction it's sufficient to note that Cleland actually took up this issue in his own writing, looking for signs of monstrosity in tribade and sodomite alike, and in both cases calling into question the theory of sexual deviance as a function of bodily disorder and deformation.

'Deviance', of course, is itself a loaded term, and one that Cleland's writing actually undermines, as I hope to show; but certainly in the eighteenth century homoerotic relations were a deviation from an at least putative norm, and Cleland's texts always start from that premise. His translation of an Italian medical history of a cross-dressing female adventurer and lady's man, Catterina Vizzani, subjects the figure of the tribade to the same scrutiny as, in the *Memoirs*, he turns on the figure of the sodomite, and in both cases he is trying to work out the precise relationship between illicit desires and the bodies that enact them. In doing so, he sets himself at variance with both the moralistic and medical understandings I have referred to in this introduction, and thus offers a usefully alienated perspective on the historical transformation this volume as a whole addresses. By reading Cleland's narratives of same-sex desire in relation to contemporary juridical accounts of sodomitical practice as well as Havelock Ellis's synthesis of later nineteenth-century scientific studies of inversion (male and female) as a pathological condition, I seek to chart the historical and theoretical distance between two dominant explanatory models of sexual abnormality while offering a third model – implicit in Cleland's writing – in which normality itself is turned inside-out, exposing its essential emptiness.

Sodomy could mean many things in the eighteenth century, but what it almost always *did* mean, as a matter of law, was sex between men involving anal penetration.[6] The phrase that crops up so often in trial reports –'the heinous and detestable Sin of Sodomy, not to be named among Christians' – refers exclusively to this. The legal requirement for a guilty verdict on a charge of sodomy was two-fold: both penetration and emission had to be proved, and that by two witnesses. In one case from 1721, one witness testified that the accused, George Duffus, 'turned me upon my Face, and forcibly enter'd my Body about an Inch, as near as I can guess; but in struggling, I threw him off once more, before he had made an Emission, and having thus forced him to withdraw, he emitted in his own Hand, and clapping it on the Tail of my Shirt, said, *Now you have it!*' A second witness then testified, of another incident, that Duffus 'got upon me, kept me down, and thrust his Yard betwixt my Thighs, and emitted' (*Select Trials* I, pp. 106–7). Here there are two witnesses, penetration and emission, but, evidently because the two latter events could not be shown to have occurred together, Duffus could be found guilty (upon retrial) only on the lesser charge of attempted sodomy: 'The Spermatic Injection not being prov'd, the Court directed the Jury to bring in their Verdict *Special*' (*Select Trials* I, p. 107).

Not all judges and juries were so punctilious in their adherence to the letter of the law, and the evidence required for conviction seems, from the not-always-reliable record of the trial reports, to have varied from case to case. In any event, even conviction on the charge of attempted sodomy, for which the punishment was pillorying instead of hanging, could be fatal if the crowd of spectators were hostile enough.[7] Such popular hostility was a useful adjunct to the campaign against London's molly houses orchestrated by the Societies for the Reformation of Manners, culminating in the battery of police roundups and trials of 1726.

These molly houses, as is now well-known, were coffee-houses or taverns where sodomites, or mollies, as they were variously named in the period, could meet; and the pogrom of 1726, as Alan Bray has called it, was designed to scour this network of meeting-places from the city.[8] The criminal trials of individuals, then, were in large part the vehicle of a more ambitious undertaking, a project of cultural purification.

Given the straightforwardness of the legal requirements for conviction, it is striking how little of the testimony reported in the *Select Trials* and other accounts actually pertains to them. Instead, much of the evidence taken in court describes what could almost be called sodomitical folkways – customs and practices that have no obvious bearing on the criminal charges in question. Indeed, sexual acts seem at times almost incidental. The featured eyewitnesses – constables, rent boys, betrayers – describe a form of life at which the reader is solicited to peep in appalled fascination. If the evidence in the 1721 Duffus case quoted above is experiential and tactile – the witnesses describe what they *felt* on and in their own bodies – most criminal cases depended on third-party visual evidence of sexual crimes, since apart from cases of rape those personally involved would not have been likely to testify. But rather than limit themselves to establishing the two necessary physical proofs, the witnesses often shift their (and their audience's) attention to the milieu within which prohibited acts could – indeed, were almost certain to – occur. So, for example, in the 1726 trial of Thomas Wright, who kept a molly house in the City, a constable testified that:

> In a large Room there we found one a fiddling, and eight more a dancing Country Dances, making vile Motions, and singing, *Come let us — finely*. Then they sat in one another's Lap, talked Bawdy, and practiced a great many Indecencies. There was a Door in the great Room, which opened into a little Room, where there was a Bed, and into this little Room several of the Company went; sometimes they shut the Door after them, but sometimes they left it open, and then we could see part of their Actions.
>
> (*Select Trials* II, p. 368)

It is precisely at the point where visual evidence matters – the point at which the presumably criminal 'Actions' should be brought to light – that the text stops short. There is no way of knowing whether the testimony in court was any more explicit, but in its reported form the absence of detail both calls on the reader to imagine unimaginable scenes and adds to the sense of nightmarish indeterminacy. As in much of the anti-sodomite literature of the time, the object of horrified attention is an underworld, a way of life, not a single, provable crime.

Collectively, the trial reports assume an almost ethnographic function, detailing this strange world's rituals, language, and kinship structures as they map its interior and exterior spaces. Sex may have been, as Alan Bray writes, 'the root of the matter', but it was at least equally the world-upside-down atmosphere, the signs of *collective* perversity, that disturbed moralistic observers.[9] In the criminal trial of Margaret Clap, for example, on charges of 'keeping a disorderly

House, in which she procured and encouraged Persons to commit Sodomy', one witness testifies that:

> On *Sunday* Night, the 14th of *November* last, I went to the Prisoner's House in *Field-lane*, in *Holborn*, where I found between 40 and 50 Men making Love to one another, as they call'd it. Sometimes they would sit in one another's Laps, kissing in a lewd Manner and using their Hand indecently. Then they would get up, Dance and make Curtsies, and mimick the Voices of Women ... Then they'd hug, and play, and toy, and go out by Couples into another Room on the same Floor, to be married, as they call'd it.
>
> (*Select Trials* III, p. 37)

Magnified by 'between 40 and 50', the lewd kisses, indecent hand gestures, cross-gender mimicry, and parody-enactments of heterosexual norms produce a saturnalian, chaotically unsettled flux of bodies. The *disorder* inside Mother Clap's house is collective, contagious, and, worst of all, taken for granted: these are the customary practices of an alternative, alien culture the more alarming for being diffused through the whole city, everywhere at home.[10]

Virtually all the moral commentators on the supposed growth of sodomy from early to mid-eighteenth century endeavour to justify the campaign against it on the basis of the danger it poses to Britain; it is a crime not so much against nature as nation. That is, while it is, of course, everywhere against nature, sodomy is suited to the unnatural inhabitants of other nations, but has (or should have) no purchase here. Yet it flourishes:

> 'Till of late Years, *Sodomy* was a *Sin*, in a manner unheard of in these Nations; and indeed, one would think where there are such *Angelic Women*, so foul a Sin should never enter into Imagination: On the contrary, our *Sessions-Papers* are frequently stain'd with the *Crimes* of these *beastly Wretches*; and tho' many have been made Examples of, yet we have but too much Reason to fear, that there are Numbers yet undiscover'd, and that this *abominable Practice* gets Ground ev'ry Day.[11]

The *abominable Practice* is an import, a sin 'Translated', in the words of another author, 'from the *Sadomitical* [*sic*] Original, or from the *Turkish* and *Italian* Copies into *English*'.[12] In still another text, the figure of *transplantation* is substituted for that of *translation*:

> Since that most detestable and unnatural Sin of *Sodomy*, which but rarely appears in our Histories, and that among Monsters and Prodigies, has been of late transplanted from the hotter Climates to our more temperate Country, and has dared to shew its hideous Face among a People that formerly had it in the utmost Abhorrence; it is now become the indispensable Duty of the Magistrate to attack this horrible Monster in Morality, by a vigorous Exertion of those good Laws, that have justly made that vile Sin a Capital Crime.[13]

But if sodomy is not only unnatural but naturally un-English – if it has always been held here in the 'utmost Abhorrence' – what can account for this modern infestation?

Despite the invocation, in this last passage, of prodigies and monsters, their role has become purely figural, a nostalgic appeal to an earlier state in which sodomites were as rare as two-headed calves. Instead, as in the other two texts from which I have quoted, sodomy is represented as a form of contagion, a visitation or plague whose mode of transmission is (perhaps paradoxically) not bodily but cultural. It comes from the East, from Sodom itself by way of Turkey and, almost always, Italy. In some texts it comes uninvited, an insidious and contaminating vice (this is likely the sense of 'transplanted' in the passage above); in others, more commonly, it comes as the bad effect of cross-cultural emulation. This model is implicit in the notion of *translation* either from an ancient original or 'from the *Turkish* and *Italian* Copies into English', and is fully elaborated in the 1749 *Satan's Harvest Home*:

> But of all the Customs *Effeminacy* has produc'd, none more hateful, predominant, and pernicious, than that of the Mens *Kissing* each other. This *Fashion* was brought over from *Italy*, (the *Mother* and *Nurse* of *Sodomy*); where the *Master* is oftner *Intriguing* with his *Page*, than a *fair Lady*. And not only in that *Country*, but in *France*, which copies from them, the *Contagion* is diversify'd, and the Ladies (in the *Nunneries*) are criminally *amorous* of each other, in a *Method* too gross for Expression.[14]

Kissing is not only repellent in itself (the pamphlet's author equates it with 'slavering' and 'slopping') but it is 'the first *Inlet* to the detestable Sin of *Sodomy*' and thus a vehicle for the corruption of youth. If the custom were abolished, 'the Sons of *Sodom* would lose many *Proselytes*, in being baffled out of one of their principal Advances; for under Pretence of extraordinary Friendship, they intice unwary Youth from this first Step, to more detestable Practices, taking many Times the Advantage of their Necessities, to decoy them to their Ruin'.[15] As with the broader 'translation' of sodomy from the Middle East to Turkey to Italy to England, the mode of transmission within England today is emulation: the neophyte imitates the customs he sees and is drawn to, and so insensibly falls into more 'detestable Practices'.

The fashion of men kissing one another, then, compared unfavourably to the 'more manly, more friendly, and more decent' custom of shaking hands, is a predatory form of initiation or schooling in vice, and the schoolboy often appears in anti-sodomite literature as an emblem of moral vulnerability. Sometimes the threat was from dissolute schoolmasters or tutors (the future Attorney General Dudley Ryder wrote in 1716 that 'it is dangerous sending a young man that is beautiful to Oxford'[16]); at other times from men who loitered in the vicinity of schools, as in the 1760 case against Richard Branson, found guilty of attempted sodomy against a poor scholar at God's Gift College in Dulwich. In his summation to the court, the Council for the Crown 'demonstrated the fatal

Consequence of this wicked Attempt': had Branson 'prevailed with this Lad, now Sixteen Years old, to commit this horrid and most detestable Crime, he would have infected all the others; and, as in Course of Years they grew big enough, they would leave the College to go into the World and spread this cursed Poison, while those left behind would be training the Children to the same vitious Practices'.[17] Sodomitical inclination is infectious, then, and seemingly irresistible once it gains a foothold; it passes from schoolboy to schoolboy and then friend to friend, or older to younger; but while this transmission involves bodily intimacy, the inclination itself is imitative rather than rooted in bodily anomaly. There is nothing about this crowd of schoolboys that sets them apart, that somehow marks them as specially susceptible; the presumption is that, once exposed, every schoolboy is a sodomite.

Such a notion of universal susceptibility coexists uneasily with an essentialising discourse that, during the same period, configured the sodomite as not only perverse but of a different species or race – a discourse visible in several of the passages I have discussed here, from the use of such stock phrases as 'the Sons of *Sodom*' to the representation of sodomy as a transplant 'from the hotter Climates to our more temperate Country'. This unstable mix of tendencies to read sodomy as alien to or, contrarily, latent in 'our' natures is an integral feature of eighteenth-century anti-sodomite writings, whose very incoherence on this question only added to the anxiety aroused by a propensity both far-reaching and invisible. For it transpires in case after case that there are no outward signs of illicit desire – nothing to awaken the suspicions even of the sodomites' occasional bedfellows. In the trial of Gabriel Lawrence, one of six witnesses for the defense, Henry Yoxan, testifies that 'I am a Cow-keeper, and the Prisoner is a Milk-man. I have kept him Company, and served him with Milk these eighteen Years. I have been with him at the *Oxfordshire-Feast*, where we have both got drunk, and then come Home together in a Coach, and yet he never offered any such Indecencies to me' (*Select Trials* II, p. 363). In another case from the same year, the reporter states that 'the Prisoner, in his Defence, called some Witnesses, who had been his Bedfellows. They deposed, that he never offer'd any Indecencies to them, and that he had a Wife and Child, and took care of his Family' (*Select Trials* III, pp. 36–7). In a third case, from 1745, the fellow-servant of one of he accused testifies that 'I have lain with Davis upwards of sixteen months, and never saw any unhandsome action by him'.[18] There is, it seems in all three cases, nothing to see: no deformity, no defect, no effeminacy of manner. That the accused were all nevertheless found guilty shows unmistakably that perverse desire is not locatable upon (though it may be performed by) the body.

Something over a century later, the young Italian army physician Cesare Lombroso 'beguiled [his] ample leisure with a series of studies of the Italian soldier'. In the course of these, he was 'struck by a characteristic that distinguished the honest soldier from his vicious comrade: the extent to which the latter was tattooed and the indecency of the designs that covered his body'.[19] Although Lombroso did not, in 1864, grasp the import of this observation, it would prove in retrospect the first intimation of the new science of criminal anthropology, whose relationship with the equally new science of sexology over the ensuing decades was close if not always easy. As Jane Caplan has written, both can be understood as 'discourses of "social hygiene"', attempts 'to find means of management appropriate to dangers that were now grasped in terms of morbidity rather than morality; they subsumed a range of strategies to protect and cleanse society from the abnormal, the deviant, the unfit'.[20] And as Caplan also notes, the figure who most clearly demonstrates the affiliations between the two sciences, despite his ambivalence over some aspects of Lombroso's work, was the author of the monumental *Studies in the Psychology of Sex*, Henry Havelock Ellis.

One of Ellis's earlier books, *The Criminal* (1890), was in fact undertaken in order to bring Lombroso's ideas to an English audience. Lombroso's central theoretical claims – for which he found support in the voluminous data he accumulated from the measurement of criminals' and lunatics' crania, and the cataloguing of their facial and bodily anomalies – were that criminality is congenital; that the born criminal is a biological throwback, 'an atavistic being who reproduces in his person the ferocious instincts of primitive humanity and the inferior animals'[21]; and that the criminal type can be recognised by the presence of specific physical traits or stigmata, the outward signs of congenital abnormality. While Ellis had reservations about Lombroso's atavistic claims, and gave greater weight than did Lombroso to the social conditions that foster criminal behavior, he was powerfully affected by the contention that deviance is congenital and can be clinically diagnosed from external symptoms. One suggestive passage from *The Criminal* shows how closely allied were the two projects of criminological and sexological categorisation: discussing the physical traits associated with various types of deviance, Ellis writes that 'in those guilty of sexual offenses, Lombroso finds the eyes nearly always bright; the voice either rough or cracked; the face generally delicate, except in the development of the jaws, and the lips and eyelids swollen; occasionally they are hump-backed or otherwise deformed'.[22] Ellis does not comment on this catalogue of peculiarities, but much of his later writing on the nature of sexual inverts is grounded in a similar search for visible correspondences to psychic disturbances that would otherwise remain hidden.

For Lombroso, the tattoo was an especially significant marker of criminal or sexual deviance, precisely because it manifested on the body the subject's otherwise secret desires. In Gina Lombroso-Ferrero's 1911 *Criminal Man*, her English presentation of her father's most significant findings, she writes:

> Tattooing often reveals the psychology, habits, and vices of the individual. The tattooing on pederasts usually consists of portraits of those with whom they have unnatural commerce, or phrases of an affectionate nature addressed to them. A pederast and forger examined by Professor Filippi was tattooed on his forearm with a sentimental declaration addressed to the

object of his unnatural desires; a criminal convicted of rape was covered with pictorial representations of his obscene adventures. From these few instances, it is apparent that these personal decorations are of the utmost value as evidence of hidden vices and crimes.[23]

Tattoos, in this example, are a kind of secondary sexual characteristic – not a congenital deformation but a willful form of disfigurement that signals a (perverse) erotic disposition. They act as both a record of sexual practice and an advertisement of availability, and they even, Lombroso believed, provide evidence for the atavism hypothesis, in that tattooing is a custom belonging to a more primitive stage of cultural development.

In his own work, Ellis evinced no interest in tattoos, and notwithstanding the role they played in leading Lombroso to his theory of stigmata, they might seem to raise more questions for that theory than they answer, being neither involuntary nor innate but rather a product of cultural imitation and transplanting. But in Ellis's writings on inversion, too, the visible symptoms of perverse desire – a desire often unacted on by the unhappy and guilt-ridden subjects of his sexual case histories – are also a mixture of somatic traits and imitative behaviours. In a discussion of the physical abnormalities typical of inversion, Ellis writes:

> The greater part of these various anatomical peculiarities and functional anomalies point, more or less clearly, to the prevalence among inverts of a tendency to infantilism, combined with feminism in men and masculinism in women. This tendency is denied by [the German sexologist Magnus] Hirschfeld, but it is often well indicated among the subjects whose histories I have been able to present, and is indeed suggested by Hirschfeld's own elaborate results; so that it can scarcely be passed over.[24]

Among the recurrent characteristics Ellis enumerates in the male inverts he has studied are well-developed breasts; '"menstrual" phenomena, physical and psychic, recurring every four weeks' (p. 290); broad hips and rounded arms; lack of skill in throwing a ball; hairless bodies; left-handedness (though he is unsure if the incidence is really higher among inverts); a high feminine voice; and an inability to whistle. (This last trait is among the most frequently cited in nineteenth-century studies of inversion; as Ellis notes, it was 'first pointed out by [Karl Heinrich] Ulrichs' and analysed by Hirschfeld. 'Many of my cases', he goes on to write, 'confess to this inability, while some of the women inverts can whistle admirably' [p. 291].) Ellis states that 'the sexual characters of the handwriting are in some cases clearly inverted, the men writing a feminine hand and the women a masculine hand' (p. 290). Child-like faces are found with equal frequency among male and female inverts. One of Ellis's anonymous correspondents (these included John Addington Symonds and Edward Carpenter) writes:

> I have noticed little abnormal with regard to the genital formation of [male] inverts. There are, however, frequent abnormalities of proportion in their

figures, the hands and feet being noticeably smaller and more shapely, the waist more marked, the body softer and less muscular. Almost invariably there is either cranial malformation or the head approaches the feminine in type and shape.

(p. 293)

Ellis offers no comment on the Lombrosian drift of this final observation, but seems disinclined to pursue anthropometric inquiries, preferring albeit tentatively to suggest that inversion originates in 'the stimulating and inhibiting play of the internal secretions' (p. 316) or hormones.

If the overriding pattern in this catalogue of physical abnormalities is a combination of arrested development and the manifestation of bodily traits found normally in the other (or opposite) sex, some of the peculiarities he lists – the inability to whistle, for example, or the adoption of a feminine or masculine 'hand' – are likely to seem incongruous or bizarre, as Ellis indirectly acknowledges, writing that:

they by no means necessarily imply inversion. [The poet] Shelley, for example, was unable to whistle, though he never gave an indication of inversion; but he was a person of somewhat abnormal and feminine organization, and he illustrates the tendency of these apparently very insignificant functional anomalies to be correlated with other and more important psychic anomalies.

(p. 291)

Gender-inappropriate behaviours, then, including the incapacity to whistle or throw a ball correctly, while probably not themselves congenital, may be imitatively acquired as a result of an anomalous psychic identification, based on hormonal imbalance, with the sex one is not. The same may be true, although it is not easy to be sure, of another trait – 'a preference for green garments' (p. 299). As Ellis writes:

This decided preference for green is well marked in several of my cases of both sexes, and in some at least the preference certainly arose spontaneously. Green (as Jastrow and others have shown) is very rarely the favorite color of adults of the Anglo-Saxon race, though some inquirers have found it to be more commonly a preferred color among children, especially girls, and it is more often preferred by women than by men.

(p. 299)

That children and especially girls tend to like green links this sartorial preference in inverts to infantilism and, at least for male inverts, to what Ellis calls feminism, and so suggests that the trait is congenitally derived. Yet his discussion of this propensity becomes less clear as it goes on. Ellis notes, first, that 'some years ago a band of pederasts at Paris wore green cravats as a badge', which suggests that the custom is not physiological but cultural in origin; and then, after observing that 'the favourite colour among normal women' is red, tells us that 'of recent years there has been a fashion for a red tie to be adopted by inverts as their badge' (p. 299). Quoting an American correspondent, himself inverted, Ellis writes that 'male prostitutes who walk the streets of Philadelphia and New York almost invariably wear red neckties. It is the badge of all their tribe' (p. 300). The discussion is incoherent on a number of levels. A paragraph that begins as a commentary on inverts' tendency to wear green ends up with them wearing red neckties (and painting their rooms red as well). An initial preference for green that signals the infantilism of male and female inverts alike gives way to a preference for red that signals male inverts' imitation (conscious or unconscious) of female adults. A discussion whose overall burden is to demonstrate the congenital basis of inversion leads to an example of emulation as a form of (sub)cultural signalling.

This intellectual or discursive incoherence is not accidental, but an outgrowth of Ellis's method and of the mixed origins of *Sexual Inversion*, the 1897 volume he produced in uneasy and unequal collaboration, beginning in 1892, with J. A. Symonds.[25] Although much of what Symonds contributed to that volume was excised from the re-edited text that eventually became part of *Studies in the Psychology of Sex*, his interest in the historical and cultural dimensions of sexual inversion, and, perhaps more importantly, the collection of first-person case histories he supplied Ellis, left a considerable imprint on the final work – in part, I think, because of Ellis's own ambivalence on the subject. Ellis's methodological reliance on first-person accounts, whether passed on to him by Symonds or obtained from a wide network of female and male inverts that included many of his closest friends (among them his wife Edith), meant that while he continued to give priority to the theoretical claim that inversion is a congenital anomaly–or, indeed, a 'pathological abnormality' (p. 321) – he also provided a textual forum within which inverted subjects, including Symonds, could offer their own very different readings of their experience. Ellis acknowledges that 'a large majority (including all the women)' of his subjects are 'emphatic in their assertion that their moral position is precisely the same as that of the normally constituted individual' (p. 300), and that they regard their inclinations as, for them, no less normal. It is also evident from the histories that most of the speakers share Symonds's conviction that their own desires were powerfully affected by the people around them, by their education and cultural milieu, by the (ironically, perverse) norms of public school or philosophy tutorial.[26] Ellis recognises, as in the case of the red neckties, that there is a culture of inversion in 1890s England and America as there had once been a culture of *paiderastia* in ancient Greece, and that it manifests itself in the self-conscious imitation of historically contingent (and contagious) forms of homosexually-coded behaviour.

And yet: culture is always secondary in Ellis's theory of inversion. If he gave greater weight than Lombroso or Krafft-Ebing to the contexts in which the variant forms of sexual desire can develop, and rejected their classifications of inversion as atavistic or degenerate, he nevertheless held fast to the idea that deviance is rooted in bodily 'deformity' (p. 321) and that it can, theoretically, be diagnosed even without knowing the subject's history. When he writes that 'the sexual invert may thus be roughly compared to the congenital idiot, to the instinctive criminal, to the man of genius' (p. 317), he might be fancied to be paying tribute, in that last phrase, to Symonds (one of 'the intellectual aristoc- racy of inversion', who 'have found consolation in the example of the Greeks' [p. 301]), even as he pays his debt to the biological determinism of Lombroso, and in the process, however tolerantly, labels his erstwhile partner a pathological case.

If congenital malformation is, for Ellis and his fellow sexologists, the definitive basis of same-sex desire, the deformity in question is but seldom located where one might expect to find it, in the sexual organs themselves, although on this point there is a real if not absolute difference between male and female cases. Among the males, of the few whose genitals are described at all, there is some (unsurprising) variation in size, but Ellis remarks that 'it is doubtful whether [these variations] possess as much significance as the tendency to infantilism of the sexual organs in inverted women' – even if, as he goes on to argue, these are less important than 'the deviations found in the general conformation of the body' (pp. 289–90). Why the arrested development or infantilism Ellis regarded as a defining trait of male and female inverts alike should manifest itself more often in the female sexual organs than the male, he never explains.[27] But in making this general claim, for which he finds confirmation in the studies of Krafft-Ebing and Hirschfeld, Ellis represents a scientific shift away from an older if still commonly-held belief in an oversized clitoris as the locus of female homoerotic desire. 'An enlarged clitoris', Ellis writes, 'is but rarely found in inversion and plays a very small part in the gratification of feminine homosexu- ality' (p. 258). A long history of equating female bodily excess to excess of desire, and especially desire for other women – a history embodied in the mon- strous and unruly figure of the tribade – gives way in late nineteenth-century sexology to another but equally tendentious equation, that of female inversion to bodily immaturity or lack; but in either case, the task of the anatomist is to locate the physiological signs that, whether causal or symptomatic, attest to the presence of deviant impulses.[28]

The search for a physiological *explanation* of perverse desire is the subject of a text John Cleland produced in 1751, two years after the publication of the *Memoirs of a Woman of Pleasure*; but before I turn to it I need to return to a question I left suspended in the opening pages of this essay. That is, why did eighteenth-century discussions of female same-sex desire focus on physiological aberrations (the monstrous excess of the tribade) while discussions of male same-sex desire did not? There are two principal ways of approaching the ques- tion: from the point of view of the prosecutor, or from that of the anatomist. In law, as I observed earlier, sodomy had come by the eighteenth century to be defined as an act of penetrative sex, and in England there is no record of a woman being tried for the crime; in any event, according to the implicit logic of

the definition, sex between women could only be imagined in cases either of cli-
toral enlargement or of what Valerie Traub calls 'prosthetic supplementation' –
that is, the use of a dildo.[29] For men, on the other hand, bodily anomaly –
eunuchism, effeminacy and the like – would call into question the very possibility of sodomitical activity.

In the realm of medicine, the considerable literature on tribadism going back
to the late sixteenth century had produced consensus on the principle that, to
quote Traub again,

> Clitoral size correlates with quantity of desire... Anatomists also agreed
> that some kind of motion (whether internal humoral flux, as suggested by
> Sharp, or external 'fretting' by clothing or fingers, as suggested by Crooke
> and Bartholin) could cause the clitoris to grow. Due to excessive bodily
> heat, the clitoris becomes engorged with fluids and gravitates outward, imi-
> tating the extension of the penis, and seeking, almost with a will of its own,
> to penetrate other bodies. Other than locating such growth within a humoral
> economy, however, medical writers failed to distinguish whether an
> enlarged clitoris incited unnatural lust or sexual 'abuse' of the clitoris
> caused it to grow monstrously large.[30]

Whether excess of lust produces bodily deformation or deformity arouses perverse desires, neither can be found in the absence of the other: for the tribade,
bodily anomaly is the sign of illicit desire. For the male sodomite, by contrast,
any visible change in the direction of a female conformation–and such cases
were often discussed in medical texts – would, again, by the very definition of
the term, appear to rule sodomy out. Unnatural desires are thus linked, for the
sodomite, to a visibly normal body; for the tribade, to a visibly aberrant one.

An unruly woman's body is at the centre of Cleland's 1751 text, titled *An
Historical and Physical Dissertation on the Case of Catherine Vizzani*, which
offers an unusually well-documented and detailed opportunity to test the physiological model of female perversity outlined above. Cleland's pamphlet is a translation of an Italian text of 1744 by Giovanni Bianchi, Professor of Anatomy at
Siena, with extensive emendations and commentary by Cleland.[31] Catherine
Vizzani had passed for eight years (from the age of 16) as a man, conducting
love affairs with a number of women until, having eloped with two sisters, she
was wounded in the thigh by pursuers and brought to the hospital in Siena,
where she soon afterwards died. It was only when the hospital servants were
removing the body that they discovered two signs of 'Giovanni's' true nature:
the first, 'her prominent Breasts' (p. 37), and the second, 'a leathern Contrivance, of a cylindrical Figure', which, Bianchi later infers, had been 'fastened
below the Abdomen, and had been the chief Instrument of her detestable Impos-
ture' (p. 34). Alerted to this discovery, Bianchi writes, 'I went again to the Hospital, and caused an Incision to be made in the Body, and the Parts of Generation
to be disseevered with the nicest Exactness, which were carried to my House to
be thoroughly examined by a regular Dissection' (p. 42). The purpose of this

post-mortem examination of Vizzani's body was, of course, to discover whether any physiological abnormality was at the root of her deviant sexual and social identity – although it is possible to interpret the 'dissevering' of the 'parts of generation' and the carrying them from the hospital to the surgeon's house as a form of retribution for the libidinous excesses of Vizzani's life.

As it turns out, however, the body explains nothing. From the evidence of Bianchi's post-mortem, Vizzani died a virgin – that is, with an intact hymen – and in fact this is enough reason for some of the townspeople to want to proclaim her a saint, as she had 'preserved her Chastity inviolate' (p. 40) despite having often, disguised as a male servant, shared beds with other men. But for Bianchi this physiological fact is morally insignificant: 'her making love, and with uncommon Protervity, to Women, wherever she came, and her seducing at last two young Women to run away from their Uncle, were flagrant Instances of a libidinous Disposition' (p. 41). Moreover, contradicting the dominant medical theory as to the physiological traits of 'those Females, who, among the *Greeks*, were called *Tribades*, or who followed the Practices of *Sappho*', Bianchi reports that Vizzani, in fact, was physiologically unremarkable: 'The *Clitoris* of this young Woman was not pendulous, nor of any extraordinary size, as the Account from *Rome* made it... on the contrary, hers was so far from any unusual Magnitude, that it was not to be ranked among the middle-sized, but the smaller' (p. 44). Her 'parts of generation', then, are not directly commensurable with her 'erotic desires and practices'.[32] In their failure to anchor gender identity (in this case tribadic or female-masculine) in the body, Vizzani's 'parts' resemble nothing so much as the 'leathern Contrivance' mentioned before, by which Vizzani established her sexual (and thus social) status as a male, with all the prerogatives attending that status. When this 'Machine' is discovered after her death, some hospital workers, assuming it to contain 'Money, or something else of Value', rip it open, 'but they found it', Bianchi notes, 'stuffed only with old Rags' (p. 37).[33] The truth of the body, its physiological nature, does not determine the identity of the desiring subject, who manages to both usurp and undermine phallic authority by putting on a 'Contrivance' with nothing of value inside.

In the commentary he added to Bianchi's history, Cleland notes with exasperation that 'it does not appear that [Bianchi] has assigned any Cause whatever, or so much as advanced any probable Conjecture on this extravagant Turn of [Vizzani's] lewdness, notwithstanding it surprized him so much' (pp. 52–3). So, relying on the evidence of the post-mortem exam, Cleland draws his own inference: deviant sexual identity originates not in the body, but in 'some Disorder or Perversion in the Imagination' (p. 53). 'There, indeed, if closely attended to, it will be found that more monstrous Productions are to be met with than have exercised the Pens of such as have addicted themselves to write of strange Births, and such like Prodigies' (p. 54). What, then, produced this disorder or perversion in the imagination of Catherine Vizzani? Her imagination was corrupted, Cleland writes, either by 'obscene Tales that were voluntarily told in her Hearing' as a youth, or 'by privately listening to the Discourses of the Women, who are too generally corrupt in that Country' (p. 54). Sexual identity, the argument runs, originates in overheard fictions, and seems as unfixed by nature as a body that can 'be' male or female at will. Vizzani's deviant impulses are a product of cultural contagion, effected not by literal seduction, as in the hypothetical case of the Dulwich schoolboys, but by 'obscene Tales', by literature.

Among Italian women, Cleland asserts, echoing the defensive nationalism of the anti-sodomitical texts then circulating in Britain, corruption is the norm; but this is not the case among us. Indeed, as translator of the original text he has had to excise some of the 'nauseous Detail of her Impostures' which Bianchi provided his Italian readers, for 'these, if agreeable to the *Italian Goût*, would shock the Delicacy of our Nation' (p. 9). The editorial comment proves disingenuous, however, when checked against what Cleland has actually chosen not to translate, for the passage in question contains nothing that is not spelled out explicitly later in the English text.[34] By pretending to draw a curtain over obscenities too shocking to translate but then translating them just the same, Cleland is making a rather complex rhetorical move: presenting himself as a guardian of national morality even as he tantalizes the reader to fill in the textual lacunae with his or her own 'nauseous' imaginings. If we are somehow able to imagine the shocking details that Cleland felt obliged to cut out, we delicate British reader-subjects thereby reveal ourselves to be infected by a 'Disorder or Perversion in the Imagination' not unlike Catherine Vizzani's, and originating, like hers, in stories passed from hand to hand.

Certainly the reader's imagination is replete, by the end of the *Dissertation*, with 'flagrant Instances of a libidinous Disposition' (p. 41), 'leathern Machines' (p. 37), and the like, so that like the young Catherine, the reader – 'her Head being thus filled with vicious Inclinations' (p. 55)–comes away from the text with 'Incitements' that 'might prompt her to those vile Practices, which being begun in Folly, were continued through Wickedness' (p. 55). Those 'Incitements', of course, have been put into our heads by Cleland's text. Yet he goes on to maintain that the *Dissertation*:

> affords (if that were at all necessary) a new Argument for suppressing those scandalous and flagitious Books, that are not only privately but publickly handed about for the worst Purposes, as well as Prints and Pictures calculated to inflame the Passions, to banish all Sense of Shame, and to make the World, if possible, more corrupt and profligate than it is already. We are very certain that all Things of this Sort must have a very bad Tendency.
>
> (pp. 63–4)

But as Emma Donoghue asks, reasonably enough, 'is *Catherine Vizzani* not one of these "scandalous books?" '[35] I would say that it is, and that Cleland knows that it is, and that if so, a writer as rhetorically supple and insidious as Cleland shows himself to be in the *Memoirs* is setting a trap here, disavowing any intent to 'inflame', so that the reader, again, is left to assume any guilt for the passions elicited by reading. 'The only Reason that can justify the making Things of this

Sort public', Cleland argues, 'is to facilitate their Discovery, and thereby prevent their ill Consequences, which indeed can scarce be prevented any other Way' (p. 62). The 'making Things of this Sort public', then, is both incitement and warning, or more precisely a warning against the very incitement it provides; and it is not only among Italian women, but everywhere in this 'corrupt and profligate' world, that disorders and perversions of the imagination are likely to take hold. Not only perverse desire, but desire itself, is second-hand, instilled as an involuntary effect of reading, listening, watching; and so a susceptibility to deviance is implicit in the capacity to desire at all.[36]

Catherine Vizzani's 'extravagant' desires stem not from any malformation of the body but from obscene 'discourses' whose promptings she then acts out in the flesh; but Cleland does entertain the possibility that the body might itself be materially altered by the subject's libidinous excesses: 'nor is it at all unreasonable to believe', Cleland writes, 'that, by Degrees, [these] might occasion a preternatural Change in the animal Spirits, and a Kind of venereal Fury' (p. 55) that in time could debilitate the physical constitution. Yet Bianchi's investigation has already established that her illicit actions left no imprint on Vizzani's body at all: 'venereal Fury' is a fever of the imagination, not an organic disturbance. As Cleland presents it, the Vizzani case is ultimately about the circulation of perverse desire as fantasy, as communal narrative, as moral contagion – not about deficient, excessive, or otherwise remarkable bodies. It is only when we become aware of what others want, by way of stories inciting desire, that we begin to conceive what we want ourselves.

The same apprehension of the imitative structure of desire runs throughout the *Memoirs of a Woman of Pleasure*, nowhere more disturbingly for the novel's narrator and protagonist Fanny Hill than in her encounter with the sodomites.[37] This encounter comes as the last in a series of three episodes in which Fanny's narrative approaches, inexorably and as if unconsciously, a previously unimagined species of sexuality which, when she finally does witness it, provokes a moralistic outrage so extreme it threatens to undo her. In the first of these episodes, Fanny is picked up in the street by a young sailor, 'tall, manly-carriag'd, handsome of body and face' (p. 140). As their sexual encounter approaches its climax, things take an unexpected turn: the sailor, Fanny writes, 'bares my naked posteriours to his blind, and furious guide: it forces his way between them, and I feeling pretty sensibly that it was going by the right door, and knocking desperately at the wrong one, I told him of it: "Pooh, says he my dear, any port in a storm"' (p. 141). The already familiar association of sodomy and sailors is evoked in the midst of an ostensibly heterosexual encounter as a figure of potential danger, disrupting Fanny's settled notions of the proper sites of sexual desire. Inverting the more familiar pattern of boys' school, prison, and pirate narratives, in which the 'submissive' male is feminized by sodomitical penetration, the danger from Fanny's perspective is that it will make a boy of her.

In the second episode, Emily, a fellow-prostitute of Fanny's, attends a masquerade in the guise of a shepherd boy, and is accosted by 'a gentleman in a very handsome domino' (p. 154). As Fanny observes of Emily, 'nothing in nature could represent a prettier boy than [she] did', but Emily fails to realize that the domino 'took her really for what she appear'd to be, a smock-fac'd boy', and so takes 'all those addresses to be paid to herself as a woman, which she precisely ow'd to his not thinking her one' (p. 154). Soon after, as Emily reports, 'when they were alone together, and her *enamorato* began to proceed to those extremities which instantly discover the sex, she remark'd that no description could paint up to the life, the mixture of pique, confusion, and disappointment, that appear'd in his countenance, which join'd to the mournful exclamation, "By heavens a woman!" ' (p. 155). Nevertheless, he eventually presses on; but as Fanny writes, 'he was so fiercely set on a mis-direction, as to give the girl no small alarms for fear of losing a maiden-head she had not dreamt of; however her complaints, and a resistance gentle, but firm, check'd, and brought him to himself again; so that turning his steed's head, he drove him at length in the right road' (p. 155). In this scene, too, the ostensible 'normality' of the encounter is relentlessly undermined by an apprehension that the real is only a simulacrum: the would-be sodomite is only able to be 'brought to himself again', to enact heterosexual desire, by an imaginary substitution of the boy Emily seems to be for the woman she 'naturally' is. As Fanny has it, 'his imagination having probably made the most of those resemblances that flatter'd his taste, he got with much ado whip and spur to his journey's end' (pp. 155–6). The gentleman's performance of normal masculinity is as much a travesty as Emily's shepherd-boy get-up.

The 'unnaturalness', in this scene, of heterosexual normality seems not to register with Fanny, whose only response is to say 'that I could not conceive how it was possible for mankind to run into a taste, not only universally odious, but absurd, and impossible to gratify, since, according to the notions and experience I had of things, it was not in nature to force such immense disproportions' (p. 156). It is not until some months later that Fanny's questions are answered, by 'occular demonstration' (p. 156), when she spies on two young fellows, aged 19 and 17, who have been shown into the room next to hers in a public house.[38] After 'piercing' a hole in a patch in the wainscoting, through which she can look only if she stands on a chair, Fanny, motivated purely by 'a spirit of curiosity', begins to monitor their actions:

> For now the elder began to embrace, to press, to kiss the younger, to put his hands in his bosom, and give such manifest signs of an amorous intention, as made me conclude the other to be a girl in disguise, a mistake that nature kept me in countenance in, for she had certainly made one, when she gave him the male stamp. In the rashness then of their age, and bent as they were to accomplish their project of preposterous pleasure, at the risque of the very worst of consequences, where a discovery was nothing less than improbable, they now proceeded to such lengths as soon satisfied me, what they were.

(pp. 157–8)

Echoing her response to Emily's earlier adventure, Fanny comments that the older boy's 'engine' was 'very fit to confirm me in my disbelief of the possibility of things being push'd to odious extremities, which I had built on the disproportion of parts' (p. 158); yet she soon sees that their desire is anything but 'impossible to gratify': 'the first streights of entrance being pretty well got through, every thing seem'd to move, and go pretty currently on, as in a carpet-road, without much rub, or resistance' (p. 158).

Fanny's first speculation is that the younger of the boys is really 'a girl in disguise', which would make this a repetition of Emily's story; but even when she sees that this is not the case, she contends that nature 'had certainly made one [a girl], when she gave him the male stamp'. Yet there is no visual evidence to support this in Fanny's fanatically detailed testimony. When she first describes the boy in question, she writes that he 'could not be above seventeen, fair, ruddy, compleatly well made, and to say the truth, a sweet pretty stripling: He was, I fancy too, a country lad, by his dress' (p. 157). Nothing marks either boy as different from the innumerable Wills and Charleses and Good-Natur'd Dicks on whom Fanny has gazed with desire and with whom she has then gratified the desire that the eye awakened. Even the hermaphroditic sense of such observations as (of the younger boy) 'if he was like his mother behind, he was like his father before' (p. 158), fail to differentiate him from the two males (Will and Charles) who are the recipients of Fanny's most enraptured gaze, consistently rendered as desirable precisely for their androgynous beauty.[39] What seems most to disturb Fanny in this scene is that her (voyeuristically aroused) desire for them is superfluous and unreturned.

Fanny's denunciation of sodomy as odious, absurd and impossible depends on her belief that 'it was not in nature to force such immense disproportions'; yet in claiming this, she actually subsumes all desire under the heading of sodomy. For immense disproportion has been, from the beginning, the keynote of Fanny's representations of heterosexuality as well, at least in relation to herself as a desiring subject. Early in the *Memoirs*, Fanny watches a heterosexual couple having sex as she hides in a dark closet.[40] When asked for her reactions to what she observed, she says that 'having very curiously and attentively compared the size of that enormous machine, which did not appear, at least to my fearful imagination, less than my wrist, and at least three of my handfuls long, to that of the tender, small part of me which was framed to receive it, I could not conceive its being possible to afford it entrance there' (p. 27). And this inconceivability, which is articulatcd in almost the same terms as in Fanny's diatribe against sodomy, persists as a constitutive feature of her most pleasurable enactments of heterosexual desire. When she first undresses the young footman Will, for example, she notes:

> with wonder and surprize, what? not the play-thing of a boy, not the weapon of a man, but a may-pole of so enormous a standard, that had proportions been observ'd, it must have belong'd to a young giant ... and it now fell to my lot to stand his first trial of it, if I could resolve to run the risques of its

disproportion to that tender part of me, which such an over-siz'd machine was very fit to lay in ruins.

(pp. 72–3)[41]

If immense disproportion is the mark of the unnatural, Fanny's accounts of heterosexual desire consistently denaturalise it, recast it as another kind of sodomy. Hence her 'burning ... with rage, and indignation' (p. 159) all the time she stands glued to her peep-hole spying on the boys. In making manifest what has always been implicit in her own experience of desire, the spectacle of perversity in the next room disrupts the secure distinction Fanny wishes to maintain between natural and unnatural tastes, and suggests that normality is a narrative or ideological 'contrivance' as empty as the leather one discovered on Catherine Vizzani's corpse.

Fanny's friend Mrs Cole tries to reaffirm her faith in an impermeable border separating the deviant from the normal with her talk of plague spots 'visibly imprinted on all that are tainted with it' (p. 159).[42] But as she continues speaking, the point doesn't seem so clear: 'among numbers of that stamp whom she had known, or at least were universally under the scandalous suspicion of it, she could not name an exception hardly of one of them whose character was not in all other respects the most worthless and despicable that could be' (p. 159). Is the plague spot a literal mark, or just a metaphor for the social circulation of rumours, calumny and suspicion? In his 1753 *Dictionary of Love*, Cleland introduces another possible meaning of 'plague spot' in his article on 'fribble', which he defines as 'one of those ambiguous animals, who are neither male nor female; disclaimed by his own sex, and the scorn of both'.[43] After noting the fribbles' tendency to give women advice on how to dress, Cleland writes: 'Nor is their own dress neglected: the muff, the ermin-facing, a cluster-ring, the stone-buckle, and now and then a patch, that on them does not always suppose a pimple, are the plague-spots, in which the folly of these less than butterflies breaks out'. Here, the plague spot is explicitly not a bodily mark. In fact the one item on Cleland's list that looks as if it could be such a mark – the 'patch, that on them does not always suppose a pimple' – is a sign that points to an absent object it only pretends to conceal. The mark 'visibly imprinted' on the sodomite is just a bauble that can be put on or taken off on a whim – nothing to do with 'air and climate', or with the body, at all. In fact these plague spots seem rather like Havelock Ellis's red neckties: badges of subcultural identification. In his narratives of same-sex desire, Cleland breaks with both the moralism of the anti-sodomites and the model of congenital deformity urged by the sexologists in favour of an understanding of desire as always – whatever the object – perverse, imitative, susceptible to the 'incitements' of scandalous persons and texts.

Notes

1 *Select Trials at the Sessions-House in the Old-Bailey* [1742], facsimile edition, 4 vols, New York: Garland, 1985, II, p. 362. Subsequent references will be cited parenthetically in the text.

2 On the probable reasons for Cleland's arrest, see David Foxon, *Libertine Literature in England, 1660–1745*, New Hyde Park: University Books, 1965, p. 61. I have discussed the censorial prosecution of Cleland in my article 'Obscenity, Censorship, and the Eighteenth-Century Novel: The Case Against John Cleland', *The Wordsworth Circle*, 35:3, 2004, 134–41.

3 Henry Merritt, 'A Biographical Note on John Cleland', *Notes and Queries*, 28, August 1981, 305–6.

4 John Cleland, *Memoirs of a Woman of Pleasure* (1749), edited by Peter Sabor, Oxford: Oxford University Press, 1985 [reissued with new bibliography 1999], p. 159. Subsequent references will be cited parenthetically in the text.

5 On the persistence of (one might have hoped) archaic discourses of perversion and monstrosity in the representation of AIDS from the mid-1980s on, see Simon Watney, *Policing Desire: Pornography, AIDS and the Media*, London: Methuen, 1987 and Douglas Crimp (ed.), *AIDS: Cultural Analysis/Cultural Activism*, Cambridge: MIT Press, 1988.

6 On the multiple possible meanings of 'sodomy' in the early modern period, see Valerie Traub, *The Renaissance of Lesbianism in Early Modern England*, Cambridge: Cambridge University Press, 2002, p. 42. By the eighteenth century, the definition had narrowed, and the term was, in a legal context, applied only to males; see Tim Hitchcock, *English Sexualities, 1700–1800*, New York: St. Martin's Press, 1997, pp. 60–1. On the 'invisibility' of lesbianism under the law in Britain, see Traub, *Renaissance*, pp. 167–8 and Hitchcock, *English Sexualities*, p. 80.

7 Ibid., p. 73; David Greenberg, *The Construction of Homosexuality*, Chicago: University of Chicago Press, 1988, p. 339.

8 Alan Bray, *Homosexuality in Renaissance England*, second edition, London: Gay Men's Press, 1988, p. 91. On the molly houses in general, and the 1726 campaign to close them down, see ibid., pp. 81–114, and Rictor Norton, *Mother Clap's Molly House: The Gay Subculture in England 1700–1830*, London: Gay Men's Press, 1992, esp. pp. 49–105.

9 Bray, *Homosexuality*, p. 84.

10 On the ubiquity of molly-house locations and cruising grounds, see ibid., pp. 81–114 and Norton, *Mother Clap*, pp. 49–105.

11 *Reasons for the Growth of Sodomy*, published as the second part of *Satan's Harvest Home: or the Present State of Whorecraft, Adultery, Fornication, Procuring, Pimping, Sodomy, and the Game at Flatts* [London, 1749], facsimile edition, New York: Garland Publishing, 1985, p. 52.

12 *The Tryal and Condemnation of Mervin, Lord Audley* [London, 1699], facsimile edition reprinted in *Sodomy Trials: Seven Documents*, New York: Garland, 1986, [sig. A3r].

13 'Reformation Necessary to Prevent Our Ruin, 1727', in Rictor Norton (ed.) *Homosexuality in Eighteenth-Century England: A Sourcebook*. Updated 29 April 2000, amended 24 July 2002. Online. Available at: www.infopt.demon.co.uk/1727ruin.htm (accessed 15 August 2005).

14 *Reasons for the Growth of Sodomy*, p. 51.

15 Ibid., pp. 51, 52, 54.

16 Norton, *Mother Clap*, p. 159.

17 *The Trial of Richard Branson* [London, 1760], facsimile edition reprinted in *Sodomy Trials: Seven Documents*, New York: Garland, 1986, pp. 24–5.

18 'The Trial of Richard Manning and John Davis, 1745', in Rictor Norton (ed.), *Homosexuality in Eighteenth-Century England: A Sourcebook*. 25 January 2001, updated

1 March 2003. Online. Available at: www.infopt.demon.co.uk/1745mann.htm (accessed 15 August 2005).

19 Cesare Lombroso, 'Introduction' to Gina Lombroso-Ferrero, *Criminal Man, According to the Classification of Cesare Lombros*, London: G. P. Putnam's Sons, 1911; reprint ed. Montclair: Patterson Smith, 1972, p. xxii.

20 Jane Caplan, ' "Educating the Eye": The Tattooed Prostitute', in Lucy Bland and Laura Doan (eds), *Sexology in Culture: Labelling Bodies and Desires*, Chicago: University of Chicago Press, 1998, p. 105.

21 Lombroso, 'Introduction', p. xxv.

22 Henry Havelock Ellis, *The Criminal*, London: Walter Scott, n.d. [1895], p. 83.

23 Lombroso-Ferrero, *Criminal Man*, pp. 232–3. On nineteenth-century studies of tattooing among female prostitutes, also strongly influenced by Lombroso's theory of criminality as atavistic, see Caplan, '"Educating the Eye":', pp. 100–15.

24 Henry Havelock Ellis, *Sexual Inversion*, third edition, published in *Studies in the Psychology of Sex*, I, part 4, New York: Random House, n. d. [1942], pp. 291–2. Subsequent references will be cited parenthetically in the text. On Ellis's mutually problematic collaboration with John Addington Symonds to produce the first (1897) edition of *Sexual Inversion*, see Joseph Bristow, 'Symonds's History, Ellis's Heredity: *Sexual Inversion*', in Bland and Doan (eds), *Sexology in Culture*, pp. 79–99. Much of the material contributed by Symonds was excised from later editions including the one I have cited, bringing it into closer conformity to Ellis's overall theoretical orientation.

25 See Bristow, 'Symonds's History', and Ellis, *Studies*, I, pp. xi–xxi.

26 Ellis, *Studies*, I, pt. 4, pp. 82, 173–9.

27 Siobhan B. Somerville argues that Ellis finds genital abnormality more frequently among his female cases because he looks more anxiously for it: 'To Ellis, the seemingly imperceptible differences between "normal" and "abnormal" intimacies between women called for greater scrutiny into the subtleties of their anatomy'. Somerville, 'Scientific Racism and the Invention of the Homosexual Body', in Bland and Doan (eds) *Sexology in Culture*, p. 66.

28 On early modern definitions and theories of tribadism, see Traub, *Renaissance*, pp. 45–8 and 188–228.

29 On the legal history, see Hitchcock, *English Sexualities*, p. 77; on prosthetic supplementation, see Traub, *Renaissance*, pp. 195–7.

30 Ibid., pp. 213–14.

31 Giovanni Bianchi, *Historical and Physical Dissertation on the Case of Catherine Vizzani*, London, 1751. The attribution of the English translation to Cleland was first made in Roger Lonsdale, 'New Attributions to John Cleland', *Review of English Studies*, New Series, XXX, no. 119 (1979), 268–90. All subsequent references will be cited parenthetically in the text. The case is also discussed by Emma Donoghue in *Passions Between Women: British Lesbian Culture 1668–1801*, New York: Harper Collins, 1995, pp. 80–6.

32 Traub, *Renaissance*, p. 191. On this question of the putatively self-evident 'commensurability of body parts to erotic desires and practices', see also pp. 226–8.

33 Many commentators have been struck by the symbolic suggestiveness of this valueless, emptied-out phallus. See Ian McCormick (ed.), *Secret Sexualities: A Sourcebook of Seventeenth- and Eighteenth-Century Writing*, London and New York: Routledge, 1997, p. 176; Donoghue, *Passions*, p. 83. Catherine Vizzani's 'contrivance' could be taken as an illustration of Thomas Laqueur's claim that in the early modern period:

> biological sex, which we generally take to serve as the basis of gender, was just as much in the domain of culture and meaning as was gender. A penis was thus a status symbol rather than a sign of some other deeply rooted ontological essence: *real* sex. It could be construed as a certificate of sorts, like the diploma of a doctor or lawyer today, which entitled the bearer to certain rights and privileges.

Thomas Laqueur, *Making Sex: Body and Gender from the Greeks to Freud*, Cambridge, MA: Harvard University Press, 1990, pp. 134–5. See also Traub, *Renaissance*, p. 196:

> Early modern women's prosthetic supplementation of their bodies is, I would argue, both additive and substitutive: as a material addition to the woman's body and as a replacement of the man's body *by* the woman's, prosthesis not only displaces male prerogatives, but exposes 'man' as a simulacrum, and gender as a construction built on the faulty ground of mutually exclusive binaries.

34 The excised passage runs as follows in Italian: 'Anzi per parere uomo da vero un bel Piuolo di Cuojo ripieno di Cenci s'era fatto, che sotto la camiscia teneva, e talora, ma sempre coperto a suoi Compagni per baldanza di soppiatto mostrava, per cui in Anghiari in poca d'ora corse fama che Giovanni nel fatto delle femmine più d'ogni altro valesse, la qual fama egli a caro grandemente avea che si spargesse' (Giovanni Bianchi, *Breve Storia della Vita di Catterina Vizzani, Romana* [Venice, 1744], p. 8). In rough translation, this might run: 'Indeed, in order to seem like a real man she had made herself a nice leather [Piuolo] which she kept under her shirt, and sometimes she would half show it to her companions, though always covered up, so that within a few hours the rumor spread throughout Anghiari that when it came to pleasing women Giovanni had it over anyone else, a rumor it was her dearest wish to have spread around'. Equivalent passages can be found in Cleland's text on pp. 10–11, 34–5, and 37. Thanks to Corrinne Harrol for providing me with a photocopy of Bianchi's text.

35 Donoghue, *Passions*, p. 85.

36 In his idiosyncratic *Institutes of Health* (1761) – a compilation of rules for living a salubrious life – Cleland argues that all forms of excessive desire – from libertinism to a taste for rich foods – are not properly our own, but imitations of the desires we see others acting on. The libertinism of the 'arrantest sensualist. . . a taste he suffers to drive him with as much fury as if it was a passion of nature', is, 'in fact, nothing more than the suggestion of false, absurd, and fashionable opinion' (p. 32).

37 On the many recent critical readings of this scene, see Peter Sabor's review essay, 'From Sexual Liberation to Gender Trouble: Reading *Memoirs of a Woman of Pleasure* from the 1960s to the 1990s', in *Eighteenth-Century Studies*, 33:4, 2000, 561–78.

38 According to Cleland's later recollections, although the *Memoirs* were published in 1749, when he was near 40, the book was largely written in collaboration with a friend, Charles Carmichael, when Cleland was 19 years old and Carmichael 17 – in the immediate wake of the sodomy trials of the late 1720s. See Peter Sabor, 'Introduction' to the *Memoirs*, pp. xiii–xiv.

39 See, for example, Cleland, *Memoirs*, pp. 34–5 and 44–5 (for Charles) and 70–2 (for Will). Donald H. Mengay notes that virtually 'all the male characters [in the *Memoirs*] are Ganymedes of sorts, patterned after Zeus' catamite who was abducted . . . "on account of his beauty" ' ('The Sodomitical Muse: *Fanny Hill* and the Rhetoric of Crossdressing', in Claude J. Summers (ed.), *Homosexuality in Renaissance and Enlightenment England*, New York: Haworth, 1992, p. 190).

40 Initiating the pattern of voyeurism that runs throughout the novel and culminates in the sodomite episode, Fanny describes herself getting in position to watch: 'I instantly crept softly, and posted myself so, that seeing every thing minutely, I could not myself be seen' (p. 24).

41 For other examples of disproportion as a vital constituent of desire, see pp. 30, 40 and 162.

42 Lisa L. Moore, in *Dangerous Intimacies: Toward a Sapphic History of the British Novel*, Durham,: Duke University Press, 1997, pp. 72–4, reads Cleland's treatment

of sodomy in the *Memoirs* in the context of works like *Satan's Harvest Home* that represent sodomy as a foreign import, although her reading of the 'plague spot' passage differs from mine.

43 The attribution of the *Dictionary* to Cleland was made in Roger Lonsdale, 'New Attributions' pp. 285–7. All quotations are taken from the British Library copy of the 1753 first edition; there are in that edition no page numbers, but the entries are arranged alphabetically.

4 'Wonderful Effects!!!'

Graphic satires of vaccination in the first decade of the nineteenth century

Suzanne Nunn

Can any person say what may be the consequences of introducing a *bestial* humour into the human frame after a long lapse of years? Who knows, besides, what *ideas* may rise in the course of time from a *brutal* fever having excited its incongruous impressions on the brain? Who knows, also, but that the human *character* may undergo strange mutations from *quadrupedan* sympathy, and that some modern Pasiphae may rival the fables of old?[1]

In this characteristic example of early nineteenth-century anti-vaccination rhetoric, Dr Benjamin Moseley expresses the fear that Edward Jenner's method of vaccination against smallpox using cowpox threatened the distinction of the human species. Vaccination brought into sharp focus concerns about the tenuousness of the boundary between animal and human and it articulated a specifically modern dread of chaos from the breaking down of distinctions between self and other. The risk of mental and physical degeneration through the amalgamation of bovine and human characteristics was the main argument mobilised against vaccination by its opponents. Evidence for extreme reactions to vaccination was readily presented to support their view. The anti-vaccinationist Mr Stuart, for example, found, 'a child at Peckham, who, after being inoculated with the cow-pox, had its former natural disposition absolutely changed to the *brutal*; so that it ran upon all fours like a beast, bellowing like a cow, and butting with its head like a bull'.[2] Ludicrous as these claims may seem to us, and indeed at the time the well respected *Edinburgh Review* was highly sceptical, accusing the anti-vaccionationists of preferring to rely 'on hearsay evidence, and on the authority of ignorant mothers'[3] rather than actual observation, such stories nevertheless formed the substance of much anti-vaccinationist propaganda. Vaccination divided medical and lay opinion, it was the focus of sermons and parliamentary debate, the subject of plays, poems and graphic satires, it spawned numerous medical papers and the invective that supporters and detractors heaped on each other coloured the pages of the medical press for over a decade.

Retrospective histories of the medical profession have tended towards representing vaccination in terms of the linear progress of modern medicine towards the greater good and as Ludmilla Jordanova has demonstrated portraits of

Edward Jenner contributed to this model of medical heroism.[4] Recent challenges to these celebratory histories have looked beyond the great men and great events to interrogate medicine as a discursive practice.[5] Drawing in the main on Marxist concepts of alienation and Foucauldian theories of discipline through surveillance such analysis tends to present too comprehensive a picture and ignore the transgressive potential of popular cultural texts as both sites of resistance and important conduits in the negotiation of cultural meaning. Furthermore, by continuing to interrogate written 'official' accounts the permanent remains privileged over the ephemeral leading to a loss of valuable context. In his seminal article 'Seeing the Past', Roy Porter outlined the difficulties that 'reading' graphic satire posed for historians, arguing that the interpretation of visual material should be extended beyond the narrowly evidential.[6] Most recently Ludmilla Jordanova has cautioned against the simplistic interpretation of images, and demonstrated that visual material has its own logic and contains many complex layers of meaning which can be most comprehensively interpreted by adopting an interdisciplinary methodology.[7]

This chapter focuses on two graphic satires on the subject of vaccination, James Gillray's print *The Cow-Pock – or – the Wonderful Effects of the New Inoculation!* (1802), Figure 4.2 and *Vaccination* – attributed to Charles Williams (1808) – Figure 4.3. Both prints have been thoroughly described by M. Dorothy George in the British Museum *Catalogue of Political and Personal Satires*,[8] and the Gillray print has been frequently reproduced as an 'illustration' in the context of medical history. This chapter extends the understanding of these prints beyond narrowly evidential interpretations by adopting a visual cultural perspective and interpreting them both in terms of the practice of art and the practice of medicine at the beginning of the nineteenth century. By positioning graphic satires on vaccination as a point of intersection between conflicting attitudes to the body it becomes possible to appreciate these ephemeral texts as part of a set of communicative practices that made shared anxieties about the body and medicine meaningful in a unique and vibrant way. Graphic satires on vaccination, as I demonstrate, were both sites of resistance to the disciplining of the body and important conduits in the negotiation of medical authority over the diseased body and its representation. Medicine at the beginning of the nineteenth century had as yet no automatic authority over the ways in which the diseased body could be represented, and graphic satires reveal the body as a contested territory over and through which old and new attitudes to the body were articulated and negotiated.

In Foucault's account of the development of medical knowledge in Paris he identifies the establishment of the clinic and the publication of Xavier Bichat's *General Anatomy* (1801) as a turning point in the conceptualisation of the body and disease.[9] As N. D. Jewson has argued, the advent of scientific medicine marked a transformation from a person-centred cosmology of illness to an object-centred cosmology,[10] and the differences between medical illustration and medical graphic satire testify to this ideological struggle. For example, the engraving of the cowpox pustules on Sarah Nelmes's arm, Figure 4.1, scruti-

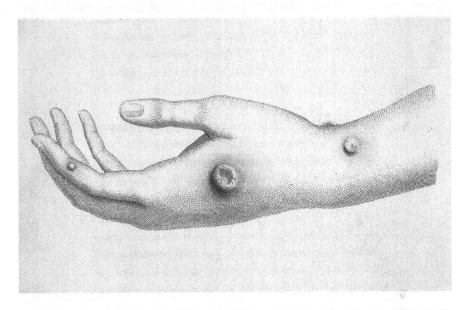

Figure 4.1 An Inquiry into the Causes and Effects of the Variolae Vaccine, 1798 (Well-
    come Library, London).

nises the part and exemplifies the impersonal medical gaze which ushered in the
possibility of clinical detachment. In complete contrast are the bacchanalian
transformations and the brutalising results of vaccination depicted in the two
graphic satires discussed in this chapter. These graphic satires relocate and re-
orientate medical discourses, by reducing them to the lowest common denomi-
nator: the flesh. The emphasis in early nineteenth-century medical graphic satire
is unrelentingly focused on the body, and bodily functions and they stand in
opposition to medical images which utilise the standardised healthy body.
Medical publications position medical practice in the discourse of science,
which brings the unruly body back into the symbolic order, and this is appropriate since medicine, as a professional discourse, tries to distance itself from disorder. By emphasising the chaos of the diseased body graphic satire deconstructs
medicine by deliberately stripping away the gloss of science and refusing the
clean and proper body.[11] Graphic satires use the grotesque as a category of
explanation, as a way of exploring conflicting ideas about the body, and to question medical progress and medical authority at the beginning of the nineteenth
century.

   Smallpox is one of the most highly contagious diseases, and with the demise
of leprosy it had become the most common cause of facial disfigurement in the
eighteenth century. It was a disease unknown in ancient times and became
specifically associated in medical and religious thinking, along with measles and
scarlet fever, with the mass of urban poor.[12] Smallpox had been distinguished
from other general rashes and the 'great' or 'French pox' in the sixteenth

century. It was a disease that became endemic in the dirty and overcrowded urban environment, but also periodically swept through rural towns and villages. The first symptoms are a high fever and a rash that develops after a few days into separate 'pocks'. These pocks, which are about the size of a pea, become enlarged as they develop into pustules full of yellow matter that emit a foul odour. The fever returns, often accompanied by delirium or coma, and the pustules dry out and form scabs which itch. As the scabs fall away the sufferer is left with characteristic depressed white scars. There was no cure, but inoculation, or more specifically variolation using pus from mature smallpox pustules, had been practiced in Britain since the 1720s and many practitioners had amassed considerable fortunes from this practice both at home and in the newly-founded colonies.[13] The visitation of disease was still considered by many to be a sign of Divine displeasure, with the corruption of the surface of the skin providing a tangible reflection of the modern spiritual condition, and it bore the mark of Cain.

The surface of the body – the skin – is the place where inside and outside meet and ruptures to this surface; the mouth, the vagina, the anus and open wounds all have psychological significance as the places where self and other merge. As the anthropologist Mary Douglas argues, these bodily openings require extensive policing through purifying rituals to neutralise their potential dangers.[14] The stability of meaning, reliant for definition on its opposite, becomes challenged if these divisions become indistinct. In her writing on Levitical abominations Douglas argues that the physical expression of holiness was represented by the 'clean and proper body', its smooth surface devoid of openings. Since the ravages of smallpox distressed the surface of the skin, we can conjecture that, in preventing this distress, vaccination not only preserved health but, on the surface at least, returned humanity to its immaculate state. Douglas continues, 'Holiness requires that individuals shall conform to the class to which they belong. And Holiness requires that different classes of things shall not be confused'.[15] Vaccination's merging of animal and human, then, presented a direct contravention of God's law, in Douglas's terms it was 'polluting'. Merging with the 'other' threatened the very identity of the modern self.

The half human/half animal exemplifies Julia Kristeva's concept of abjection by which she means 'that which does not respect borders . . . [and] disturbs identity, system, order'.[16] The abject threatens the distinction of the self because it is situated at the point where meaning collapses, and strategies therefore need to be in place to maintain order. In medical texts, illustrations of the diseased body are sanitised through visual codes that deny the status of the body as 'subject', thus bringing the unruly body back into the symbolic order. The illustration of the pustules on Sarah Nelmes's arm, Figure 4.1, for example, blossom on the underlying immaculate marble-like skin, and refer to the fusion of anatomical with classical iconography established by the anatomist Andreas Vesalius in the *Humani Corporis Fabrica* (1543). This fusion neutralises the grotesque aspect of the corporeal body within the register of the clean and proper body of classical sculpture. As an abstracted part, Nelmes's arm is in a sense a picture without a narrative and yet the relaxed pose of the hand suggests acquiescence to the scrutiny of the medical gaze. Graphic satire, in contrast to medical illustration, flagrantly relocates the unruly diseased body in its entire grotesque and transgressive aspects to centre-stage. The humour fully engages with the body's capacity to offend but it does so in such a way that it is pleasurable, thus neutralising the threat of the unruly body through laughter. The offensive and offending body of the patient in late eighteenth and early nineteenth-century graphic satire, vomiting, bleeding, defecating, erupting with boils, and even dying, can be said to conform to the older grotesque body of the carnivalesque:

> The artistic logic of the grotesque image ignores the closed, smooth, and impenetrable surface of the body and retains only its excrescences (sprouts, buds) and orifices, only that which leads beyond the body's limited space or into the body's depths . . . the image consists of orifices and convexities that present another, newly conceived body.[17]

In visual representations of vaccination the conflict between the older grotesque carnivalesque body and the 'modern' medical body find their full expression. The different printing techniques used, engraving for illustration and etching for graphic satire, further distinguish the message by virtue of the different implicit political meanings embedded in the quality of the line. The engraved line is cut into the metal plate and the resulting image is created from a series of marks of various thicknesses. The representation of skin that could be achieved by engraving, through the contrast between the dark engraved line and the white paper was unique to that medium, and as Barbara Maria Stafford has argued, engravings of the dissected body were predicated on the monumental.[18] In contrast the etching processes use acid to 'bite' into a resist which created a much 'softer' overall appearance that closely resembled watercolour paintings and did not rely on hard edges to demarcate surfaces. The mobile and flowing quality of the etched line, a line that trails off and disappears and hints at excess, is of itself expressive of the grotesque and transgressive aspects of bodies and spaces.

Medicine in 1800 was an eclectic mix of science, tradition and blatant fraud. The public was regarded as generally gullible and specifically ignorant by all factions of the medical profession: while the public for its part made little discrimination between the physician and the mountebank. The public was well used to a variety of specifics,[19] in the form of potions, lotions and apparatus which all claimed to produce 'wonderful effects', when Edward Jenner privately published *An Inquiry into the Causes and Effects of the Variolae Vaccine* (1798). The *Inquiry* presented details of observed cases whereby the inflammation and swelling of horses' heels known as 'the grease' was transmitted to the udders of cows by human contact, where in Jenner's words the disease became 'modified' and was then known as cowpox, which may be contracted by humans. The human form of cowpox presents itself as inflamed circular pustules on the hands with the attendant symptoms of stiff joints, lassitude and vomiting. Over several years Jenner observed that contracting cowpox in this way seemed to provide immunity from the highly contagious human disease smallpox, to which it bore a striking similarity. The *Inquiry* then goes on to describe how in 1796 Jenner inoculated a young boy with some matter taken from the cowpox pustule of Sarah Nelmes who had contracted the disease while milking. Six weeks later Jenner inoculated the boy again, this time with lymph taken from a smallpox pustule but the disease did not develop. Jenner had made what he believed to be the vital connection between cowpox and its more virulent human form, and proved that the deliberate introduction of cowpox from an infected cow into the human body would provide immunity from smallpox.[20]

Jenner was confident of the importance of his discovery and in an age when 'puffing' was the norm he proved to be a formidable self-publicist. He sought and secured the support of the aristocracy and in 1800 he was presented to King George who granted permission for the second edition of the *Inquiry* to be dedicated to him.[21] In 1802 Jenner had begun to seek support in Parliament to promote vaccination and outlaw variolation, but in spite of the support of William Wilberforce nothing came of the campaign until 1807 when a Government commissioned report by the Royal College of Physicians endorsed the practice of vaccination.[22] As a result of this report a Bill 'To Prevent the spreading of the Infection of the Small Pox' was presented to parliament in 1808.[23] Jenner was also acutely aware of the importance of popular support for his discovery and he sought validation in the public sphere through the medium of the popular press by commissioning poetry to be written in his and vaccination's honour.[24] In the Government Select Committee Report on vaccination (1801), many eminent medical witnesses endorsed vaccination as 'the greatest discovery',[25] but a vociferous opposition continued. Branding it as quackery, vaccination's opponents argued that the incorporation of bovine matter risked the degeneration of the human species. 'The brutalisation of the noblest work of creation', as Jenner's main critic Dr Benjamin Moseley phrased it.[26]

In the first decade of the nineteenth century the *Edinburgh Review*, an influential Whig periodical, published two significant articles on vaccination. The first, 'Willan and Others on Vaccination' (1806)[27] begins with the assertion that although medical subjects were properly left to medical journals, vaccination was of 'such incalculable importance, and of such universal interest'[28] that an exception should be made. With this proviso the *Review* presented its 12,000–14,000 subscribers with a detailed account of both the vaccination process and the acrimonious controversy it had excited in medical circles. Evidently supportive of vaccination, the *Review* was opprobrious of the conduct of medical men and condemned the 'coarseness, illiberality, violence, and absurdity, as is here exhibited by gentlemen of sense and education, discussing a point of professional science'.[29] In the second article, 'Pamphlets on Vaccination' (1810),[30] the *Review* specifically criticised, what it described as, the 'violence and disregard for accuracy'[31] indulged in by the anti-vaccinationists. The use of 'nicknames, handbills, squibs and caricatures' the *Review* complained were 'too successfully employed, where they were calculated to do most mischief – among the weak and ignorant'.[32] The *Review* stated that the 'disgusting caricatures of mangy girls and oxfaced boys', that were used to reinforce the anti-vaccinationists claims, 'have done more to prevent the universal adoption of vaccination, than any doubts of its efficacy'.[33] These comments imply, from the *Review's* point of view, that not only were the anti-vaccinationists employing tactics that discredited the medical profession, but also that caricature was a powerful formulator of opinion, particularly amongst those who were less educated than the *Review's* target audience.

The *Review's* comments, however, seem somewhat inconsistent with the realities of public life, since at the beginning of the nineteenth century, 'nicknames, handbills, squibs and caricatures' were part of the political currency of the day. This is the period in which the graphic satirist James Gillray (1756–1815) produced some of his most incisive and sardonic commentaries on domestic and foreign policies, and the commissioning of graphic satires against one's political or professional opponents was commonplace. The hybridisation of animal and human, or vegetable and human forms was an established feature of the political graphic satirical repertoire and had its roots in popular and classical mythology and heraldry. The *Review's* concerns regarding the depiction of 'mangy girls and oxfaced boys', then, need to be understood in terms of the broader anxieties generated by the vaccination process itself, which through the deliberate incorporation of bovine matter into the human body called into question the stability of the boundary between animal and human. As the historian Keith Thomas states:

> Wherever we look in early modern England, we find anxiety, latent or explicit, about any form of behaviour which threatened to transgress the fragile boundaries between the man and the animal creation . . . 'Beasts are more hairy than men', wrote Bacon, 'and savage men more than civil'.[34]

Whether the deeply cynical James Gillray was being ironic when he engraved *The Cow-Pock – or – the Wonderful Effects of the New Inoculation!* (1802), Figure 4.2, it is impossible to say, but he was certainly familiar with anti-vaccination rhetoric. Although this print seems to endorse anti-vaccinatinist views about the potential 'brutalization of the noblest work of creation', following the title in small print is inscribed 'Vide – the publications of ye Anti-Vaccine Society', suggesting the possibility that this highly exaggerated image was ridiculing the arguments of Moseley and his followers. Whatever its intention the image utilises the issue of vaccination to present an extraordinary visualisation of broader contemporary concerns about the control of the body and the fear/fantasy associated with the body of the 'other'. The crowded interior is a representation of the Smallpox and Inoculation Hospital at St Pancras as the 'St Pancras' charity school badge on the sleeve of the ragged boy in the foreground testifies, he also has a pamphlet entitled 'Benefits of the vaccine process' protruding from his pocket. His crooked limbs are indicative of rickets and, like others in the room, he has the collapsed nasal bridge specifically symptomatic of syphilis. The low sloping forehead of the boy and others in the room was a

Figure 4.2 James Gillray, *The Cow-Pock – or – the Wonderful Effects of the New Inoculation!*, 1802 (Wellcome Library, London).

physiognomy typically associated with the lower classes. The source of this physiognomy lies with the work of two men, Johan Caspar Lavater who attributed physiognomy to moral constitution rather than the consequences of social conditions, and the Dutch anatomist Pieter Camper who used the 'facial angle' to assess an individual's evolutionary proximity to the ape, claiming the 'angle' as scientific evidence of a primitive or animal nature.[35] Gillray had used similar faces in his political prints to represent the moral degradation of the Jacobins.[36] The boy holds a bucket of 'Vaccine Pock hot from ye Cow' for the doctor standing behind. 'Hot' refers not only to temperature but also indicated freshness, and it was used generally to mean a high level of sexual desire, with particular reference to the lustfulness of animals. The doctor is Edward Jenner, easily recognised from contemporary portraits and he is not caricatured. Indeed the physiognomical contrast between Jenner and some of his patients is so marked that he seems to almost be a different species. Gillray deliberately distinguishes Jenner from both the patients and the assistants and this may imply that Gillray was endorsing vaccination by not ridiculing its discoverer.

Jenner is in the act of vaccinating a buxom woman whose ornate straw hat suggests that she has pretensions to gentility, but the near exposure of her left breast evidences how fragile the control of her sexual passion actually is. Her possibly hard won respectability is now in jeopardy as repressed animal instincts threaten to gain the ascendant once the containing surface of her skin is breached. As the blood flows, under Jenner's knife, the sexual connotations are palpable. It is small wonder she is anxious as she bears witness to the 'Wonderful Effects' that the 'New Inoculation' has produced in the preceding patients. Next to her a horrified man desperately clasps his buttocks in a vain attempt to prevent the spontaneous excretion of a small cow, while he watches in horror as another erupts from his forearm. A butcher in the background has grown horns, a traditional sign of the cuckold, and there may be an oblique reference here to the equation in the popular consciousness between butchers and surgeons. On the far right a woman in a ragged apron, who may be the butcher's cuckolding wife, vomits one small cow, while giving birth to another. There are clear associations here with well known theories of maternal impressions associated with monstrous births, and even with bestiality which was a capital offence until 1861. She may represent the modern Queen Pasiphae that Dr. Moseley had warned of in the opening quotation to this chapter.[37] This woman is set in juxtaposition to the seated matron, and perhaps represents the matron's potential future once animal passions, signified by the man between them, become ascendant.

There are no speech bubbles but it is obvious that these events would be accompanied by a cacophony of shouting, mooing, farting and retching. The image reflects and endorses hierarchical readings of bodily organs whereby the lower classes are equated with the lower stratum of the body.[38] Details on the far left below the dandified assistant, administering 'opening mixture' with a ladle, all relate to bodily evacuations, there is a bottle labelled 'vomit', a syringe, a type of commode called a close-stool and of course the prime satiric signifier for late eighteenth and early nineteenth century medical practitioners, the ubiquitous clyster. The grotesque body, open, excessive and metonymic, dominates this image. It presents a dramatic challenge to the discourse of vaccination which sought amongst other things to create a smooth unblemished surface. These are bodies manifestly out of control. The incorporation of the bovine 'other' initiates a bacchanal of qualitative and quantitative transformation that precipitates a return to chaos. The painting on the wall behind, depicting the idolatrous worship of the golden calf by naked revellers, warns of the consequences for a culture that has substituted the worship of ideas and objects for its God. These transgressive bodies, being both animal and human, also pose a threat to the developing capitalist economy with its ultimate reliance on the disciplined working body. At a time when revolutionary ideas were prevalent throughout Europe the undisciplined working body presented a very real challenge to the power of the dominant institutions. If this image is read in a broader social and political context, then, the lower classes as collective and individual bodies are 'revolting' in every sense.

Gillray's work was well-known and highly popular but the *Edinburgh Review* did not refer to this Gillray print in its articles on vaccination. The *Review* did however single out a more obscure and less accomplished print as one of the most 'disgusting caricatures', this was *Vaccination* (Figure 4.3) used as the frontispiece to an anti-vaccinationist publication entitled *The Vaccine*

Phantasmagoria by Ferdinand Smyth Stuart Esq., who, the title page claimed was Physician, barrack master and great grandson to King Charles II. When this book was published in 1808 the vaccination debate was again very much to the fore, following the establishment of the Vaccine Institution in 1807 with Government support,[39] the reward of £20,000 to Jenner by the Government for promulgating his discovery, and the passage through Parliament of a Bill to prevent the spreading of the infection of the smallpox.[40] In Figure 4.3 the pastoral is made strange, presenting a stark contrast to the contemporary vogue for representations of the English landscape informed by the precepts of the Picturesque. This is a violated landscape peopled not by simple country folk but by rampant vaccinationists and their monstrous cow. The beast, an incongruous hybridisation of a cow, a lion and a dragon is a Chimera, the fabled monster of Greek mythology and part of the popular grotesque iconography of the Middle Ages.[41] Figuratively the Chimera was used to refer to a horrible fear inspiring phantasm, an unreal creature of the imagination – literally the stuff of nightmares. Technically the Chimera is theriomorphic – something or someone having the form of a beast – whereas the vaccinators, who will be discussed later, are terianthropic – combining the form of beast and human.[42]

As a metaphor the Chimera therefore exposes vaccination as a mere wild fancy, as an unfounded conception. As a monstrous hybrid the beast testifies to

Figure 4.3 Charles Williams, *Vaccination*, 1802 (Wellcome Library, London).

the nightmarish vision of amalgamation evoked in anti-vaccionationist rhetoric. The Chimera is covered with suppurating ulcers inscribed 'pestilence', 'plague', 'fetid ulcer' and 'leprosy', all ancient diseases that manifested themselves as disfigurement of the surface of the skin. The ulcers on the hide of the Chimera are strongly reminiscent of the illustration of the cowpox pustule on Sarah Nelmes's arm in the *Inquiry* (Figure 4.1), thus collapsing the boundary between medical and popular illustration. 'Pandora's box' is inscribed above an incision in the creature's belly, not only invoking mythology to signify the potential dangers of birthing progressive medical techniques, but also referring to the importance of the stomach in Galenic regimes of health, where the proper evacuation of waste was deemed essential. Digestion is the assimilation of something that is not part of oneself, so the stomach is at the centre of a system of exchanges between the inside and outside world.[43] Digestion was therefore both a useful metaphor for the assimilation of the 'other', with the belly as noted in relation to the Gillray print (Figure 4.2), referring to the lower orders of society. The contagious aspect of the poor was becoming well documented in medical treatise which can be linked to fears of the 'mob' following the Terror in France. The poor were also constructed through animal metaphors, Edmund Burke in *Reflections on the Revolution in France* (1790) famously referred to the French proletariat as 'a swinish multitude'. Although the setting is pastoral, the urban poor as pollution were becoming a source of increasing anxiety and the seeping belly may allude to the introduction of smallpox into rural areas by visitors from the towns. Medicine at this time begins to be concerned with distancing itself from the grotesque and the re-emergence of the grotesque Chimera therefore signifies a regressive rather than a progressive movement, as does the return of leprosy and plague which had become less significant diseases during the eighteenth century. Where the ulcers on the Chimera refer to the illustration of the pustule on Sarah Nelmes's arm, the reference to Pandora undermines the trustworthiness of Jenner's scientific method and directly associates vaccination with the spread of evil rather than good on a global scale.

Feeding the insatiable beast with baskets of naked infants are purposeful vaccinationists, rendered diabolical or bovine by horns and tails. Steve Baker argues that, 'the pictorial form of a polluting person will be characterized by the troubling in-between-ness of therianthropism', and he goes on to state that visualising someone in this way is an 'effective means of stereotyping them, of objectifying them, and of rendering them inferior'.[44] The paper in the coat pocket of the main figure has £10,00[0] inscribed on it, telling the viewer that this is Edward Jenner who was awarded a parliamentary grant of that sum in 1802. The vaccinatinists throw infants into the gaping maw of the beast, these are then excreted with horns and tails, and a lone figure at the back shovels the transformed infants into a dung cart. The man with the spade is either Robert Thornton or William Woodville the chief physician at the St Pancras Dispensary, both of whom wrote pamphlets in support of vaccination and were, in addition, acclaimed botanists. In 1803 Thornton had published *Facts Decisive in Favour of the Cow Pock*, which he dedicated to Jenner, and a lavishly illustrated work entitled *New Illustrations of the Sexual System of Linnaeus* (1807), while William Woodville wrote a four volume work entitled *Medical Botany* (1790–1794). The man is standing on a book with the legible title 'Lectures on Botany' but since there is no definitive caricaturing it is impossible to say with certainty which candidate he is. Within late eighteenth-century scientific circles, botany had become a truly shocking science, once plants were discovered not to exercise sexual restraint. Linnaean botany emphasised that flowers were the sexual organs of plants and went beyond biological analogies importing social analogies onto his descriptions of plant life. Botany became a discourse with a radical edge as flowers were used as a metaphor to address questions about sexuality and class as in Erasmus Darwin's *The Loves of the Plants* (1789) and Mary Wollstonecraft's *Vindication of the Rights of Woman* (1792). Botany also initiated a new sort of pastoral, 'a Golden Age before human beings had fallen into sexual division and conflict, subject to lust and unsatisfied desire'.[45] In Figure 4.3 such a nostalgic vision is deluged with excrement and trampled under foot. Excrement is the 'other' in the tranquil countryside, a waste product but nevertheless vital for its life-giving and regenerative force. This is demonstrated in the image by its proximity to the book on botany, and may be a reference to changing agrarian practice and the conflict between scientific understanding and rural wisdom. Jenner's research had been stimulated by the Gloucestershire folk tradition that dairymaids and cowherds, although they caught cowpox, had uniquely unblemished skin, and the *Inquiry* had provided a scientific rationalisation of this vulgar knowledge.

There is a marked horizontal division of Figure 4.3 into chaos in the foreground and order in the background. On top of the distant mountain stands the 'Temple of Fame', the classical circular form of this building with a colonnade and hemispherical dome was a popular feature in gardens and parks. The Temple of Fame was also a common symbol used in graphic satire since the mid-seventeenth century and had its roots in a much earlier emblematic tradition. Appearing over the horizon are the anti-vaccinationists in heroic mode. They brandish swords inscribed 'Truth' and carry shields bearing a single identifying letter; their surnames Mosley, Squirrell, Rowley, Birch and Lipscomb, being inscribed in full on a commemorative obelisque. Benjamin Mosely, physician at the Royal Hospital, Chelsea, published many controversial tracts on cowpox including a long dissertation against vaccination in *A Treatise on Sugar* (1799). Robert Squirrell wrote *Observations on the Cowpox,* John Birch, surgeon at St Thomas's, published *Serious Reasons for Uniformly Objecting to the Practice of Vaccination* (1806) and William Rowley, man-midwife and general surgeon at the Queen's Lying-in Hospital, published several pamphlets in opposition to vaccination including *Cow-pox Inoculation no Security Against Small-Pox infection* (1805). In the same year George Lipscomb, house surgeon at St Bartholomew's, published *A Dissertation on the Failure and the Mischiefs of the Disease called Cow-Pox.* Although they opposed vaccination on scientific and philosophical grounds the anti-vaccinationists all agreed with the principle of inoculation and had made handsome livings from variolation both home and abroad. Ostensibly the pending battle will be fought on the specific issue of vaccination, but ultimately it was an expression of the infighting between different factions of medical practice over the body of the patient.

These caricature bodies, as 'fictions' or narratives of vaccination, are themselves embodiments of established artistic tropes and cultural practices. The focus was on personalities and the graphic satirists response was reflexive rather than reflective, they presented a 'knee-jerk' reaction to events through an established and understood visual medium embedded in the radical tradition. The particular visual language of British graphic satire, developed by William Hogarth (1697–1764) from the European broadside tradition on the theme of the 'World Upside Down' and seventeenth-century emblems, enabled the engagement with contemporary events in a way that 'spoke' to and about contemporary society. Graphic satires seize on popular symbols in order to exploit them, and graphic satires on vaccination play on the continuing tension between self and other and anxieties about self control. The simultaneous presentation of medical and lay attitudes to the body in the picture plane, while it dissolved the boundary between them, paradoxically highlighted this tension. In Figures 4.2 and 4.3 grotesque and civilised bodies are juxtaposed and yet they coexist; it worth noting that in both prints the civilised body is accorded to selected medical men. Graphic satire could call to account the instability and inherent fragility of the early modern self constructed through the other by virtue of its position on the periphery of the artistic sphere. The Royal Academy established in 1768 explicitly excluded engravers, and the commercial imperative of graphic satire encouraged the view that its practitioners were hacks. Diana Donald argues that the exclusion of engravers created a counter-culture of artists working outside and independently of the Academy, and for Donald this was a fundamental factor in graphic satire's ability to create 'a vision of politics as seen from below'.[46] Gillray's *Wonderful Effects* (Figure 4.2) presents bodies that are out of control, but comedy works to neutralize the 'real' fears of degeneration articulated in this image. These fears are not mediated through humour in quite the same way in *Vaccination* (Figure 4.3), except perhaps through the ludicrousness of excess and it is uncertain, given its context in a medical treatise, just how funny this image was supposed to be. The incorporation of bovine matter into the human body brought into sharp focus the potential instability of the boundary between animal and human and raised important questions about the role of medicine in the lives of the populace.

By positioning graphic satire as a point of intersection between lay and medical attitudes to the body and deconstructing the layers of meaning within the print it is possible to demonstrate that they provide a unique and historically specific commentary for the control over meaning by different social groups. The two graphic satires discussed in this chapter testify to the importance of ephemeral texts in the process of cultural negotiation, existing as sites where resistance to the medical disciplining of the body could be articulated. However, analysis of these images in terms of a definitive resistance is frustrated by their inherent paradoxes. Since, although the grotesque degrades medicine's pretensions as a 'high' discourse by continually reasserting the body's predisposition to excess, the maintenance of opposition between the grotesque and the civilised body also confirmed that opposition. By accepting paradox as a condition of existence, and working with it, the graphic satirist was able expose for the viewer the limitations of different cultural discourses as a way of understanding and structuring their world.

Notes

1 Dr Benjamin Moseley (1798) quoted in 'Willan and others on vaccination', *Edinburgh Review*, 9, 1806, 37. Italics in original.
2 Mr Stuart quoted in 'Pamphlets on vaccination', *Edinburgh Review*, 15, 1810, 339 (italics in original).
3 Ibid., 330.
4 Ludmilla Jordanova, *Defining Features: Scientific and Medical Portraits 1660–2000*, London: Reaktion Books, 2000.
5 For example, Mary Poovey, *Making a Social Body: British Cultural Formation, 1830–1864*, Chicago: Chicago University Press, 1995; Frank Mort, *Dangerous Sexualities: Medico-Moral Politics in England since 1830*, London: Routledge, 2000.
6 Roy Porter, 'Seeing the Past', *Past and Present*, 118, 1988, 186–205.
7 Ludmilla Jordanova, *History in Practice*, London: Arnold, 2000.
8 Frederick Stephens and M. Dorothy George, *Catalogue of Political and Personal Satires preserved in the Department of Prints and Drawings in the British Museum*, 11 vols, London: British Museum, 1870–1954, [hereafter *BM*] viii, catalogue nos. 9924 and 9925.
9 Michel Foucault, *The Birth of the Clinic: An Archaeology of Medical Perception*, London: Routledge, 1989.
10 N. D. Jewson, 'The Disappearance of the Sick-Man from Medical Cosmology 1770–1870, *Sociology* 10, 1976, 225–44.
11 The term 'clean and proper body' is used by Mary Douglas. See her *Purity and Danger: An Analysis of Concepts of Pollution and Taboo*, London: Routledge & Kegan Paul, 1969.
12 Barbara Maria Stafford, *Body Criticism: Imaging the Unseen in Enlightenment Art and Medicine*, Cambridge: MIT Press, 1991, p. 291
13 See Charles Creighton, *A History of Epidemics in Britain*, 2 vols., Cambridge: Cambridge University Press, 1891–94, II, pp. 434–631. J. R. Smith, *The Speckled Monster: Smallpox in England 1670–1970, with particular reference to Essex*, Chelmsford: Essex Record Office, 1987, pp. 40–67. Peter Razzell, *Smallpox: The Impact of Inoculation on Smallpox in Eighteenth Century Britain*, Sussex: Caliban Books, 1997. See also David E. Shuttleton's chapter above and the references there cited.
14 Douglas, *Purity and Danger*.
15 Ibid., p. 53.
16 Julia Kristeva, *Powers of Horror: An Essay in Abjection*, New York: Columbia University Press, 1982, p. 4.
17 Mikhail Bakhtin, *Rabelais and His World*, trans. Helene Iswolsky [1965], Bloomington: Indiana University Press, 1984, p. 318.
18 Stafford, *Body Criticism*.
19 For example, Solomon's 'Balm of Guilead', 'Perkins Tractors', James Graham's 'Electrical Aether', 'Nervous Aetherial', 'Elixir of Life', 'Imperial Pills' and the 'Grand Celestial Bed' guaranteed to cure impotence at a cost of 500 guineas a night. Roy Porter, *Quacks, Fakers and Charlatans in English Medicine*, Stroud: Tempus 2000.

20 See Peter Razzell, *Edward Jenner's Cowpox Vaccine: The History of a Medical Myth*, Sussex: Caliban Books, 1980. Razell argues, through a close analysis of Jenner's case notes, letters and papers that the original strain was lost, and that since 1799 when Jenner used lymph sent to him by William Woodville he was actually vaccinating with a strain of attenuated smallpox.

21 Vaccination was made compulsory in the army and navy as part of wider hygiene initiatives. See Tim Fullford and Debbie Lee, 'The Beast Within: The Imperial Legacy of Vaccination in History and Literature', *Literature and History*, 9, 2000, 1–23.

22 *Report of the Royal College of Physicians of London on Vaccination*, 1807 (14) II, 55.

23 Vaccine Inoculation, *Parliamentary Debates* (House of Commons) 9 June 1808, 1st series, xi, 803, 841–4.

24 Jenner commissioned poems by Robert Bloomfield (The Suffolk Poet), Samuel Taylor Coleridge, Robert Southey and John Williams. See Tim Fullford and Debbie Lee, 'The Jenneration of Disease: Vaccination, Romanticism, and Revolution', *Studies in Romanticism*, 39, 2000, 139–63. In 1810 a comic pro-vaccination play entitled *The Cow Doctor* was performed on the London stage. This play, dedicated to Rev. T. Pennington and K. Kingsdown chaplain to the Rt. Hon. Edward Lord Ellenborough, is a blatant piece of vaccination propaganda. The opening of the play advocates that the clergy should play a role in the promotion of vaccination and this is followed by a prologue in the form of a poem that eulogises Jenner as the saviour of humankind. Through its rather tortuous plot the play charts the conversion of Crimp, an unscrupulous apothecary of doubtful morals, from variation to vaccination, after which he embraced a Christian life, enjoyed increased income and domestic bliss.

25 *Report from the Committee on Dr. Jenner's petition, respecting his discovery of vaccine inoculation*, 1801–2 (75) II, 267.

26 Dr Benjamin Moseley quoted in *Edinburgh Review* 15, 1810, 339.

27 'Willan and Others on Vaccination', *Edinburgh Review* 9, 1806, 32–66.

28 Ibid., 32.

29 Ibid., 39.

30 'Pamphlets on Vaccination' *Edinburgh Review*, 15, 1810, 322–51.

31 Ibid., 325.

32 Ibid.

33 Ibid., 338.

34 Keith Thomas, *Man and the Natural World: Changing Attitudes in England 1500–1800*, London: Penguin, 1984, pp. 38–9.

35 See Mary Cowling, *The Artist as Anthropologist*, Cambridge: Cambridge University Press, 1998.

36 For example, James Gillray, *The London Corresponding Society, alarm'd*, etching with aquatint,1798, *BM* no. 9202.

37 Pasiphae in Greek Mythology was the wife of Minos King of Crete. She mated with a bull and gave birth to the Minotaur. To humanist philosophers of the Renaissance Pasiphae represented the deliberate flouting of natural and divine law, and the overthrow of reason for animal passion.

38 Michael Schoenfeldt, 'Fables if the Belly in Early Modern England', in David Hillman and Carla Mazzio (eds) *The Body in Parts: Fantasies of Corporeality in Early Modern Europe,* London and New York: Routledge, 1997, p. 248.

39 London Vaccine Institute, *Parliamentary Debates* (House of Commons) 2 June 1808, 1st series, xi, 803; Vaccine Inoculation, *Parliamentary Debates* (House of Commons), 9 June 1808, 1st series, xi, 841–4.

40 The Bill set out extensive restrictions on the practice of variolation – which it calls the Suttonian Method. *Bill to Prevent the Spreading of the Infection of the Smallpox*, 1808 (278) I, 645.

41 In Greek mythology the Chimera was killed by Belerephon: *Illiad* 6: 155–203. Mikhail Bakhtin states: 'Most characteristic is the role of the chimera, this quintessence of the grotesque, which invades every sphere of painting' (*Rabelais and His World*, p. 96).

42 See Steve Baker, *Picturing the Beast: Animals, Identity and Representation,* Manchester: Manchester University Press, 1993, pp. 108–11.

43 Schoenfeldt, 'Fables of the Body', p. 248.

44 Baker, *Picturing the Beast*, p. 113.

45 Alan Bewell, '"Jacobin Plants": Botany and Social Theory in the 1790s', *The Wordsworth Circle*, 20, 1989, 132–9.

46 Diana Donald, *The Age of Caricature: Satirical Prints in the Reign of George III,* New Haven: Yale University Press, 1996, p. 51.

Part II
Controlling disabled bodies
Medicine, politics and policy

5 Disciplining disabled bodies

The development of orthopaedic medicine in Britain, *c*.1800–1939

Anne Borsay

Although the treatment of fractures and dislocations featured in surgical texts from the Hippocratic era,[1] the term 'orthopaedics' was first coined by the eighteenth-century French physician, Nicholas Andry, from the combination of two Greek roots, 'orthos' meaning straight and 'pais' meaning child.[2] His concept acquired new cultural and historical significance in 1975, when Michel Foucault used an image from *Orthopaedia: or, the Art of Correcting and Preventing Deformities in Children* (1743) as an illustration for *Discipline and Punish*, his ground-breaking study of the birth of the prison. Andry's bent tree – bound to a straight stake – exemplified the pursuit of normality through an ongoing and routinized regime of disciplinary power that for Foucault was the hallmark of modern societies.[3] This chapter explores how orthopaedic medicine was applied to the disciplining of disabled children in Britain between 1800 and the outbreak of the Second World War. It is argued that from the early twentieth century, a *social* brand of orthopaedics – quite distinct from its medical or surgical counterparts – came to monopolize the surveillance of impairment and the repair of disabled bodies incapable of participating in the labour market. Three main themes are examined to support this thesis: the transition in orthopaedic knowledge from 'deformity' to science; the capture of voluntary organizations for disabled people by social orthopaedists; and the principles of medical holism through which this programme of treatment and reform was implemented.

From 'deformity' to science

David Le Vay has identified three roots for the treatment of orthopaedic conditions: bone-setting, truss-making, and medical orthopaedics. As well as dealing with the obvious business of fractures and dislocations, bonesetters handled patients with club foot and other 'deformities' for whom truss-makers also crafted appliances. In contrast to this diverse multitude of practitioners, medical orthopaedics had one trailbreaker: Dr Robert Chessher (1750–1831) from Hinkley in Leicestershire whose patients, according to the *Gentleman's Magazine* of 1810, 'were loud in his praise for the benefits which they had received ... after they had vainly tried all other means'.[4] But, however gifted, Chessher's use of 'friction, massage, motion and splintage' and his construction of 'machines' to correct 'deformities' were almost without parallel among 'regular' practitioners who, in orthopaedic matters, typically deferred to 'irregular' bonesetters and truss-makers. Though the Medical Act of 1858 outlawed such collaboration, the 'irregulars' were themselves beginning to discern the advantages of professional recognition.[5] Therefore, Hugh Owen Thomas (1834–1891) – a descendant of the legendary bonesetter, Evan Thomas, who as a child in the mid-1700s was shipwrecked on the rocky north Wales coast – attended Edinburgh University, qualified at University College Hospital, London, and spent a short time studying French surgery in Paris.[6]

Medical orthopaedists like Hugh Owen Thomas brought together their 'hereditary craft with the knowledge gained in the medical schools',[7] but mainstream medicine was also developing a *surgical* response to broken bones and damaged muscles. General voluntary hospitals – a creation of the early eighteenth century – were already providing artificial legs for patients whose limbs had been amputated, in addition to opening orthopaedic departments and purchasing equipment to meet orthopaedic needs.[8] In 1817, however, the first hospital dedicated to orthopaedics was established in Birmingham for 'the relief of Persons labouring under Bodily Deformity'. Although 'spinal diseases' and 'contractions and distortions of the limbs' were treated, the management of club-foot was especially promoted. Every year there were 50 children born in the town with club-feet, the annual general meeting of 1862 was told:

> Each one costs in instruments alone, £2 and requires almost constant attention for at least a year. But this year we will send forth 50 human beings who instead of being cripples will, in the majority of cases have no evidences of their deformity remaining.[9]

Club foot was emphasized because in the late 1830s a surgical operation became available that promised to overcome the impairment. William Little, who set up an Infirmary for the Cure of Club Foot in London in 1838, learnt the procedure after undergoing it himself in Hanover. Two further metropolitan infirmaries, opening in 1851 and 1864, joined Little's foundation, and the three institutions merged in 1905 to form the Royal National Orthopaedic Hospital.[10]

The introduction of anaesthesia and antisepsis from the mid-nineteenth century helped to extend the therapeutic range of surgical orthopaedics,[11] sterile conditions being of particular importance where metal was permanently implanted.[12] From the 1860s, surgeons began to practise 'subcutaneous osteotomy – a technique for cutting and dividing bones under the skin'. Designed to prevent 'post-operative blood poisoning' by avoiding the exposure of tissues, this method enabled a raft of treatments for diseased and deformed bones, tendons and ligaments.[13] It was 20 years before it was replaced by 'antiseptic osteotomy' in which 'open operations were used for the correction of deformity and restoration of function to … limbs weakened by disease or injury'.[14] Orthopaedic hospitals were proud of the clinical profile that these surgical strategies generated. At Birmingham, for example, the medical officers reported in 1874/1875 that of the 759 new cases presenting themselves, '506 have been *cured*, 189 *relieved*, and 64 remain under treatment, and very satisfactory improvement is going on'. In achieving these results, 'upwards of 300' operations were performed, over and above to the 'numerous patients ... treated suffering from every variety of Contraction, Distortion, and Disease producing Deformity'.[15] A similar tally of operations was undertaken in 1895. Furthermore, the medical committee was gratified that 'there was absolutely no mortality attending these procedures. During the year there occurred only one death – a little girl aged four – sinking from extensive spinal disease'.[16]

Irrespective of its alleged successes, surgical orthopaedics easily slipped into defensive mode. As early as the 1840s, the London Orthopaedic Institution was contemplating 'the admission of a limited number of in-patients by election' to demonstrate the treatment of a greater variety of conditions than those recruited 'by order of the Governors'.[17] And three decades later the venerable Birmingham and Midlands Counties Orthopaedic Hospital felt compelled to justify the existence of specialist institutions.[18] By this stage, however, a specialist literature was evolving. In 1871, for instance, Bernard Brodhurst published a series of lectures delivered at St George's Hospital, London in which he defined orthopaedic surgery as 'the treatment of deformities of the trunk, neck, and extremities'. Congenital deformities, he contended, arose from one of two causes. Either they were due a 'morbid nervous influence on the muscular system', where just a 'short spasm' could lead to 'structural shortening' because foetal growth was rapid. Alternatively, an 'arrest of development' was capable of producing 'deformity, or even monstrosity', 'occurring as it may in a limb whilst growth elsewhere proceeds in a normal manner'. 'Disordered nervous influence' was also the 'prevailing cause' of non-congenital deformities, by far the more common. During infancy, for example, 'spasmodic action ... [was] very frequently occasioned by dental and by intestinal irritation', whilst paralysis before the age of two was 'often caused by exposure to cold' due to throwing off bedding or sitting on a stone seat. Additionally, however, non-congenital deformities were triggered by 'local inflammation' due to burns, punctured wounds and gunshot, and by 'debility' due to disabling employment, rickets, and scrofula or tuberculosis.[19]

Brodhursts's title – *Deformities of the Human Body* – locked surgical orthopaedics into the mindset of the early nineteenth-century. By the 1890s, A. H. Tubby, whose appointments included surgeon to the National Orthopaedic Hospital, was complaining that 'The practice of orthopaedic surgery in England does not include all phases of diseases of the bones and joints, such as ... arthritis of the hip and knee, on what grounds it is difficult to understand'. Nevertheless, his treatise, aimed at practitioners and advanced students, was not only called *Deformities* but also replicated Brodhursts's epistemology with sections on the spine, the upper and lower extremities, and other parts of the body.[20] By his second 1912 edition Tubby was lauding the 'immense progress' that had been made in orthopaedic surgery. 'New methods of treatment, based on clearer conceptions of pathogenesis and rendered possible by recent advances in *technique*, have come into vogue, and in a measure supplanted the older ones'. Therefore, he had rejected 'the less scientific regional classification, adopted in the first edition' and was 'grouping ... the various subjects on aetiological and pathological bases'.[21] However, it was only in third edition of 1924 that Tubby finally abandoned the title *Deformities* for *The Advance of Orthopaedic Surgery*, whilst simultaneously expanding the parameters to embrace the economic as well as the physical 're-education' of 'cripples'.[22]

The capture of the voluntary sector

The *social* orthopaedics into which Tubby plugged went back to the turn of the century. Notwithstanding the enhanced scientific status of surgery, medical orthopaedics was gaining ground as orthopaedic hospitals were increasingly marginalized by their concentration on a narrow range of techniques confined to the foot.[23] At the same time, the commencement of state schooling from 1870 – which became compulsory ten years later – made visible children who had previously 'all been mixed together in school or remained at home', and put them 'under public supervision and assessment for the first time'.[24] The voluntary sector reacted enthusiastically to this expanded pool of young 'cripples' and by 1914 over 40 agencies had been formed. At first, their ethos was sentimental. In 1888, however, the Invalid Children's Aid Association was founded as branch of the Charity Organization Society (COS), and five years later the parent body published an influential report that extended its rabid brand of personal responsibility to disabled people; charitable assistance was to be confined to the 'deserving' poor who were predisposed towards self-help, leaving the Poor Law to deal with the 'undeserving'.[25] But this stance was increasingly out of step with a state seeking partnerships with the voluntary sector. Therefore, organizations like the Nottingham District Cripples' Guild – established in 1908 as part of the new guilds of help movement[26] – operated in collaboration with government agencies whilst endorsing the COS's stringent moral code when processing the requests for assistance.[27]

The emphasis on self-help underpinning this code challenged the assumption of the sentimental charities that impairment was irremediable and prepared the way for an alliance with orthopaedists unhappy that philanthropy was preoccupied with education and occupational training at the expense of medical intervention.[28] Robert Jones (1857–1933) began bridging the gap in 1899 when he opened the first British hospital for the long term treatment of crippled children.[29] Apprenticed to his uncle, Hugh Owen Thomas, before qualifying at the Liverpool School of Medicine in 1878, Jones practised in the city throughout his career.[30] But it was at the Salop Convalescent Home for Women and Children – founded in 1900 by Agnes Hunt (1867–1948) at Baschurch near Oswestry in Shropshire – that his work became most famous.[31] The First World War, during which Jones served for a period as Director of Orthopaedics for the Army, enhanced the stature of his specialty because at least a half of all battle injuries involved the 'impairment of locomotor function and usefulness of limbs'. However, retaining peacetime control of the 20 orthopaedic centres that had grown up to treat military cases proved more difficult.[32] Therefore, on return to civilian life, orthopaedic surgeons advocated 'an ambitious scheme to recreate the . . . glory of their military empire' by organizing a national programme for the 'crippled' children with whom they had started to work before the war.[33]

Since health policies were in the grip of fragmented local authorities, the orthopaedists turned to the Central Council for the Care of Cripples: a voluntary body set up in 1919 with representatives from medicine, education, and welfare. Based on the arrangements at Baschurch,[34] their National Scheme proposed a network of central orthopaedic hospitals, allied to a series of affiliated local after-care clinics. The central orthopaedic clinic provided the 'crippled' child with skilled surgery and nursing, a good diet and 'the benefits of the sun and the open air . . . for as long as his physical disability demands'. The local after-care clinics supplied a 'short-cut' to accurate diagnosis and hospital admission, enabled 'the surgeon to supervise his own handiwork . . . and to realize the end results'.[35] It was through this programme that social orthopaedics matured. By 1936 the Central Council was coordinating a network of 40 orthopaedic hospitals to which were attached 400 out-patient clinics.[36] Some of the charities participating in the Scheme were inaugurated specifically for the purpose, but others adapted their mission to the changed circumstances. Therefore, the Nottingham District Cripples' Guild had dropped moral for medical surveillance by the mid-1920s, appointing an honorary orthopaedic surgeon to lead its clinic activities and putting its weight behind the campaign for an orthopaedic hospital for Nottinghamshire and the East Midlands that opened in 1929.[37]

The healing power of nature

The vehicle for this transition from moral to medical surveillance was the holistic approach to healthcare that from 1900 was slowly losing its marginality. Holism had dominated Western medicine until the end of the eighteenth century, absorbing mechanical and chemical theories into the humoral framework inherited from the classical era that emphasized the interaction between persons and their environments.[38] From 1800, however, localized pathology went into the ascendancy, displacing humoralism with an impersonal focus on individual organs.[39] The growth of laboratory science and an increasing reliance on technology not only compounded this fragmentation but also, in conjunction with the bureaucratization of healthcare through the National Insurance scheme, 'subverted' clinical authority at the bedside and made 'obsolete clinical skills that were the basis of the physician's identity' and the traditional doctor-patient relationship. The revival of medical holism was a reaction against confining 'research, diagnosis, and therapy . . . [to] a single organ, cause, or problem'. Resonant with contemporary trends in philosophy, history, the social sciences and the arts, it rejected the atomistic reductionism that had emerged in the economic, social and political context of industrialization and understood society as a collection of discrete individuals. Advanced instead were strategies that envisaged patients and their environments as organic and interconnected wholes.[40]

Nineteenth-century medical orthopaedics bequeathed three aspects of this holistic philosophy to the National Scheme of hospitals and clinics: a minimalist approach to clinical intervention; a comprehension of the interface between mind, body and society; and a commitment to exploit that interface through strategies for social and economic discipline. Clinical minimalism was manifest in a resistance to surgery; an enthusiasm for fresh air; and a conviction that left to its own devices, the body would 'repair tissues damaged by inflammation, injury or fatigue'.[41] The eighteenth-century teachings of John Hunter had not only recommended cautious use of the scalpel but also realized 'the curative value of fresh air, rest, the immobilization of injured limbs' and the sparing prescription of drugs.[42] As a medical student at Edinburgh, however, Hugh Owen Thomas, the Liverpool orthopaedist, was appalled by the number of amputations carried out for diseases of the joints: conditions that his father – an unqualified bonesetter – had treated successfully without resort to surgery. Two teachers reinforced this disquiet: Professor Hughes Bennett at Edinburgh, and John Hilton at University College, London.[43] Writing in *On Rest and Pain* (1877), Hilton urged surgeons to remember 'the physiological truth that Nature has a constant tendency to repair the injuries to which her structures have been subjected, and that the reparative power becomes more conspicuous when the disturbing cause has been removed'. In Thomas's copy of the book, this passage was underlined.[44]

Upon return to Liverpool, these ideas were implemented. Thomas did not abandon surgery. Far from it, he kept pace with innovation and adopted antisepsis following the publication of Lister's 'successes'. Three years later, however, he went back to his original open technique. The new method was 'but the old method made safe and harmless'. The results were no better, and may have been worse.[45] Above all, excessively 'mechanical' intervention was encouraged. Thomas maintained in his *Principles of Treatment of Fractures and Dislocations* (1886) that 'since the discovery of antisepsis ... even recent fractures are at once drilled or pegged in the surgery of fractured bones'. But 'if we are thoughtful of the fact that it is living matter we have to influence, interference will seldom be required'. Indeed, 'such operations are sometimes a hindrance, rather than an aid, to repair'.[46] He was equally critical of the common insistence on absolute rest, which was said to reduce 'deformity' and lead to more rapid and effective cure.[47] But immobility also caused stiffness, leading some doctors to recommend only temporary rest and even remove splints to allow movement. Over a period of 15 years, Thomas tackled this problem. A talented engineer, he started 'to devise splints which would ensure the maximum possible rest of diseased joints', whilst simultaneously enabling the patient to remain ambulatory and hence capable of some kind of work.[48] Therefore, though accused of leaving 'rehabilitation to take its own course after removal of splintage',[49] his protagonists are adamant that he practised it before the word was invented, 'not at the end of treatment but throughout treatment'.[50]

Complementing these conservative treatments was a belief in the therapeutic properties of fresh air. From the 1880s Hugh Owen Thomas was placing babies and young children from the Liverpool slums in makeshift beds *outside* their homes, chaining the orange or soapboxes to the railings for security.[51] The virtues of fresh air were also more generally cherished. In 1894/1895, for instance, the Medical Committee of the Birmingham Orthopaedic and Spinal Hospital repeated their call for 'a suitable Convalescent Home', not only to increase the throughput of patients but to confirm and enhance 'the good results of in-patient treatment . . . by a short sojourn in healthful and beautiful surround-ings'.[52] Subsequently, the Cadbury family donated an estate on the outskirts of the city.[53] The Royal National Orthopaedic Hospital, which acquired rural premises in the early 1920s, likewise boasted that even the use of balconies – 'reserved for children with tuberculous joints' from 1892 – 'produced as good results . . . in the heart of London as . . . could . . . [be] wished for in the country'. Indeed, the children 'became quite brown and fit, and lying there they were often the means of attracting donations from passengers in the more leisurely days of the horse-bus'.[54]

Fresh air fused with conservative treatments most dramatically at Agnes Hunt's Baschurch Convalescent Home. Physically impaired since childhood by an arthritic hip joint, Hunt's initial experience of nursing was at the Alexandra Hospital in Rhyl on the north Wales coast. She then trained at the West London Hospital and at the Salop Infirmary, and qualified as a district nurse. However, it was her period in Rhyl, where Hugh Owen Thomas was honorary consultant, which proved most formative. For 'cripples', fresh air and happiness were regarded as the principal remedy; and children well enough were carried onto the sands to play with their buckets and spades, whilst the less fit were pushed outside to watch summer seaside entertainments. Nevertheless, when the Baschurch Home ventured into open-air treatment, it was more by accident than design. After recruiting a number of disabled children in its first year, Hunt recalled a conversation at the foot of the staircase leading to the 'ambitiously entitled wards':

> This is too dangerous. We shall probably kill one of the children, and most certainly ourselves. The doctor always says that fresh air and sunshine are essential, for goodness sake let's build a shed in the garden and let them live in it day and night![55]

A later appeal for funds included – below a photograph of the open-air facilities – a list of doctors who had 'sent cases here, [and] allow us to say that they approve the treatment their patients received'.[56] However, the initial request met with only anxious consent after the doctor whose advice was sought had to concur that the stairs were more dangerous than the cold.[57]

Not all parents were convinced by open-air therapy either and in 1905 a patient was removed by his/her mother who 'preferred to follow her child to the grave than to allow it (*sic*) to sleep in an open shed'.[58] However, the reputation of the Baschurch Home was consolidated by its early successes. Children who were suffering primarily from tubercular joints were admitted 'to get up a little strength before undergoing another operation'. 'What surprised the surgeons . . . that sent them was, that the tubercular joints improved to such an extent that, in nine cases out of ten, operations were unnecessary, after a stay of two or three months'.[59] The reasons were unclear. Though city life was perceived as unhealthy, the connection between rickets, vitamin D deficiency, and lack of sunlight in narrow streets with tall buildings and smoke pollution was not appreciated until after the First World War.[60] Moreover, A. H. Tubby was still speculating in 1924 'how it is that carefully regulated exposure to the sun effects such a profound change in the child's nutrition, promotes the drying up of abscesses and the healing of diseased parts'. Despite pointing to experimental research in the formation of pigment, he concluded that credit had to be 'given to the pure air in mountain or seaside places, and to the local and general rest which the patient enjoys'.[61] But fresh air was 'an absolute heresy', 'abhorrent both to general practice and the homes of England'. Therefore, 'without the sympathetic association of Robert Jones', Frederick Watson was certain that Hunt's project in rural Shropshire 'might have perished . . . or failed to mature on scientific lines'.[62]

Watson was hardly a disinterested observer. Married to Jones's daughter, he established and edited *The Cripples' Journal* and was the 'moving spirit' behind the Voluntary Orthopaedic Association in Montgomeryshire. None-the-less, though Agnes Hunt had already encountered the ideas of Hugh Owen Thomas – Robert Jones' uncle and mentor – via the Alexandra Hospital in Rhyl, their face-to-face meeting was critical. It occurred when Hunt was advised to consult Jones about the arthritic hip with which she had lived since the age of nine. Following the operation in Liverpool in 1903, Jones paid a visit to Baschurch and offered to see patients at his clinic at the Royal Southern Hospital in Liverpool. Soon afterwards he was invited to join the staff of the Home, whereupon he began a schedule of monthly visits to Shropshire that was to last for 30 years. Operating facilities – at first primitive in the extreme – were gradually upgraded so that by 1907 Hunt was claiming that 'the Home had become a hospital'.[63] It went on to achieve international renown as an orthopaedic facility that combined conservative treatment with open-air therapy.[64]

Mind, body and society

Although the model for harvesting the healing power of nature was devised by Agnes Hunt, Robert Jones and a coterie of followers, they were able to roll out the National Scheme of hospitals and clinics because it embodied a social orthopaedics that shared its holistic principles with the concept of preventive medicine that was driving the new Ministry of Health. For George Newman, the first Chief Medical Officer, preventive medicine was no longer 'exclusively concerned with "drains and stinks", or with quarantine and the isolation of patients suffering from infectious diseases'. Nor was disease 'a dragon outside the body which we have to slay'. Rather, 'the body (including the mind)' had to be equipped and fortified 'against reactionary influence', or the environment modified 'to suit its susceptibilities'. Otherwise, 'disturbed functioning' would remain unresolved.[65]

The integration of body and mind – outlawed by Cartesian dualism since the Scientific Revolution – was central to social orthopaedics. Indeed, before the First World War the Baschurch Home had claimed to be 'a pioneer ... in the psychological treatment of the cripple', preaching 'the gospel of the cheerful heart and the danger of sentimentality'; visiting surgeons, it was declared, learnt that 'deformity is a physical and not a spiritual handicap' and were 'astonished at the atmosphere of gaiety and fun prevailing the place'.[66] This homespun psychology persisted into the interwar period. 'Deformity has always been attended by certain temperamental reactions', wrote Watson in 1930, 'and prolonged treatment due to an ever-advancing skill in operative technique made it essential that recovery of the body should not be jeopardized by impatience or despondency of mind'.[67]

Attitudes were to refine during the decade which saw 'the influence of psychoanalysis ... more strongly felt' in Britain[68] and, by the commencement of the Second World War, the discipline of psychology – which in the 1930s had increasingly become concerned about social problems[69] – was in 'agreement that personality maladjustment results from crippling'. But 'how it actually occurs' was contested, with one school assuming that 'the presence of any sort of ... physical handicap is sufficient in itself to occasion ... disorder' and the other maintaining that the child 'has been subject to unwise family influences'.[70] By 1937, Norman Ross Smith – an orthopaedic surgeon at the Cornelia Hospital in Poole, Dorset – was identifying with the first school of thought. For him, the psychological aspects of orthopaedic work were 'most important'. The crippled child, he posited, 'soon realizes that he is different from other children, in that he cannot play or work like others, and he may be an object of pity or even ridicule'. Consequently, there was a risk that from this 'he may develop a feeling of helplessness or inferiority, which is as serious a handicap to his progress in life as his physical disability'. Regardless of the inroads made by psychology, Ross Smith perceived that physical and mental impairment was still confused. 'Crippled children are not necessarily, as is popularly supposed, intellectually inferior to other children ... in most cases since their crippling was acquired by injury or disease, such children are of normal intelligence'.[71]

The psychological thinking that orthopaedics had absorbed by the late 1930s interpreted physical impairment as a personal pathology to which the individual had to adjust, overlooking how material and attitudinal environments subjected disabled people to social discrimination and oppression.[72] But despite lacking this insight – promoted by the disability movement from the 1960s – orthopaedics did acknowledge a degree of social responsibility for the causation of 'crippling' conditions. Therefore, Charles Dickens was accused of being 'quick to see the emotional appeal of crippled children' but as 'only a sob'. 'Crippledom' was a social problem – 'an indictment' of manufacturing processes, domestic and industrial, that brutalized body and mind. Domestic industries 'carried out in crowded rooms of insanitary cottages [had] produced men and women crippled in body, frequently blind and totally uneducated, and unfamiliar with the most elementary things of human existence'. 'The outstanding social abuses of the industrial system', on the other hand, 'were bad housing, unhealthy working conditions, low wages, and the prolonged labour of women and children. All these produced then and now their heavy toll of the crippled in lungs, heart and limbs'.[73]

In recognizing that physical impairment had structural causes, social orthopaedics positioned itself along the spectrum of eugenic ideas, so popular in the early twentieth century that they were an implicit cultural assumption in Western societies.[74] Until the 1880s, it was widely assumed that the capitalist economy would deliver jobs to all who genuinely wanted to work. The relative decline of the British economy after an extended reign of international pre-eminence shook this confidence, whilst a new theoretical orientation towards trade cycles and labour markets within the discipline of economics qualified the past obsession with voluntary unemployment.[75] The net effect was a sharper differentiation between the 'respectable' poor – regarded as victims of a volatile economy – and the underclass or 'residuum' – perceived as physically and mentally degenerate.[76] This bifurcation was underpinned by the new science of eugenics, which applied biological principles to the improvement of the human race. Feeding on the long term 'cultural and social pessimism' that afflicted late Victorian Britain, eugenics had widespread political currency. Consequently, for the Right, it supplied a 'scientific rationalization' with which to resist social reforms that flouted 'the laws of natural selection'; whereas for the Left, it offered a progressive agenda with which to plan and guide social reforms in a progressive way.[77]

Although more often associated with 'mental deficiency', eugenics also infused approaches to physical impairment,[78] surviving the alleged social cohesion of the Second World War.[79] In 1942, for instance, the Child Guidance Council suggested that there were no grounds for believing that rickets influenced mental maturation. On the other hand, rickets was:

> a slum disease and the inhabitants of slums tend to be of the lowest ranges of human society. Amongst these are many dullards and high grade defectives, who pass on their dullness and feeblemindedness to the next generation. It will, therefore, be found that many rickety children are dullards but their dullness is an inheritance from their dull parents and not a result of their disease.[80]

Social orthopaedics was less deterministic in its attitude to rickets and other physical impairments. In the first place, hospitals acknowledged that 'much credit is often due to the mothers' of long term patients 'for their patience and perseverance, the children frequently having to be brought to the Out-Patient Department two or three times a week'.[81] Furthermore, the debilitating effects of deprived environments were noted, albeit with racial connotations. As Frederick Watson conceded, 'in the airless, sunless single rooms of a slum family, ill-nourished and without the sanitary liberties of aborigines, tuberculous infection is unavoidable, rickety children are a commonplace, and the whole fibre and resistance of the human body deteriorate year by year'.[82]

In spite of this concession, social orthopaedics did not shun blaming impoverished parents for the impairments of their children. Thus rickets was caused by poor feeding as well as lack of sunlight because the missing vitamin D was present in maternal milk:[83] 'that criminal resource of the selfish mother'. Furthermore, whilst not automatically assuming that 'the slum population will carry their environment wherever they go', poverty begat 'laxity [and so] ... to provide a new house is not to bestow a new sense of the responsibilities of parenthood or civic life'. The 'malign influence of alcohol' was a major aggravating factor. 'Any substantial reduction of the drink evil makes easier the solution of the slum problem; with the passing of both, many of the worst features of child crippledom would disappear'. This fusion of social with family responsibility encouraged orthopaedic surgeons to acquiesce in existing inequalities, accepting that they 'cannot remove the social conditions from which their patients arrive any more than they can shield the industrial worker in the factory or the pedestrian on the street'.[84] However, it was entirely compatible with the organic understanding of society to which both social orthopaedics and preventive prescribed. Mass movements, whether communist or fascist, were not the answer to social malaise. Rather, collective progress would ensue from the improvement of the individual.[85] Therefore, a comprehensive medical regime was designed to survey disabled children and subject them to the disciplinary rigour of the orthopaedic hospital.

Orthopaedics and social discipline

The social discipline imposed by orthopaedics was grounded in what David Armstrong has called 'surveillance medicine', which monitored the social body as a whole and 'spread its gaze over the normal person to establish early detection ... and to enable the potentially abnormal to be adequately known'.[86] At the community level, statistical methodologies were used to investigate the local prevalence of physical impairment. Thus military surgeons at the Prince of Wales Hospital in Cardiff – opened in 1917 for limbless soldiers and sailors in Wales and Monmouthshire[87] – decided to calculate 'the number of civilians who had lost limbs in peace time at home'. To their surprise, 'it worked out to be no less than 1 in 810 in a population of nearly two million of whom we received a record. Applied to England and Wales, this "datum-line" produced a figure of 46,722 civilian limbless cripples alone to deal with'.[88] Statistical evidence was also used to make the case for orthopaedic institutions. Lamenting in a letter to *The Cripples' Journal* that expert advice was only available in large centres, Lionel Meredith Davies – Medical Officer of Health for Aberystwyth – set the frequency of 'deformity' against the child population. In his county of Cardiganshire, 5.5 per 1,000 school children had 'deformities' due to tuberculosis and ten per 1,000 had 'deformities' due to other causes; yet for neighbouring

Breconshire the ratios were 0.4 and 2.9 respectively. Such disparities were indicative of a neglect of impairment that pointed up the need for rural counties to combine and organize an efficient orthopaedic scheme for Wales similar to those in England.[89]

From the outset, early detection was a major objective of social orthopaedics and in 1920 Agnes Hunt's Baschurch Home was expressing gratitude to 'the Medical Practitioners of Shropshire, the School Doctors, Health Visitors and Child Welfare Workers' for their diagnostic work. Thanks to this prompt diagnosis, 'cases of tubercle, rickets and infantile paralysis' were being referred 'before any deformity has occurred' and, as a consequence, surgical operations were 'unnecessary', lengths of stay in hospital were cut, and 'the ultimate recovery quicker and infinitely more complete'.[90] The network of satellite clinics that grew up around the fledgling orthopaedic hospitals complemented the surveillance of these public and private services.[91] By 1930 the Central Council for the Care of Cripples was reporting that 'as the more serious cases of crippling (the result of long neglect) are cleared from the hospitals, it is becoming ever easier to make room for the treatment of less severe deformities and to deal with all cases at an earlier age and therefore more effectively'. Indeed, even the Minister of Health claimed in his *Annual Report* for 1934 that there had been a sharp fall in the incidence of severe disablement in areas where the national orthopaedic scheme had blossomed.[92]

Once detected, patients had to be persuaded of the 'need' for clinical intervention, which in the case of disabled children meant negotiation with the family. Not all relatives were compliant. Therefore, during 1929, the Princess Elizabeth Hospital in Exeter – founded two years earlier under the auspices of the Devonian Association for Cripples' Aid[93] – resolved that in the case of minors 'for whom the surgeon strongly recommended treatment which the parents refuse to sanction', the matter should be referred to the local authority for a decision on whether legal action was appropriate 'after all possible enquiry and persuasion' had been undertaken.[94] In practice, this procedure was selectively applied and towards the end of 1930 the management committee agreed to take 'no further action' after a father had failed to materialize for several interviews to explain why he objected to his daughter receiving anaesthesia.[95] Perhaps enforcement was too draconian. In any event, the committee adopted a lesser penalty in 1931 when it resolved that – unless the medical staff made a special case – surgical shoes and appliances would not be supplied to children whose parents declined in-patient treatment.[96] A boy was subsequently refused boots, 'pending [his] parents consent to Hospital treatment recommended as urgent by [the] Surgeon'.[97]

Disciplinary measures were also enacted outside the hospital to counteract the 'more careless and casual atmosphere' of the family.[98] Agnes Hunt recalled how, working as a district nurse in London, she visited a child with a double club foot who was crawling without a 'much prized splint', which his mother fetched from a cupboard still wrapped in tissue paper.[99] Equally 'maddening' was the experience of sending:

a child home in splints, walking beautifully, only to have it (*sic*) brought back again in six months rather worse than when first admitted, because the splint had broken, and the parents, in all honesty, considered this was the Almighty's way of showing it was no longer required![100]

The after-care clinic was devised to overcome these problems. Although the nurses who served as after-care superintendents were expected to inform hospital staff where 'conditions exist rendering the discharge of a patient ... inadvisable',[101] full checks were impractical and surveillance relied on 'exceptional circumstances' coming to light when the child was admitted. Cases of suspected child abuse were reported to the National Society for the Prevention of Cruelty to Children.[102] For the most part, however, after-care services sought to stop families from 'undoing ... all the hospital work'.[103] There were two strategies. First, treatment was 'conveniently arranged ... , their interest ... sustained and encouraged and their confidence retained' through friendly but expert support.[104] Second, 'instruction ... in the common laws of health' was delivered:[105] in Agnes Hunt's words:

open windows, need of sunshine, wholesome food, the value of vegetables, general cleanliness, the undesirability of putting cobwebs on cut fingers, and dummies in children's mouths, the avoidance of certain foods and the value of clean milk from a tested herd of cows.[106]

Orthopaedics and economic discipline

The ultimate purpose of the social discipline that orthopaedics applied to disabled children was economic discipline: to turn them into financially independent adults. Enlightenment political arithmetic had valued the economic efficacy of a low death rate and a healthy workforce.[107] However, population growth from the mid-eighteenth century weakened the purchase of this synergy and neither the 1896 nor the 1912 edition of A. H. Tubby's *Deformities* made reference to the economic rehabilitation of patients.[108] In the years leading up to the First World War, some orthopaedists did experiment with the idea of a curative workshop in which employment was understood as 'valuable in social terms as a means to reconstitute ... [the] sense of individual and communal worth'.[109] But it was the war itself that put work on the orthopaedic map. As Robert Jones reflected in 1918, the 'hasty discharge' of wounded soldiers had to 'cease – not only from the point of view of national economy, but also from the point of view of military conservation of man power'.[110] In an effort to staunch this wastage, the War Office invited Jones to take over up to 400 beds at Alder Hey – a requisitioned poor-law infirmary in Liverpool. However, his flagship institution was the Shepherd's Bush Military Hospital in London, which opened in May 1916 with 800 beds in the old Hammersmith Workhouse.[111]

The occupational ethos at Shepherd's Bush was transmitted to other curative military hospitals, their employment programmes being geared to the regional economy. At Cardiff's Prince of Wales Hospital, for instance, the garden – dubbed 'Miniature Wild Wales' – contained 'pits for the men to practice loading course gravel and sand, a miniature coal mine, and appliances for training in the use of shovels, mattocks, pickaxes, colliers' picks, mandrels, axes and saws, and wheelbarrows'. In addition, a forge and workshops for steel workers, carpenters, glass blowers and leather workers were constructed.[112] The lessons of wartime rehabilitation were less compelling in a peacetime economy where unemployment was high and the curative workshop was only resuscitated by the labour shortages of the Second World War.[113] However, social orthopaedics carried forward the economic message for disabled children. Post-war governments thus urged the 'business community' to remember that expenditure on the treatment of 'crippled' youngsters was 'a sound investment'; it meant that 'thousands . . . who would otherwise grow up to be a burden on their relatives and the community will become useful, self-supporting citizens'.[114] Furthermore, mainstream orthopaedics was also warming to the personal and communal returns of the workshop ethos. Therefore, in his 1924 edition, Tubby extolled the virtues of comprehensive rehabilitation as his specialty moved 'from simple re-education of structures to a problem of great economic significance, namely, the education of cripples'. The objective, he went on, was to 'direct such energy and powers' as the 'cripple' possessed as 'to enable him to realize that he can lead a useful and happy life and become a valuable citizen'.[115]

By the late 1930s, 'the restoration of . . . patients to normal useful life' was being identified as the 'test of the work of an orthopaedic organization'.[116] Yet the older moral strictures survived. Tubby thus prescribed 'sympathy' for disabled people in an effort 'to see and realize the personality . . . behind the handicap'; by showing them the scope for useful occupation, 'their morale . . . [was] raised, and from being depressed they . . . [became] serene and cheerful'.[117] This patronizing stereotype easily collapsed into moral disapprobation if the work ethic went unfulfilled. Robert Jones had insisted that employment should be 'curative' of the disabled person's 'physical disability, and especially keep him from becoming an incurable idler'.[118] Frederick Watson was similarly worried that compensation for injured workmen was an incentive to permanent economic inactivity; payments, he insisted, should be 'utilized to restore an industrial cripple to health and occupation, not to fling him on charitable funds for rehabilitation or allow him to decline into a tramp'. Watson had a novel solution. The countryside was 'once more becoming a wilderness'. Not every 'partially disabled man could restore agricultural prosperity or . . . [was] even suited for it'. However, 'new markets, such as animal husbandry and intensive market gardening . . . [were] worth exploration'.[119] In being bridled to police the economic ambitions of the modern state, orthopaedic medicine was tapping into its holistic tradition.

Conclusion

In this chapter, we have teased out the ways in which orthopaedic medicine evolved into a science for disciplining disabled bodies. Preoccupied with the treatment of 'deformities' for much of the nineteenth century, *surgical* orthopaedics lost ground to *medical* orthopaedics from around 1900. With its roots in the craft skills of 'irregular' bonesetters, medical orthopaedics pursued a conservative strategy in which surgery was regarded as a last resort and the therapeutic properties of fresh air were harnessed. These ideas came to fruition at Agnes Hunt's Edwardian Convalescent Home at Baschurch in Shropshire. In the aftermath of the First World War, however, orthopaedists managed to mastermind a National Scheme of charitable hospitals and after-care clinics, primarily targeting disabled children. Partly due to success with battle injuries, this coup was also possible because from the early years of the twentieth century orthopaedics began to identify its economic potential: an initiative that reached its apotheosis in the wartime curative workshop. A *social* version of orthopaedics – embracing physical but also economic rehabilitation – thus won collateral by aligning itself with the holistic notion of preventive medicine that after 1919 was informing the new Ministry of Health under George Newman. Though the environmental causes of impairment were conceded, social progress was believed to reside in the individual. As a result, orthopaedic medicine subjected disabled children and their families to close surveillance and robust policing calculated to render them economically productive citizens.

Notes

1 L. Klenerman, 'Setting the scene – the start of orthopaedic surgery', in L. Klenerman (ed.) *The Evolution of Orthopaedic Surgery*, London: Royal Society of Medicine, 2002, p. 1.

2 J. Menzies, *The Heritage of Oswestry: The Origin and Development of the Robert Jones and Agnes Hunt Orthopaedic Hospital, Oswestry (1900–1961)*, no place of publication, publisher or date, p. 16. See also N. R. Smith, *Elements of Orthopaedic Surgery*, Bristol: J. Wright, 1937, p. 1.

3 M. Foucault, *Discipline and Punish: the Birth of the Prison*, trans. Alan Sheridan, Harmondsworth: Penguin, 1977, pp. 167, 198–200.

4 E. Muirhead Little, 'Orthopaedics before Stromeyer', in H. Milford (ed.) *The Robert Jones Birthday Volume: A Collection of Surgical Essays*, London: Oxford University Press, 1928, p. 14.

5 David Le Vay, *The History of Orthopaedics: An Account of the Study and Practice of Orthopaedics from the Earliest Times to the Modern Era*, Carnforth, Lancashire: Parthenon, 1990, pp. 73–89.

6 A. Keith, *Menders of the Maimed: The Anatomical and Physiological Principles Underlying the Treatment of Injuries to Muscles, Nerves, Bones and Joints*, London: Hodder and Stoughton, 1919, pp. 39–40; Oxford Dictionary of National Biography, 'Hugh Owen Thomas'. Online. Available at: www.oxforddnb.com/articles/38/38058-article.html (accessed 15 August 2005); F. Watson, *Hugh Owen Thomas: A Personal Study*, London: Oxford University Press, 1934, pp. 1–8, 28–36.

7 D. Power (ed.) *British Masters of Medicine*, London: Medical Press and Circular, 1936, p. 163.

8 See, for example, T. G. Davies, *Deeds Not Words: A History of the Swansea General and Eye Hospital, 1817–1948*, Cardiff: University of Wales Press, 1988, p. 60; H. Osmond-Clarke, 'Half a Century of Orthopaedic Progress in Great Britain', *Journal of Bone and Joint Surgery*, 1950, vol. 32-B, 630; J. Reinarz, *The Birth of a*

Provincial Hospital: The Early Years of the General Hospital, Birmingham, 1765–1790, Stratford: Dugdale Society, 2003, p. 28.

9 W. M. White, *Years of Caring: The Royal Orthopaedic Hospital*, Studley: Brewin, 1997, pp. 15, 18–19.

10 J. A. Cholmeley, *History of the Royal National Orthopaedic Hospital*, London: Chapman and Hall, 1985, pp. 1–3.

11 W. F. Bynum, *Science and the Practice of Medicine in the Nineteenth Century*, Cambridge: Cambridge University Press, 1994, pp. 121–3, 132–7.

12 Osmond-Clarke, 'Half', 639–42.

13 R. Cooter, *Surgery and Society in Peace and War: Orthopaedics and the Organization of Modern Medicine, 1880–1948*, Basingstoke: Macmillan, 1993, pp. 18–24.

14 Menzies, *Heritage*, pp. 16–17.

15 Birmingham and Midland Counties Orthopaedic Hospital, *58th Annual Report* (1875) pp. 10–12.

16 Royal Orthopaedic and Spinal Hospital, Birmingham, *Annual Report* (1894/1895) p. 17.

17 *Fourth Annual Report of the Orthopaedic Institution or Infirmary for the Cure of Club Foot and Other Contractions, presented at the Fourth Public Meeting* (23 February 1843) p. 13.

18 Birmingham and Midlands Counties Orthopaedic Hospital, *58th Annual Report*, p. 12.

19 B. E. Brodhurst, *Deformities of the Human Body: A System of Orthopaedic Surgery*, London: J. and A. Churchill, 1871, pp. 1–5, 7, 16, 18–22, 25.

20 A. H. Tubby, *Deformities: A Treatise on Orthopaedic Surgery Intended for Practitioners and Advanced Students*, London: Macmillan, 1896, p. viii.

21 A. H. Tubby, *Deformities, including Diseases of the Bones and Joints: A Text-Book of Orthopaedic Surgery*, London: Macmillan, 2nd edn, 1912, pp. vii–viii.

22 A. H. Tubby, *The Advance of Orthopaedic Surgery*, London: H. K. Lewis, 3rd edn, 1924, p. 125.

23 Cooter, *Surgery*, pp. 15–17.

24 L. McCoy, 'Education for Labour: Social Problems of Nationhood', in G. Lewis (ed.) *Forming Nation, Framing Nation*, London: Routledge, 1998, p. 121. See also W. B. Stephens, *Education in Britain, 1750–1914*, Basingstoke: Macmillan, 1998, pp. 79–80.

25 Cooter, *Surgery*, pp. 54–9; S. Koven, 'Remembering and Dismemberment: Crippled Children, Wounded Soldiers, and the Great War in Great Britain', *American Historical Review*, 99, 1994, 1173.

26 K. Laybourn, 'The Guild of Help and the Community Response to Poverty, 1904–*c*.1914', in K. Laybourn (ed.) *Social Conditions, Status and Community, 1860–c.1920*, Stroud: Sutton, 1997, pp. 9–11, 13–15, 19, 28.

27 Nottingham Cripples' Guild, *Seventh Annual Report* (1914), p. 2; Nottingham Cripples' Guild, *Eight Annual Report* (1915), pp. 3–4, 6–7, 8.

28 Cooter, *Surgery*, pp. 54, 60.

29 F. Watson, *The Life of Sir Robert Jones*, London: Hodder and Stoughton, 1934, pp. 108–9, 110–2.

30 Menzies, *Heritage*, pp. 34–6, 38–41; Le Vay, *History*, pp. 137–41; Oxford Dictionary of National Biography, 'Sir Robert Jones'. Online. Available at: www.oxforddnb.com/articles/34/34237-article.html (accessed 15 August 2005); Watson, *Hugh Owen Thomas*, pp. 58–63; Watson, *Life*, pp. 45–6.

31 The Baschurch Home became known as a Home and Hospital in 1905 after surgical cases were treated and moved to a former military hospital near Gobowen outside Oswestry in 1921 where it was called the Shropshire Orthopaedic Hospital. After the death of Robert Jones in 1933, the Hospital was renamed again and became the

Robert Jones and Agnes Hunt Orthopaedic Hospital. See M. Carter, *Healing and Hope: 100 Years of the 'Orthopaedic'*, Oswestry: Robert Jones and Agnes Hunt Orthopaedic and District Hospital NHS Trust, 2000, pp. 10, 21, 35.

32 R. Jones, *An Address on the Orthopaedic Outlook in Military Surgery*, London: British Medical Association, 1918, p. 3. See also Cooter, *Surgery*, pp. 105–6.

33 Cooter, *Surgery*, p. 153.

34 A. Hunt, *Reminiscences*, Shrewsbury: Wilding, 1935, pp. 125, 128, 130.

35 G. R. Girdlestone, *The Care and Cure of Crippled Children*, Bristol: J. Wright and S. Marshall, 1924, p. 3.

36 J. Anderson, *A Record of Fifty Years Service to the Disabled by the Central Council for the Disabled*, London: Central Council for the Disabled, 1969, p. 29.

37 Nottingham District Cripples' Guild, *Annual Report* (1924) pp. 5–9; Nottingham District Cripples' Guild, *Thirty-Second Annual Report* (1939) p. 7.

38 N. D. Jewson, 'Medical Knowledge and the Patronage System in Eighteenth-Century England', *Sociology*, VIII, 1974, 371–2.

39 C. Lawrence, 'Democratic, Divine and Heroic: the History and Historiography of Surgery', in C. Lawrence (ed.) *Medical Theory, Surgical Practice: Studies in the History of Surgery*, London: Routledge, 1992, pp. 20–3. See also Bynum, *Science*, 1994, pp. 32–3.

40 C. Lawrence and G. Weisz, 'Medical Holism: The Context', in C. Lawrence and G. Weisz (eds) *Greater Than The Parts: Holism in Biomedicine, 1920–1950*, New York: Oxford University Press, 1998, pp. 2–7, 10–12.

41 G. Thomas, 'Liverpool and the Origins of Orthopaedic Surgery', in J. A. Ross (ed.) 'Collected Papers Concerning Liverpool Medical History', 8th British Congress on the History of Medicine held in Liverpool 1971, Liverpool: unpublished typescript, 1977, p. 43.

42 Cooter, *Surgery*, p. 20. See also Keith, *Menders*, pp. 3–4, 17; G. Newman, *Health and Social Evolution*, London: Allen and Unwin, 1931, pp. 161–3.

43 Menzies, *Heritage*, pp. 32–3; Thomas, 'Liverpool', pp. 39–40

44 Le Vay, *History*, p. 109. See also H. O. Thomas, *Diseases of the Hip, Knee and Ankle Joints*, London: J. & A. Churchill, 1875, pp. 138–43.

45 Thomas, *Diseases*, pp. 183–4.

46 Le Vay, *History*, p. 117; Keith, *Menders*, p. 61.

47 White, *Years*, pp. 50, 53.

48 Thomas, 'Liverpool', pp. 42–4.

49 Le Vay, *History*, pp. 115–16.

50 Thomas, 'Liverpool', p. 44.

51 Ibid.; F. Watson, *Civilization and the Cripple*, London: John Bale, 1930, p. 18.

52 Royal Orthopaedic and Spinal Hospital, Birmingham, *Annual Report* (1894/1895), p. 18.

53 White, *Years*, p. 134.

54 A. Morley, 'Orthopaedic Centres, III: the Royal National Orthopaedic Hospital', *The Cripples Journal*, I, 1924, 191, 193.

55 A. Hunt, 'Baschurch and after, I: The Birth of a Pioneer Hospital', *The Cripples Journal*, I, 1924, 18. See also Hunt, *Reminiscences*, pp. 4, 64–6, 69, 73, 77; Oxford Dictionary of National Biography, 'Dame Agnes Hunt'. Online. Available at: www.oxforddnb.com/articles/34/34054-article.html (accessed 15 August 2005).

56 Shropshire Records and Research Service, Shrewsbury (SRRS) 1387/1, 'Salop Convalescent Home for Women and Children', no date.

57 Hunt, 'Baschurch and after, I', 18.

58 Carter, *Healing*, p. 5.

59 Hunt, 'Baschurch and after, I', 20.

60 A. Hardy, 'Rickets and the Rest: Child-care, Diet and the Infectious Children's Diseases, 1850–1914', *Social History of Medicine*, 5, 1992, 397–8. See also S. Sturdy,

'Hippocrates and State Medicine: George Newman Outlines the Founding Policy of the Ministry of Health', in Lawrence and Weisz (eds) *Greater Than The Parts*, p. 121.

61 Tubby, *Advance*, pp. 129–30.

62 Watson, *Civilization*, p. 16.

63 A. Hunt, *This Is My Life*, London: Blackie, 1938, pp. 139, 143, 154, 205.

64 Watson, *Civilization*, pp. 16–17; Watson, *Life*, p. 121.

65 Newman, *Health*, pp. 69–70, 170. See also G. Newman, *The Rise of Preventive Medicine*, London: Oxford University Press, 1932, pp. 227–9; G. Newman, *The Building of a Nation's Health*, London: Macmillan, 1939, p. 436.

66 Menzies, *Heritage*, p. 55. See also Girdlestone, *Care*, p. 30.

67 Watson, *Civilization*, p. 20.

68 K. Woodroofe, *From Charity to Social Work in England and the United States*, London: Routledge and Kegan Paul, 1962, p. 147.

69 M. Roiser, 'Social Psychology and Social Concern in 1930s Britain', in G. C. Bunn, A. D. Lovie and G. D. Richards (eds) *Psychology in Britain: Historical Essays and Personal Reflections*, Leicester: British Psychological Society, 2001, pp. 174–5.

70 R. C. Kammerer, 'An Exploratory Psychological Study of Crippled Children', *Psychological Record*, 4, 1940, 47.

71 Smith, *Elements*, p. 4.

72 P. Hunt (ed.) *Stigma: The Experience of Disability*, London: Geoffrey Chapman, 1966; Union of the Physically Impaired Against Segregation, *Fundamental Principles of Disability*, London: UPIAS and Disability Alliance, 1976; M. Oliver, *The Politics of Disablement*, Basingstoke: Macmillan, 1990.

73 Watson, *Civilization*, pp. 7–8, 10, 12. See also Watson, *Life*, pp. 244–5.

74 D. Marks, *Disability: Controversial Debates and Psychosocial Perspectives*, London: Routledge, 1999, p. 35.

75 I. Gazeley and P. Thane, 'Patterns of Visibility: Unemployment in Britain during the Nineteenth and Twentieth Centuries', in Lewis (ed.) *Forming Nation*, pp. 184–8; L. Hollen Lees, *The Solidarities of Strangers: The English Poor Laws and the People, 1700–1948*, Cambridge: Cambridge University Press, 1998, pp. 287–9.

76 G. Stedman Jones, *Outcast London: A Study in the Relationship Between Classes in Victorian Society*, Harmondsworth: Penguin, 1971, pp. 281–314.

77 R. A. Soloway, *Democracy and Degeneration: Eugenics and the Declining Birthrate in Twentieth-Century Britain*, Chapel Hill: University of North Carolina Press, 1995, pp. xvii, xxiv. See also M. Freeden, 'Eugenics and Progressive Thought: A Study in Ideological Affinity', *Historical Journal*, 22, 1979, 658–9.

78 Koven, 'Remembering', 1173.

79 See, for example, P. Addison, *The Road to 1945: British Politics and the Second World War,* London: Pimlico, 1994, pp. 280–92.

80 *The Mind of the Cripple: An Introduction to the Study of the Behaviour of the Physically Handicapped Child for Nurses and Others Working in Orthopaedic Hospitals and Clinics*, Bath: Child Guidance Council, 1942, p. 17. For a survey of the early years of child guidance clinics in Britain, see O. C. Sampson, *Child Guidance: Its History, Provenance and Future*, London: British Psychological Society, 1980, Chapters 1 and 2.

81 Royal Orthopaedic and Spinal Hospital, Birmingham, *Annual Report* (1914/1915), p. 19.

82 Watson, *Civilization*, pp. 80–1.

83 Smith, *Elements*, p. 61. See also Girdlestone, *Care*, p. 12; N. Moore, *The Cause and Treatment of Rickets*, London: Bradbury, Agnew & Co., 1876, pp. 30–2; Watson, *Life*, p. 251.

84 Watson, *Civilization*, pp. vii, 78, 82, 84, 87.

85 C. Lawrence, 'Still Incommunicable: Clinical Holists and Medical Knowledge in

Interwar Britain', Lawrence and Weisz (eds), *Greater Than The Parts*, pp. 94–5, 106; Sturdy, 'Hippocrates', pp. 112–13, 129–30.

86 D. Armstrong, *Political Anatomy of the Body: Medical Knowledge in Britain in the Twentieth Century*, Cambridge: Cambridge University Press, 1983, p. 9.

87 *The Hospital*, LXI, 3 March 1917, 435.

88 J. Lynn-Thomas, 'Crippledom in Wales', *The Cripples' Journal*, I, 1924, 61.

89 L. M. Davies, 'Crippledom in Wales', *The Cripples' Journal*, I, 1924, 166–7.

90 Shropshire Surgical Home, Baschurch, *Annual Report* (1920) p. 12. See also Girdlestone, *Care*, p. 20; R. Jones, 'The Surgical Treatment of Infantile Paralysis', *The Lancet*, 30 May 1914, 1521; Smith, *Elements*, p. 2.; Watson, *Civilization*, pp. 15, 77; Watson, *Life*, p. 242.

91 Girdlestone, *Care*, p. 3.

92 Anderson, *Record*, p. 19.

93 *Kelly's Directory of Devonshire 1930*, London: Kelly's Directories, 1930, p. 219.

94 Devon County Record Office, Exeter (DCRO) 2609F/HM1, Princess Elizabeth/Devonian Orthopaedic Hospital: Hospital Management and Other Committee Minutes, 16 May 1929.

95 DCRO 2609F/HM1, Princess Elizabeth/Devonian Orthopaedic Hospital: Hospital Management and Other Committee Minutes, 20 March 1930, 17 April 1930, 20 November 1930.

96 DCRO 2609F/HM1, Princess Elizabeth/Devonian Orthopaedic Hospital: Hospital Management and Other Committee Minutes, 19 March 1931.

97 DCRO 2609F/HM1, Princess Elizabeth/Devonian Orthopaedic Hospital: Hospital Management and Other Committee Minutes, 15 October 1931.

98 Girdlestone, *Care*, p. 9.

99 Hunt, *This Is My Life*, p. 145.

100 A.G. Hunt, 'Baschurch and After, III: During the War', *The Cripples' Journal*, I, 1924, 185.

101 SRRS 1387/37, Shropshire Orthopaedic Hospital and Agnes Hunt Surgical Home, Oswestry, 'General Rules and Regulations' (1929) p. 14.

102 DCRO 2609F/HM1, Princess Elizabeth/Devonian Orthopaedic Hospital: Hospital Management and Other Committee Minutes, 16 October 1930.

103 Nottingham and District Cripples' Guild, *Seventh Annual Report* (1914) p. 6.

104 Nottingham and District Cripples' Guild, *Annual Report* (1925) p. 7.

105 SRRS 1387/37, Shropshire Orthopaedic Hospital, 'General Rules', p. 15.

106 Menzies, *Heritage*, p. 70.

107 See, for example, J. Bellers, *An Essay towards the Improvement of Physick*, in G. Clarke (ed.) *John Bellers: His Life, Times and Writings,* London: Routledge and Kegan Paul, 1987, pp. 177–220.

108 Tubby, *Deformities*, 1896; Tubby, *Deformities*, 1912.

109 J. S. Reznick, 'Work-therapy and the Disabled British Soldier in Great Britain in the First World War: The Case of Shepherd's Bush Military Hospital, London', in D. A. Gerber (ed.) *Disabled Veterans in History*, Ann Arbor: University of Michigan Press, 2000, pp. 187 9.

110 R. Jones, *Address*, p. 4.

111 Watson, *Life*, pp. 143–51, 164–82.

112 R. Phelps, *The Prince and the Pioneers: The Early Work of the Prince of Wales Orthopaedic Hospital, Cardiff*, Cardiff: University Hospital of Wales and Cardiff Royal Group of Hospitals, 1993, p. 14.

113 See A. Borsay, *Disability and Social Policy in Britain Since 1750: A History of Exclusion*, Basingstoke: Macmillan, 2005, pp. 127–35; A. Borsay, ' "Fit to work": representing rehabilitation on the South Wales Coalfield during the Second World War', in A. Borsay (ed.) *Medicine in Wales, c.1800–2000: Public Service or Private Commodity?* Cardiff: University of Wales Press, 2003, pp. 128–53.

114 Girdlestone, *Care*, p. 20.
115 Tubby, *Advance*, p. 125.
116 R. C. Emslie, 'Foreword', in Smith, *Elements*, p. xi.
117 Tubby, *Advance*, p. 125.
118 Jones, *Address*, p. 6.
119 Watson, *Civilization*, pp. 96–7, 100. See also W. Mercer, *Orthopaedic Surgery*, 2nd edn, London: Edward Arnold, 1936, pp. 3–4.

6 Making deaf children talk

Changes in educational policy towards the deaf in the French Third Republic

François Buton

The aim of the paper is to analyze a specific normalizing policy, which, at the end of the nineteenth century, in the early French Third Republic, led to the banning of French Sign Language (FSL), and to the mandatory use of oral methods in schools for deaf-mute children. The paper will be organized in three parts. First, the main steps of pro-voice policy will be described. Second, an analysis of the specific social and political configuration that made such a policy possible and available in the 1880s in France will be proposed. Finally, a specific part will examine the decisive factor of the policy process, namely the past development of the State in terms of bureaucratization.[1]

A new policy

The educative sector for deaf-mute children was rather important in France – as compared to the sector for the Blind, for instance.[2] Many reasons can explain such a development. The needs were all but insignificant: thousands of deaf-mute children were under 15 years old, probably twice the population of the Blind under 15. Besides, educating deaf-mutes was considered as an important philosophical and medical issue and an educational challenge since the eighteenth century, thus arousing the interest of a large variety of actors, such as scholars, clergymen or physicians.[3] About 60 schools existed for deaf-mute children by the 1870s, educating approximately 3,000 children.[4] Most of these schools were run by Catholic congregations, such as the 'Frères de Saint-Gabriel', whose interest in the activity began in the 1820s, and grew in the 1840s and the 1850s. Nevertheless, the oldest, biggest and most prestigious institutions were two state-protected schools in Paris and Bordeaux. The Parisian school, founded by L'abbé de l'Epée in 1760, had been put under the protection of the State in 1791, two years before the school of Bordeaux. Both schools had survived different threats during the revolutionary period and the Empire, and educated more than 150 pupils any one time by the end of the nineteenth century.

Various educational methods coexisted in the 1870s, but the huge majority of educators used FSL as the basic tool for both primary and moral education. 'Discovered' by L'Epée[5] and defended by Parisian teachers, some of whom were deaf-mutes themselves, this language had two major advantages. On the one hand, it allowed easy communication with new pupils, who were ten years old when they entered school, but the majority of whom had never had the opportunity to use any conventional kind of signs. On the other hand, FSL was considered as the most adequate language to teach children to read and write – to give them the basis of primary education. Such a broad acceptance of FSL in the field of education for the deaf was recent, in so far as different actors, at different periods, tried to reduce its influence. At the end of the 1820s, the famous philanthropist Baron de Gérando and his fellow administrators of the Parisian school imposed on teachers and pupils a new mandatory course based on the imitation of speaking. In the 1850s and the 1860s, a few isolated teachers, possibly coming from abroad (German states, or Switzerland), set out to prove to French administration that their own version of oral method was appropriate to the education of deaf-mutes. But each time a few teachers, especially those of the Parisian school, had managed to turn down these proposals. Thanks to widely diffused publications and specialized reviews,[6] and by regular visits to private schools, Parisian teachers even managed in the 1860s to devise their own method, called the 'intuitive method' ('méthode intuitive'), acknowledged both by the French administration as the official one, and by the majority of their peers as being the most effective method.[7] As a result, this opened the possibility for the most brilliant pupils to become teachers in schools for deaf-mutes. Indeed, the majority of the Paris school's teachers in 1870 were deaf-mutes.

An important event occurred in the middle of the 1870s when new non-religious teachers organized themselves in order to stand up for and promote the oral method in France. The oral method was based on two techniques: the imitation of speaking ('l'articulation artificielle', literally 'artificial articulation') and lip-reading (la 'lecture sur les lèvres' or 'lecture labiale'). By the second half of the nineteenth century, these techniques, which had been elaborated by various preceptors of rich deaf-mute children between the sixteenth and the eighteenth centuries, were commonly used throughout Europe (in England, Switzerland, Italy and, above all, in the German states).[8] Despite recurrent attempts in the first half of the nineteenth century, this method had failed to find a significant place in France. But the 1870s outsiders, contrary to their predecessors, possessed powerful resources to strengthen and renew claims for the legitimacy of the oral method. Although some of them were French, they often came from foreign countries, and insisted on the international legitimacy of the oral method. Furthermore, they could count on the protection of industrial tycoons, the Pereire brothers, who owned railway, bank and transatlantic companies,[9] and were the descendants of Jacob Pereire, a famous oralist teacher and the major opponent of l'Epée in the eighteenth century. Keen to clear their ancestor's name, the Pereires gave financial support to the oralist outsiders' project and encouraged oralist teachers to write laudatory biographies of Jacob Pereire.[10] Above all, they helped to found new private and non-religious schools, and actively campaigned in favour of the oral method, mainly through their contribution to the organization of national and international congresses for the education for deaf-mutes.

These teachers' meetings were an important innovation in the sector of education for deaf-mutes – even if international congresses were a common phenomenon at this time, very frequent during World Fairs, and a useful resource for reformist actors whatever their interest (sciences and knowledge, professions, or state intervention in society).[11] During these congresses, and especially the international congress of Milan (Italy) in September 1880, the French educational reform in favour of the oral method was, if not exactly decided, nonetheless presented as necessary, and adopted by established teachers for deaf-mutes – that is clerical ones, and State-protected institutions' representatives – before eventually receiving 'universal' support.

It is not the place here to describe precisely the context, organization and development of the Milan Congress, an event considered nowadays by the majority of French deaf-mutes as the worst in their history.[12] Three major points however need to be pointed out. First, FSL was strongly condemned by the Congress – the condemnation indeed seemed to have been the only purpose of the Congress; seven out of eight of the final resolutions concerned teaching questions, almost all the participants proclaiming, rather than proving, the superiority of the pure oral method over any kind of sign language. Second, this Congress was anything but international, in so far as respectively two-thirds and one-quarter of delegates were Italian and French. Third, French oralist outsiders, in charge of the organization of the Milan Congress as they had been for the previous ones, were concretely marginalized during the debates, to the benefit of an original coalition, representing the majority of participants: French Catholic teachers and civil servants, that is to say established actors of the educative sector for deaf-mute children in France, allied with Italian Catholic teachers, themselves leaders in their own country's educative sector.

The oral method, and more precisely a 'pure' version of it, was abruptly introduced in state-protected schools in the autumn of 1880 by a governmental decision (apparently) following on from the recommendations of the Milan Congress; it also began to spread in Catholic schools at this time. In 1884, a new decision of the Ministère de l'Intérieur (French Home Office) created for the first time a certificate of aptitude for the education for the deaf (no longer called 'deaf-mutes' but 'speaking deaf people'), which all candidates had to obtain to be able to teach oralist techniques. In short, deaf-mute candidates were excluded from teaching. The banning of the FSL in schools and the banning of deaf-mutes from teaching to their fellows continued until the 1990s in France.

Making reform possible: the political and social configuration of public decisions

The historiography on the subject generally considers this reform as the success of the outsiders.[13] This interpretation can be strongly criticized, in so far as it focuses excessively on cognitive issues and fails to take into account important institutional questions. In fact, even if we consider only cognitive issues, the result of the reform differs significantly from the project of French oralists.

The 'pure' oral method defended in Milan and consequently applied in France was much more exclusive than outsiders' methods, which, unlike the demands of Italian teachers, never called for the *complete* banning of any kind of sign languages.

But the main point here is institutional: the reform was conducted by civil servants allied with clerical teachers in the name of a common institutional interest. Outsiders were actually not only oralists, but also non-religious, and even anti-clerical teachers, fighting strongly for the attachment of the education for deaf-mutes to the Ministère de l'Instruction Publique (Department for Education), in other words, the *secularization* of the activity in a republican perspective. This ambition clearly went against all established actors' interests. Catholic congregations obviously did not want to lose control of their schools; they were usually very wary of any attempt at 'republicanizing' the activities they had 'traditionally' carried out in the name of both Christian charity and moral leadership in French society. Civil servants in charge of education for deaf-mutes were obviously reluctant to see their influence reduced. The most important ones, inspectors of schools for deaf-mutes, were themselves Catholics and conservatives, whose administrative careers had been mainly carried out under the Third Empire, and who had survived, for a still undiscovered reason, the vast republican purge of higher administration at the end of the 1870s.[14] As for the republican leaders, who had just reached political power, they didn't seem to consider deaf-mute issues as important enough to take any measure on their own. On the one hand, they confirmed all the civil servants' proposals, especially since the oral method could be – and actually was – presented as a social progress, promising nothing less than to make all deaf children talk. In fact, the promise would appear impossible keep within a few years time – but the children would be blamed for this, not the method. On the other hand, it is likely that republican leaders, already in conflict with the Catholic Church about general education (that is, education for 'ordinary' children), did not wish to fight the Catholic Church on the charity field, a field in which they would later, in the 1890s, build a compromise solution, based on the complementary nature of 'bienfaisance privée' (charities) and 'assistance publique' (public assistance).[15] At this time, education for deaf-mutes was considered as part of a care policy rather than an integral part of educational policy.

One striking point about the social and political configuration that made possible such a radical reform as the complete transformation of methods in the education for deaf-mutes lies in its highly improbable composition: Catholic clerics and civil servants in the early French republic would usually rather fight each other than build any kind of alliance. However, these forces joined, for different and often contradictory reasons (philosophical, religious, health justifications) to promote the oral method. It is clear that this very surprising coalition of heterogeneous, opposed actors jointly conducted policy reform by taking over outsiders' cognitive principles as a way to prevent outsiders' organizational aims from being considered. The oral method could be attractive for established actors, providing that education structures wouldn't be changed. Moreover, the oral method could be all the more appealing since it could be presented as an element of both internal (a new method that would make the children talk) and external progress (the integration of deaf-mutes' individuals into republican society through the use of French oral language), or for the Catholics, as a means to obtain the salvation of deaf-mutes' souls (in so far as faith depends on understanding, and so on) to the educative sector.

The historical origins of a reform

Finally, it is worth raising more questions about the specific social configuration that put the reform on the agenda and led to its implementation. In terms of political sociology, the question of the motivations of social actors (why did these actors act as they did?), although of great interest, must be first examined through the question of the social conditions of the possibility of their actions (how could they act as they did?). Two highly significant, though contradictory, points about the actors involved and their roles must be given.

First, actors clearly had different roles in the reform process. The numerous Catholic teachers provided the bulk of the votes that Congress resolutions need to be adopted. Their role in strengthening the legitimacy of reform was to provide 'numbers', characterized as one of the typical legitimating resources in the construction of any social interest.[16] Even if they sometimes contributed to explain the reform in terms of progress or to define orality as a salvation good, they were mostly useful as a kind of pre-constituted majority whose vote was supposed to guarantee the representativeness of the reform in the educative sector for deaf-mutes. On the contrary, the few civil servants provided another typical legitimacy resource of social interests, namely knowledge, by the way of official reports they sent to public authorities.[17] Civil servants' knowledge was a mix of abstract 'scientific' (linguistic, medical and so on) or philosophical considerations taken from official French scholars such as Adolphe Franck, member of the Académie des sciences, and concrete administrative know-how directly based on their own practical experience in terms of legal control and educational supervising of schools for deaf-mutes.

Second, these civil servants were neither top civil servants, nor 'street-level bureaucrats'[18], but middle-rank officials: in the early 1880s, Oscar Claveau was a chief inspector of care institutions (which included state-protected schools for deaf mutes), Théophile Denis a head clerk in charge of specialized education, Louis Peyron and Adophe Franck respectively the director and one of the administrators of the National Institution in Paris. But the monopolistic presence of civil servants as members of the state and the public institutions for deaf-mutes in the reform process also meant the complete absence of teachers, who were actually not invited to give their opinion and were unable to resist a reform that went against their interests and that they generally disapproved of. Consequently, an important question about the social configuration that implemented the reform can be raised: how do we explain how middle-rank bureaucrats were able to replace teachers as the owners of specialized educational knowledge?

To fully understand the issues described above, it is necessary to consider the long term bureaucratization process of French administration and state-protected institutions. Until the 1870s, the implementation of all educational reforms had been based upon specialist expertise – in short, on teachers' reports. But teachers' access to political decisions regarding educational issues was progressively modified, and became more and more difficult; on the contrary, the role played by and given to central administration bureaucrats was strengthened by the bureaucratization process, in spite of their complete lack of practical knowledge of the matter.[19]

Teachers' loss of autonomy in designing educational principles and methods began in the 1840s, when the rather lax and non-restrictive protection of officially 'state-protected' schools evolved into a much more concrete and restrictive supervision of their functioning by chief inspectors, who had pushed for such an evolution.[20] The bureaucratization of state-protected schools had two major effects: on the one hand, it made concrete and tightened the surveillance of the schools by central administration; on the other hand, it didn't consider other (non state-protected) schools, leaving their creation and development free of any oversight and control. In other words, the process of bureaucratization created the private/public division in education for deaf-mutes by putting only public sector under the surveillance of the State inspectors. Furthermore, the public sector schools, formerly the symbolic and political centres of education for deaf-mutes, no longer tried to influence other schools' educational principles and practices after the 1850s.

Many indicators of teacher marginalization over the following three decades could be presented here. Unlike the situation that prevailed in the early nineteenth century, it became impossible for a teacher to be put at the head of state-protected school after the 1860s: all directors were civil servants. Minor reforms concerning these schools would be imposed by Home Office civil servants, in so far as the single education proposal by teachers had to be confronted to inspectors' opinions. In fact, this long term evolution did not seem to be considered by teachers as highly problematic, since it also brought them, as state employees, benefits closely connected to the emergence of what Weber calls a legitimacy based on legality.[21] In concrete terms, all teachers, including deaf-mutes teachers, were themselves subject to the bureaucratization process, and thus, from then on, saw their employment situation improved, their career progression facilitated, and the level of their wages increased. Moreover, the 1860s and the 1870s can generally speaking be described as 'golden years' for the teachers of 'public' schools from an educational point of view: their reputation was high, in France and abroad, and they could enjoy a great autonomy in their educational tasks. Nevertheless, the bureaucratization process was the silent and 'positive' evolution that made teachers in the early 1880s unable, if not unwilling, to resist an educational reform considered to a great extent as unfair and unjustified.

Two conclusions can be drawn from our analysis. The first one focuses on the consequences of the reform. These were indeed of great importance. On the one hand, the banning of FSL dramatically modified the future of thousands of

French deaf-mute children, whose access to their own language was confined to clandestine uses, and whose illiteracy rate rose dramatically during the twentieth century. On the other hand, the joining of education for deaf-mute to the social care sector – in other words, the definition of education as a charitable activity – made impossible for years the access to education for all deaf children, despite the right to education legally granted in 1882. In concrete terms, education remained a *favour* to a deaf-mute child, depending on school capacities rather than the child's abilities, and not a *right*. The second conclusion concerns the methodology of social sciences, and points out the relevance of socio-historical approaches of policies – what has been called in France 'sociohistoire du politique'.[22] It is worth underlining that our policy process analysis highlights the need for social scientists – especially political scientists – to use a diachronic point of view not only to explain the past and describe social transformations in societies, but also in order to identify historically-built conditions of possibilities of policy areas.

Notes

1 This paper is mainly based on a dissertation for the PhD of political science (Paris, EHESS, 1999), entitled 'Les corps saisis par l'Etat. L'éducation des sourds-muets et des aveugles au XIXe siècle. Contribution à la socio-histoire de l'Etat (1789–1885)' (English translation: 'Bodies Seized by the State. The Education for Deaf-mutes and for the Blind in nineteenth century. Contribution to the Socio-history of the State (1789–1885)'). I am grateful to Malcolm Eden, Anne-France Taiclet and Jay Rowell for their comments on an earlier version of this paper.

2 See Adolphe de Watteville, *Statistique des établissements de bienfaisance. Rapport au ministre de l'intérieur sur les aveugles et les sourds-muets, et les établissements consacrés à leur éducation*, Paris, 1861.

3 For comparative arguments made in favour of deaf education, and on the battle between proponents of oral methods and sign language in nineteenth-century America, see Douglas Baynton, *Forbidden Signs: American Culture and the Campaign against Sign Language*, Chicago: University of Chicago Press, 1996 (I am grateful to the editors for this reference).

4 See Jean-Jacques Valade-Gabel, *De la situation des écoles de sourds-muets non subventionnées par l'État*, [1868], Bordeaux: G. Gounouilhou, 1875, p. 5.

5 In fact, L'Epée sought to make certain signs, those used and invented by some deaf-mutes he observed in Paris, compatible with French grammar.

6 Mainly the four editions of *Circulaire de l'Institution Royale des sourds-muets de Paris à toutes les institutions des sourds-muets de l'Europe et de l'Amérique*, Paris, Imp. Royale, 1827, 1829, 1832, 1836; and the *Annales de l'éducation des sourds-muets et des aveugles* (1844–1850).

7 See Adolphe Franck, *Rapport à Son Excellence M. le ministre de l'intérieur sur divers ouvrages relatifs à l'instruction des sourds-muets*, Imprimerie Impériale, 1861.

8 On the wider influence of German methods see R. A. R. Edwards, '"Speech has an Extraordinary Humanizing Power": Horace Mann and the Problem of Nineteenth-Century Deaf Education', in Paul K. Longmore and Lauri Umansky (eds), *The New Disability History: American Perspectives*, New York and London: New York University Press, 2001, pp. 58–82 (I am grateful to the editors for this reference).

9 See J. Autin, *Les frères Péreire. Le bonheur d'entreprendre*, Paris: Perrin, 1983.

10 Three hagiographies were written by teachers directly concerned by the oralist

entreprise (members of the Pereire society): F. Hément, *Jacob Rodrigues Péreire, premier instituteur des sourds-muets en France*, Paris: Didier, 1875; M. Magnat, *Méthode Jacob-Rodrigues Péreire appliqué à l'enseignement du premier âge*, Paris: Sandoz et Fischbacher, 1876; E. La Rochelle, *Jacob-Rodrigues Péreire, premier instituteur des sourd-muets en France: sa vie et ses travaux*, Paris: P. Dupont, 1882.

11 See A. Rasmussen, 'Les Congrès internationaux liés aux Expositions universelles de Paris de 1867 à 1900', *Mil neuf cent*, 7, 1989, 23–44, and the major works of Christian Topalov: *Naissance du chômeur 1880–1910*, Paris: Albin Michel, 1995, and *Laboratoires du nouveau siècle. La nébuleuse réformatrice et ses réseaux en France, 1880–1914*, Paris: Ed. EHESS, 1999.

12 I treat the subject in more detail elsewhere. See my 'Le congrès de Milan entre mythe et réalité', *Surdités*, 4, Décembre 2001, 45–61, and, for an Italian translation, 'Il congresso di Milano tra mito e realtà', *L'educazione dei sordi*, série IX, vol CIV:4, 2003.

13 See Harlan Lane, *When the Mind Hears. A History of the Deaf*, New York: Random House, 1984, or C. Cuxac, *Le langage des sourds*, Paris: Payot, 1983.

14 On this purge, see P. Machelon, *La république contre les libertés? Les restrictions aux libertés publiques de 1879 à 1914,* Paris: Presses FNSP, 1976.

15 See C. Bec, *Assistance et République. La recherche d'un nouveau contrat social sous la IIIe République*, Paris: Les Éditions de l'Atelier/Éditions Ouvrières, 1994, and *L'assistance en démocratie. Les politiques assistantielles dans la France des XIXe et XXe siècles*, Paris: Belin, 1998.

16 For a classification of the resources available in the construction of social interests, see M. Offerlé, *Sociologie des groupes d'intérêt*, Paris: Monchrestien, 1994.

17 The most important reports were: A. Franck, *Rapport au ministre de l'intérieur et des cultes sur le Congrès international de Milan, Journal officiel* du 18 décembre 1880, Lib. des publications législatives, 1880; O. Claveau, *L'enseignement de la parole dans les institutions de sourds-muets. Rapport à monsieur le ministre de l'intérieur et des cultes*, Paris: Imp. nationale, 1880; O. Claveau, *De la parole comme objet et comme moyen d'enseignement dans les institutions de sourds-muets. Rapport à monsieur le ministre de l'intérieur*, Paris: Imp. nationale, 1881; T. Denis, *Les Institutions nationales de sourds-muets et le ministère de l'intérieur*, Paris: Berger-Levrault et Cie, 1882.

18 See M. Lipsky, *Street-level Bureaucracy: Dilemmas of the Individual in Public Service*, New York: Russel-Sage Foundation, 1980; V. Dubois, *La vie au guichet. Relation administrative et traitement de la misère*, Paris: Economica, 2003.

19 The following developments have been presented in my article 'Bureaucratisation et délimitation des frontières de l'État. Les interventions administratives sur l'éducation des sourds-muets au XIXe siècle', *Genèses*, 28, Septembre 1997, 5–28.

20 Adolphe de Watteville and Gabriel de Lurieu, chief inspectors, wrote a report of their inspection of State-protected institutions in 1840 which directly led to new and more bureaucratic legal status for these institutions in February 1841 (*Ordonnance royale du 21 février 1841 relative au mode d'organisation et d'administration des établissements généraux de bienfaisance et d'utilité publique*). The reports can be consulted under the reference F 15 3865–3866 at the *Archives Nationales* (Paris).

21 See Max Weber, *Economy and Society*, 3 vols, New York: Bedminster Press, 1968 (especially, I, 212–54).

22 About this approach, French-speaking scholars can refer to the major works of Gérard Noiriel (for instance, *Penser avec, penser contre. Itinéraire d'un historien*, Paris: Belin, 2003). See also, among numerous references, M. Offerlé, 'L'histoire des politistes', in P. Favre and J.-B. Legavre (eds), *Enseigner la science politique*, Paris: L'Harmatttan, 1998, pp. 203–16; G. Pollet, 'Regards croisés sur la construction de la loi: d'une histoire sociale à une socio-histoire de l'action publique', in J. Commaille,

L. Dumoulin and C. Robert (eds), *La juridicisation du politique. Leçons scientifiques*, Paris: LGDJ, 1999, pp. 61–80; Y. Déloye and B. Voutat (eds), *Faire de la science politique. Pour une socio-histoire du politique*, Paris: Belin, 2002; and F. Buton, 'L'Etat et ses catégories comme objets d'analyse socio-historique: les handicapés sensoriels au XIXe siècle', in Pascale Laborier and Danny Trom (eds), *Historicités de l'action publique*, Paris: PUF-CURAPP, 2003, pp. 59–78.

7 Eugenics, modernity and nationalism[1]

Ayça Alemdaroğlu

Modern eugenics, the science of biologically improving the human race, influenced the international politics of the human body in the early twentieth century. Eugenics emerged in the context of an increasing emphasis on progressivism, scientism, nationalism and racism. Its advocates believed that eugenics could guide social progress and national development, and serve to increase economic, military and governmental efficiency. In the economic and political tumult of the early twentieth century, many nation states adhere to eugenics to aid in their survival.

The origins of eugenics can be traced back to the Spartans, who feared the social implications of a declining birth rate among the noble class and the proliferation of the underclass and the slaves.[2] To protect the quality of the population, Spartans prevented emigration, penalised celibacy and rewarded fertility. The Spartans were among the first to systematically regulate marriage (celibacy, late marriages, and 'bad' marriages were punished) and they encouraged the infanticide of mentally defective, diseased, and unfit babies. The Spartans believed that the health of the pregnant woman and the quality of childcare influenced the fitness of the child. Inspired by Sparta's example, Plato formulated an early theory of eugenics. Although its intellectual foundations go back to the ancient Greeks, modern eugenics was primarily influenced by the late nineteenth century scientific developments in Europe such as Darwinism and the revival of the Mendelian and the Lamarckian theories of heredity.

The emergence of modern eugenics owes much to Charles Darwin's theory of evolution, Herbert Spencer's theory of the survival of the fittest, and Social Darwinism. 'Social Darwinist' was a loose label, which was applied to anybody who believed that Charles Darwin's theory of evolution and natural selection had implications for society. Social Darwinists believed that human beings, just as animals and plants in the wild, are engaged in a struggle for their existence and that the 'fittest' will thrive. Francis Galton, a nineteenth-century polymath and a cousin of Darwin, argued that talents and virtues of character were inherited along with physical features and offered a hereditary advantage in the struggle for existence.[3] According to Galton, society brings on its own ruin by allowing the less intelligent to out-reproduce the more intelligent. To prevent this he believed in selective breeding, i.e. that the state should encourage the rich and healthy to have many children and prevent others from doing so. Galton employed the name 'eugenics', derived from Greek, to describe the science of improving the human race. Although Galton was credited as the father of modern eugenics, similar ideas also emerged in late nineteenth century France, North America and Germany.[4] For instance, in 1850 the French scientist Prosper Lucas studied genealogically the moral and mental characteristics of criminals and concluded that the French government should discourage the perpetuation of their lineages.[5]

In the 1890s, further scientific support for eugenics came from the German biologist August Weismann (1834–1914), who argued that a part of a cell, the germ-plasm, maintained the organic continuity from one generation to the next and was independent of the environment. Moreover, the rediscovery of Gregor Johann Mendel's work by 1900, 30 years after its original publication, provided further scientific support. Mendel's work on genetically crossed plants showed that genetic elements were inherited and unchanged through many generations. A logical conclusion of Mendel's work was that his genetic principles would be equally true for humans as they were for peas. Mendel's work challenged the prevalent theory espousing the inheritance of acquired characteristics, which was associated with French naturalist, Jean de Lamarck (1744–1829). In the social context, Weismann's and Mendel's theories were interpreted to mean that neither environment nor education could help to alter the genetic composition of successive generations and buttressed state-control of human reproduction against moral objections.

Scientific developments did not naturally lead to the emergence of eugenics as a uniform international movement. Rather, eugenics was more of a social and political programme than a scientific one. A comparison of eugenics in different countries indicates that the production and application of scientific knowledge is highly dependent on political, institutional and cultural factors. Despite its claim on universality, scientific knowledge is open to interpretation. For instance, depending on the context, Mendelian theory could be interpreted to indicate that either: irrespective of social class and status, all humans could have good genes; or that those who were at the top of society had good genes. Furthermore, in many countries such as France, Mexico, Romania and Brazil, eugenics movements followed the Lamarckian theory of heredity notwithstanding its scientific decline.[6] As I will elaborate below, eugenic ideas were selected from a pool of scientific knowledge in accordance with the current political and cultural context, which, in turn, came to be influenced by eugenic policies.

The early historiography of modern eugenics usually emphasised an Anglo-Saxon origin and the widespread application in Germany and the US. In the 1990s, new studies revealed that eugenics was a far more pervasive movement, which permeated many countries. The underlying, shared motive of eugenics in different geographies was the desire to protect a nation's population from degeneration. The definition of degenerative influences, and the remedies suggested, varied according to the social texture, political history, and economic conditions of each country. In some states such as Mexico, Brazil, Romania, Japan and

Turkey, eugenic policies designed to promote the nation's health accompanied efforts to define and create a national identity and modern society.[7] Whatever form it took, by the end of the First World War eugenics was influential in many countries, including France, Sweden, Norway, Denmark and Russia.[8] In spite of their disagreements with regard to policy, all advocates of eugenics believed that national concerns should guide human reproductive decisions.

Unfortunately, an improved nation meant death or a worse life for some of its citizens: thousands of people in North America, Germany, Scandinavia and Switzerland were sterilised against their will; millions were exterminated in the Holocaust. After its association with the Nazis, eugenics fell out of political favour even though forced sterilisation was continued in Scandinavia and America until the 1960s. In the 1990s, debates on issues such as reproductive rights and euthanasia, as well as the human genome project, led to a revival of eugenics in a more individual form.

In this chapter, I will explore the eugenic discourse in Turkey, a country that was at the margins of European scientific developments, but which viewed Europe as a model of development. During 1920s and 1930s, Turkey underwent a tremendous change from an empire of multi-religious communities to a national republic with a unified national identity and culture. The modernising elite wanted to create a society with a modern secular identity and to measure up to the level of European countries in terms of wealth, military power and culture. In this context of modernisation, eugenic ideas influenced the Republican elite. Eugenic discourse in Turkey influenced the regulation of health, hygiene, marriage, reproduction and childcare. The Republican state passed laws to improve hygiene, to promote population growth and to regulate marriage and reproduction. They attacked the traditional and religious practices regarding health, marriage, reproduction and childcare. The Turkish eugenicists, who were often medical doctors, entangled Western eugenics with the agenda of Turkish modernisation and the political ambitions of the Republican regime. Eugenic discourse contributed to the physical and moral reproduction of the nation, that is, the creation of a healthy, populated and durable nation, and the reformulation of the state/individual relationship.

Here, my aim is not to write a brief history of eugenics in Turkey, but instead to describe the character of eugenic discourse and the role it had in the definition of the state/individual relationship in the production of a Turkish national identity. In this chapter, I will analyse eugenics from the point of view of the state elites, and examine the state's approach to public health, reproduction and childcare through an analysis of the primary literature of the 1930s. Before embarking on a study of Turkish eugenics, I will briefly discuss the general characteristics of the eugenic movements in Britain, France and Germany, which greatly influenced Turkish eugenicists.

The turn of the nineteenth century in Europe was marked by a belief in science, progress and nationalism. At this juncture in time, the nation state emerged as the predominate power for the realisation of social, economic, and cultural aspirations of a people. An increasingly scientific worldview, espoused in bio-medical terms, provided the nation state with a justification for controlling an individual's body. Michel Foucault explained the state's control of the human body in terms of its growing 'bio-power'.[9] According to Foucault, beginning with the late eighteenth century, a person's reproductive capacity and its measurement were seen as fundamental in determining a state's bio-power. Nicholas Rose identifies two state sponsored biopolitical strategies that were employed in early twentieth century Europe and North America, which sought to maximise the fitness of the population.[10] The first strategy was to protect the health of the population by improving hygiene through better town planning, sewage systems, medical inspection, education and moral training. The second strategy was to regulate reproduction in order to free the population from the social and economic burden of its inefficient, unhealthy, degenerated parts. Control over birth and death, sexuality and reproduction, health, family, childcare, and the quality and quantity of population became vital to the power of the state. To achieve their military, economic and political goals, the authorities undertook the management of processes fundamental to a human life. These developments were facilitated by the development of human sciences, clinical medicine and statistics, which brought many matters previously considered private under state surveillance.

Eugenics addressed both of these biopolitical strategies of the twentieth century, however its primary focus was on reproduction. Eugenics involved positive and negative measures. On the one hand, positive eugenics aimed to promote the proliferation of healthy elements in the society by promoting reproduction, marriage and childcare among the healthy groups in the society. Positive eugenics employed education, moral inculcation and material benefits such as family allowances, tax discounts and 'fitter family' competitions.[11] On the other hand, negative eugenics was based on systematic constraints and coercion, whose goal was to decrease reproduction in families having inferior hereditary qualities. Negative eugenic methods included premarital medical examinations, birth control, prenatal screening, abortion, sterilisation, and immigration restrictions. Insanity, disability, criminality, anti-social behaviour, and alcoholism were some of the targets of negative eugenics. In some cases, social 'unworthiness' was associated with ethnic minorities and immigrant populations, such as Eastern Europeans and Blacks in North America, Jews in Germany and Roma in Sweden. In the pursuit of national progress, order and efficiency, modern states employed forced sterilisation and abortion, segregation and death camps. From its milder to most violent versions, eugenics was the product of modern science and politics. The Holocaust was not a calamitous exception in the history of modernity, but as Zygmunt Bauman argued it was the product of the very project of modernity that intrinsically involved the control of the biological components of the population and the elimination of foreign ones.[12]

At the turn of the nineteenth century, the *zeitgeist* in Europe was one of decline and degeneration. Wars, declining birth rates, and poor urban living conditions generated a fear of moral and biological decline, which fed eugenics movements in Germany, Britain and France. For instance in Germany, the birth rate nearly halved between 1880 and 1925, while the decline in France was even more severe. In Germany, a deepening economic depression and increasing social unrest was coupled with political crisis, which resulted in the repeated dissolutions of the Reichstag, to deepen the feeling of national degeneration. In France, the defeat in the Franco-Prussian War of 1870–1871 and the fear of depopulation stimulated a massive literature on the causes and effects of decline and their possible solutions.[13] Industrial cities with inadequate infrastructure and an increasing number of urban poor contributed to the perception of degeneration in Europe. In pre-industrial England, for instance, more than three-quarters of the population lived in small villages, however, by the mid-nineteenth century over half of the population had moved to crowded industrial cities where disease and crime were rampant. The relatively higher birth rates among the urban poor, who were increasingly seen as the source of social diseases, generated a panic and cultural pessimism among the educated classes. The rising demands of organised labour and women in the early twentieth century further fuelled conservative reactions.

Eugenics articulated the panic and aspirations of the middle classes. More broadly, eugenics fitted well with the ambitions of a wide range of political ideologies, including liberals, socialists and conservatives. In spite of eugenics' links to early twentieth century progressivism, it also served conservatives. Whereas progressives believed that hereditary improvement was an important part of social progress, conservatives believed that the economic burden of paupers, unfits and inferior races should be reduced. Both poles of the political spectrum shared the common belief that many social diseases such as crime, alcoholism and immorality were inherited.[14]

Eugenics in Britain emerged from the professional class (such as clergymen, statisticians, and physicians), who feared being outnumbered by the urban poor, whom they believed to be a degenerate subspecies distinguished by low social worth, low intelligence and high fertility.[15] If the high fertility of the pauper class was left uncontrolled, pauperism, and its undesirable characteristics such as alcoholism, venereal diseases and ignorance, would increase and the direction of human evolution would reverse. Although class-based concerns were central to British eugenics, it was not its only motivation. The idea of preserving the position of the Empire, of protecting the English race from degeneration from immigration and miscegenation, and of defending the existing order against the demands of feminism and organised labour was also integral to British eugenics.[16] In Britain, conservative middle class professionals were not the only supporters of eugenics. Leftist social reformers, such as the Fabians, made a distinction within the poor between worthy workers and unworthy residuum, which they considered pestiferous. Despite broad political support, the British state's role in eugenics remained minimal and the proposals to legalise sterilisation between the First and Second World Wars were dismissed because of strong opposition from the church, the working class, and public health institutions. Consequently, eugenics in Britain remained limited to the activities of the

British Eugenics Society (founded in 1907) to promote public awareness of eugenic issues.

The eugenic discourse in Britain and the US during the late nineteenth and early twentieth century influenced eugenics in Germany.[17] However, Alfred Ploetz, a German social Darwinist and physician, had already formulated the German version of eugenics, 'racial hygiene', by 1895. Ploetz founded the German Society for Racial Hygiene in Society in 1905, which was earlier than its counterparts in Britain, the US and France. The notion of the purity and supremacy of the German *Volk* was central to the eugenics discourse in Germany and later to the Nazi movement. According to the Nazis, the decline of the nation and prevailing pessimism was caused by the 'illness' of the Aryan race. In 1933, a few months after seizing power, the Nazi government mandated a series of measures to increase the quality and the quantity of the German *Volk*: they prohibited the sale of contraceptives and granted interest-free loans to newly married couples with good hereditary qualities. The Ministry of Propaganda emphasised the role of women as mothers and housewives and the Nazi government limited work opportunities for married women. An ideal woman gave birth to four children or more. To encourage such behaviour, the state converted the couple's loans to grants. Also in 1933, the 'Law for the Prevention of Progeny with Hereditary Diseases' was passed to enforce sterilisation of all persons suffering from 'hereditary' defects, such as congenital feeble-mindedness, mental illness (schizophrenia and manic depression), physical deformity, epilepsy, congenital blindness and deafness, and severe alcoholism. The government charged all physicians with reporting anyone falling in the sterilisation category to the 'Hereditary Health Courts' (a judicial body composed of a judge and two health officers). Although sterilisation laws were passed in 30 states in the US, in parts of Canada, Switzerland and Denmark as early as 1907, Nazi sterilisations were the most comprehensive. In Germany by 1937 the number of sterilised people (225,000) had nearly reached ten times the number in the US in the previous three decades.[18] Finally, German eugenics espoused the elimination of non-Aryan populations, mostly Jews and Gypsies, and the Aryan 'unfits' including homosexuals and those deemed by a Nazi doctor to have mental and genetic deficiencies.

In France, eugenics emerged from a consensus for increasing the population and was closely related to the social hygiene movement. French eugenicists were primarily concerned with declining birth rates, venereal diseases, alcoholism, tuberculosis, infant mortality, poor diet and poor living conditions. In contrast to Britain and Germany, the Lamarckian theory of heredity and its emphasis on the heredity of acquired characteristics dominated French eugenics. Hence, most French eugenicists believed that if one could improve living conditions, the next generation would be better off. The Lamarckian understanding of heredity provided French eugenics with a common ground for collaboration with the natalist and social hygiene movements. Adolphe Pinard, a professor of obstetrics and the president of the French Eugenic Society, believed in the importance of the environment from the moment of conception.[19] French eugenics emphasised puericulture: the importance of a mother's health during pregnancy, breastfeeding and maternal care. Although the early work of the French Eugenic Society, established 1912, was centred on positive eugenics, by the mid 1920s the Society was campaigning for a law on premarital examination, a negative eugenic reform. However, the few attempts to introduce premarital examinations were defeated by the opposition who saw premarital examinations as a threat against individual rights and freedoms, as well as religion. Moreover, the increasing association of eugenics with racism and the repressive measures taken in the US and Germany, even if these were also evident in some French eugenicists' ideas, curtailed the support for eugenics in France.[20] However, the French Eugenic Society's proposed law mandating premarital examinations was passed by the Vichy government in 1942 and not revoked until after the Vichy government's collapse.

Although every country where eugenics emerged had its own peculiar social and political characteristics, it is still possible to talk about shared approaches of eugenic movements. First, eugenics was an elitist endeavour carried out by middle class and upper class professionals. Eugenicists had an autocratic approach, and believed that they knew what was the best for society. Although the elitism of eugenics was certainly remarkable, eugenic discourse everywhere, from the social reformist eugenics of Scandinavia (1935–1975) to today's China, adopted a collectivist discourse and required the subordination of individual rights for the greater good of the society, nation, race and so on.[21] Eugenicists, like other social Darwinists, saw society as an organism whose survival depended on the health of its parts. The dysgenic elements not only caused economic and social burdens, presumably, but also moral and racial degeneration. Another commonality of eugenic movements was racial thinking, which was integral to the political debate in the beginning of the twentieth century. The late nineteenth and early twentieth century witnessed the increasing organisation of knowledge and world affairs on the basis of racial categories. In 1881, Charles Darwin, for instance, referring to the Ottoman Russian War that ended with the defeat of Ottomans (1877–1878), observed in a letter that 'the more civilized so-called Caucasian races have beaten the Turkish hollow in the struggle for existence'.[22] Physical anthropology and anthropometric studies further strengthened the influence of race hierarchies in politics and justified the status of the powerful nations, while causing resentment in 'lower' ranked nations and peoples. Lower ranked nations, such as Japan and Turkey, also pursued eugenics with an equally race-oriented perspective. Lastly, eugenics concerned not only the physical fitness of the human body, but also its moral fitness. Eugenicists associated prostitution, crime, alcoholism and venereal diseases with congenital immorality and often attributed them to impoverished men and women whose reproduction should be curbed.

Eugenics in Turkey: the physical and moral reproduction of the nation

Turkish eugenicists' understanding of heredity was more in line with the Lamarckian theory, in spite of British and German influence. Turkish eugenicists neither critically reflected on the differences between Mendelian and Lamarckian eugenics in Europe nor explicitly affiliated themselves with French eugenics and Lamarckian theory. Instead, Turkish eugenicists pragmatically employed arguments and data from both eugenic traditions to support Republican modernisation during the 1930s. The modernisation agenda in Turkey involved a double discourse: Westernisation and nationalism. On the one hand, the Republican elite took Western Europe as a model for Turkish development; on the other hand, they advocated nationalism as a key to Turkey's political independence and cultural unity. As part of their struggle to establish an independent industrialised country with a secular-national identity, the Republican regime aspired to create a nation of 'civilised' citizens, which relinquished traditional dispositions, internalised Republican ideals and adopted modern manners, taste and daily practices.

The motto 'order and progress' defined the character of the Ottoman reformation at the turn of the nineteenth century, which influenced the spirit of the later Republican modernisation. The continuity between the Ottoman and Republican reformers was reflected not only in terms of ideas but also in terms of people. The Committee of Union and Progress (CUP), the political party of the Ottoman reformers ruling between 1908 and 1918, was founded at the Royal Medical Academy in Istanbul. The CUP combined a belief in biological materialism and evolution with the politics of social reform. For example, Abdullah Cevdet, a founding member, advocated women's emancipation by arguing that children born to enslaved women would cause racial degeneration.[23] In addition to biological materialism and scientism, reformers of both periods shared many ideological positions such as anti-clericalism, authoritarianism, intellectual elitism and nationalism. Despite overlapping ideological positions, the Republican discourse of modernisation viewed the new Republic as a clear break from the Ottoman Empire. The Republicans desired a Turkish nation of rational and secular individuals, who were loyal to the state and free from the religious loyalties and traditional practices that defined Ottoman society.

The continuous wars that brought down the Ottoman Empire and led to the emergence of the Turkish Republic caused a severe fall in Turkey's population. Epidemics, forced migration and high infant mortality multiplied the population loss in Anatolia. After the Turkish Republic was proclaimed in 1923, the Republican elite saw population growth as vital to development as well as economic and military strength. In the 1930s, natalist policies and eugenic concerns influenced the population politics, which aimed to promote rapid population growth. Guided by the Western European and North American debates, Turkish eugenicists stated that a quantitative increase in population without qualitative control would be detrimental to economic development and social order. As in France, eugenics in Turkey went hand in hand with social hygiene, natalist and childcare policies.

Atatürk, the leader of the Republican modernisation movement never mentioned eugenics as such; nevertheless, in the eyes of the eugenicists some of his famous remarks such as 'strong and sturdy generations are the essence of Turkey' and 'the nation should be protected from degenerative perils' were the basis of Turkish eugenic discourse.[24] 'Degenerative perils' referred to both biological and moral dangers and were expressed in terms of the illness of the Ottoman regime, the ignorance of the masses and the irrational health practices. Republicans drew upon science's moral authority to fight against traditional beliefs and loyalties, attacking the use of the traditional healer's methods, such as amulets, Koranic verses and ritual prescriptions.[25] In doing so, the new regime aspired to alter traditional perceptions of hygiene and to acquire a moral authority over society by employing modern scientific discourse.

One of the first institutions of the new regime, the Ministry of Health, was established in 1920, when it began to expand the state's medical infrastructure into the towns and villages of Anatolia. In order to increase the population, the Turkish Criminal Law of 1926 banned abortion and the Public Hygiene Law of 1930 (*Umumi Hıfzıssıhha Kanunu*) made the importation, manufacture and sale of contraceptives illegal.[26] No ban was put on condoms because the public hygiene regulations also aspired to curtail the spread of venereal diseases.[27]

Furthermore, the new health policies advocated preventive measures to address infant mortality and diseases such as syphilis, malaria and tuberculosis. Articles 122, 123 and 124 of the Hygiene Law mandated the premarital examination of couples: those with mental illnesses and also those with syphilis, gonorrhoea and leprosy were prohibited from marriage; and those with tuberculosis were prohibited from marriage for six months. The law also regulated wet nurses by requiring health reports for their employment and prohibiting those who had venereal diseases, leprosy or tuberculosis from breastfeeding.

The Republicans emphasised the importance of childcare and established birth and childcare clinics and the Child Protection Society, which sheltered orphans and poor children.[28] Sturdy Child Competitions were organised in the cities of Anatolia in order to promote good childcare practices. Through public education and propaganda, the Republican regime sought to teach girls rational childcare methods, i.e. that the baby should be on a strict schedule of sleeping, eating and playing. Physical fitness was also on the agenda and in 1938 the Body Discipline Law (*Beden Terbiyesi Kanunu*) was passed to regulate gymnastics and sporting activities in order to promote the development of the citizens' physical and moral abilities.[29] Article 3 of the same law mandated a youth to enrol in sports clubs and body discipline programmes in their spare time. The same article regulated a citizen's sports activities in accordance with age and season.

The primary spokesmen of eugenic discourse in Turkey were a group of medical doctors who had similar educations and political careers. The doctors had all studied in Europe and were highly influenced by the European debates and developments. The influential eugenicists were also political figures who had power over public policies regarding hygiene, childcare, city administration, and other matters. The eugenicists, like other Republicans, were critical of the ignorance of traditional society and of the Ottoman regime with regard to scientific developments concerning health, hygiene, reproduction and child breeding. By combining political power with modern medical discourse, the eugenicists defined eligibility for parenting, the bodily and social virtues of 'normal' women, the inappropriate days of conception, and the scientific methods of child breeding.

In 'Milli Nüfus Siyasetinde "Eugenique" Meselesinin Mahiyeti' (The Essence of '*Eugenique*' in National Population Policy), Fahrettin Kerim Gökay, a professor of psychiatry at Istanbul University, pointed out the significance of eugenics for development. Gökay spelled eugenics in French, but defined it, as the Germans did, along the lines of 'racial hygiene'. Gökay asserted that the protection of high racial qualities from degeneration and the creation of a mentally and physically healthy national population ought to be one of the principles of the Turkish State. In many parts of the world, he observed, eugenics became the nation state's primary concern because the issue of public health was so important that it could no longer be left to individuals. He emphasised that individuals are the most profitable capital of the state; therefore, they should be protected and managed as a matter of national economics and wealth. He supported his arguments with economic data from France, Germany and Switzerland, which depicted the burden of insane and retarded people on the state. In addition to being an economic burden, according to Gökay, these 'inferior' people were detrimental to morality and order in the society. Gökay singled out four issues as harmful to racial hygiene: mental illnesses, alcoholism, the negative impacts of modern life on the human mental condition and racial intermingling. Gökay believed that racial intermingling would bring about a schizophrenic personality that possesses two different characteristics in a single body. He argued that hybridity causes various sorts of deficiencies that were evident in the mixture of blacks and whites in Central and South America. Referring to Galton, Gökay claimed that hereditary weaknesses could not be cured but could only be avoided by controlling reproduction effectively.

In his book *Öjenizm* (1938), the medical professor Server Kamil Tokgöz, repeated Galton's concern that the increasing number of 'abnormal' people would eventually reverse evolution.[30] He divided society into three categories: the superiors, distinguished by their physical ability and morality; the mediocre, the majority of the population; and the cacogenics, the people with bad hereditary traits including lunatics, epileptics, the mute, the blind, the deaf, criminals, vagabonds, alcohol addicts, the immoral and the insane. It was the cacogenics, he claimed, who caused anxiety in society because of their abnormal characteristics and the economic and social burden they placed on the rest. Tokgöz envied the methods of dealing with cacogenics used in Western Europe and the US. He argued that all infantile defects were either hereditary or related to bad childcare and his approach to eugenics centred on childcare. Unlike Gökay, Tokgöz emphasised the social class dimension of eugenics. He argued that the material deprivation prevalent in the lower classes produces a damaging environment for the foetus or child. The upper classes, on the other hand, have the material wealth to provide proper conditions for good childcare. Therefore, Tokgöz stated, the national goal should be to increase the population in the higher classes while decreasing it in the lower ones.

Eugenicists believed children to be the most profitable capital of the state. Professor Besim Ömer Akalın, the founder of modern obstetrics and paediatrics in Turkey and author of *Türk Çocuğunu Nasıl Yaşatmalı?* (How should one make the Turkish child live?) argued that the first step towards racial improvement should be puericulture. Following the improvement of prenatal and maternal health, the state should also improve physical training, social hygiene and medical treatment. Akalın was critical of Turkish mothers' fatalism and ignorance of modern childcare and celebrated the establishment of the Department of Puericulture at Istanbul University to fight the traditional ignorance.

In 1940, the regime organised a conference series addressing eugenic concerns. Sadi B. Irmak, a professor of physiology at Istanbul University who later became a minister in the 1940s and then prime minister in the 1970s, emphasised the primary role of heredity in determining a person's ability and intelligence as well as his/her proclivity for crime and prostitution.[31] In line with Lamarckian heredity theory, he emphasised the environment's role in shaping physical and mental traits. According to Irmak, modern life had a major degenerative impact on the human race because civilised sheltering (such as apartments), the mechanisation of production, and the modern division of labour spoiled physical and mental abilities. Rural to urban migration in particular, he mentioned, paved the way to degeneration. He claimed that although migrants brought new and healthy elements into cities and improved the quality of the urban population, their good hereditary qualities would soon be spoiled by the unhealthy urban living conditions. Also, their fertility would decrease as they integrated into modern life. Moreover, Irmak argued, the modern urban life generated emotional depression, moral corruption and new social diseases such as alcoholism, which spoils good hereditary characteristics.

Although Turkish eugenicists often employed the racial language of eugenics, their use of the term 'race' was imprecise and in most of their writings, 'race', 'nation' and 'generation' were used interchangeably. The collectivist discourse during the nation-building process, which portrayed Turkey as a nation of unified, classless people sharing the same history, culture and language, was not compatible with the identification of racial or ethnic differences within the society. Accordingly, following the Kemalist[32] discourse on national unity, eugenic discourse avoided discussion of Turkey's ethnic minorities or its neighbouring populations as inferior races, focussing instead on the racial 'inferiority' of Blacks – a virtually non-existent group in Turkey.

The state's defensive racism – itself a reaction to predominant racial hierarchies of the period which placed the Turks below other European races – and the eugenics concerns were also evident in the national curriculum. As the following extract from a biology textbook shows, the Republican modernisation agenda entailed the creation of a proud, dutiful and fit nation:

> The Turkish race of which we are proud to belong has a distinguished place amongst the best, strongest, most intelligent and most competent races in the world. Our duty is to preserve the essential qualities and virtues of the Turkish race and to confirm that we deserve to be members of this race. For that reason, one of our primary national duties is to adhere to the principle of leading physically and spiritually worthwhile lives by protecting ourselves from the perils of ill health, and by applying the knowledge of biology to our lives. The future of our Turkey will depend on the breeding of high valued Turkish progeny in the families that today's youth will form in the future.[33]

Eugenics contributed to the reformulation of the state/individual relationship, in which an individual's body and choices became subsumed to the collective good. The definition of collective good was made by the Republican state, which obliged individuals to pursue physically and morally worthwhile lives. Eugenic discourse combined hygiene with morality. A part of the moral agenda addressed the relationship between the sexes as relationships out of wedlock were seen immoral and non-hygienic. Like his colleagues, Yalım (1940) saw immorality as the predominate cause of venereal diseases and advocated intense sexual and moral training to stop degeneration.[34] In line with the regime's goal of shaping a modern secular nation, eugenicists defined morality on the basis of national duty and patriotism. In the Turkish eugenics texts morality never refers to religion or tradition. Eugenics' moral framework firstly introduced the idea that breeding is more of a national duty than an individual choice; and secondly redefined with whom and under what conditions one may reproduce.

Gökay argued that contemporary motives such as love or material interest did not produce healthy marriages nor positive consequences for racial hygiene. The primary purpose of marriage should be to breed healthy generations for the sake of the nation. According to Gökay, a proper marriage is a union between a man and a woman, both in possession of good hereditary qualities, and both the woman and the man should investigate the mental and physical health of their partners to ensure a proper marriage. Likewise, Akalın believed that families should keep health records of their three past generations and use them to choose suitable marriage partners. Furthermore, Akalın argued that the state should have a significant role in promoting and regulating marriages and admired the measures taken by Hitler's Germany and Mussolini's Italy such as denying state jobs to single men, and discouraging women from working outside the home. Akalın believed these policies were compatible with the Turkish state's agenda.

Akalın was concerned about the deleterious effects of modern life on women. He observed that increased opportunities for women in education and work made them less inclined to form families, claiming additionally that images of luxury in modern novels and films raised women's material expectations from marriage, spoiled their natural characteristics as mothers and also discouraged men from getting married. Both Akalın and Gökay thought that marriage without children was a waste of a healthy man's reproductive capacity. Both disapproved of working women who are married but have no children, and claimed that those women occupy jobs that could otherwise be filled by men who had children to look after. In their eyes, a woman's natural place was in the home as mothers and housewives. However, Gökay mentioned that in Turkey working women should also get married and breed because the country urgently required a population boom.

Although the Turkish eugenicists' conservatism regarding women can be attributed to the relative emancipation of women in urban Turkey, much of the discussion echoes the German eugenic policies. In fact, their view on the nature of women was partially in conflict with the modernisation reforms. In the Republican period, the state introduced comprehensive reforms to legally and socially alter women's secondary position in society. These reforms abolished polygyny; mandated education for girls; and encouraged the participation of women in the labour market. The reforms gave many women an opportunity to pursue their interests. Nevertheless, the majority of women were still expected to contribute to modernisation by being good mothers and housewives.[35] In line with this expectation, the Ministry of Education established the Girl's Institutes in order to accustom the Republic's future mothers to more rational and 'civilised' ways. The eugenicists' discourse on women supported the modernisation agenda of creating 'enlightened' mothers in Turkey.

Although the German state's approach to gender and sexuality was well received by the Turkish eugenicists, they were hesitant to advocate for the implementation of some of the more extreme German policies such as sterilisation. In a 1934 article, Fahrettin Kerim Gökay argued that although the German's state's sterilisation policy was effective, its application in Turkey would have negative results because of technological insufficiency. In 1938, after he came back from the European Congress on Mental Health in Germany, Gökay became distant to sterilisation. A strong critique of the misapplications of German sterilisation law, such as the sterilisation of people with trivial mental disorders, at the conference influenced Gökay. He concluded that premarital examinations were proving sufficient for Turkey, 'where the number of insane and alcoholics was significantly lower than in European nations'.[36] Akalın, like Gökay, also criticised sterilisation, arguing that although sterilisation prevented degenerates from reproducing, it could not prevent poor economic and social conditions from producing new 'evils'. Turkish eugenicists believed that premarital examinations and education about degenerative factors were sufficient eugenic measures for Turkey.

In the 1930s, economic hardship, political rivalry, and the difficult task of embracing the rural majority challenged the nascent Republican regime and led it to become more authoritarian. The state aspired to create a healthy populous society in which individuals act and feel as a part of the Turkish nation. In this context, eugenics was used to aid in the physical and moral reproduction of the nation. Even if the discussion of eugenics per se remained limited to a circle of medical doctors, eugenics contributed to the reformers' definition of an individual's national duty and encouraged the state to influence areas previously left to individuals such as health, fitness, marriage, reproduction and childcare. However, in a society where the majority of people believed that deformity and disability came from the God, the spread of eugenic ideas was difficult. Yet, there is not much evidence of direct opposition to eugenics from within the medical field, nor from politicians. This can be attributed to the fact that the medicine had always been central to the influential modernising discourse and the fact that eugenic proposals in Turkey never went so far as to support forced sterilisation or abortion, which would undermine the beliefs and values of the Muslim society. Unlike in Britain, Germany and France, eugenics in Turkey did not become an organised movement and had limited popular appeal. Nevertheless, it was a component in the modernisation agenda. In conclusion, eugenic discourse dovetailed with the early Republican state's authoritarianism and collectivism, as summarised by a leading Turkish eugenicist's expression: 'one for all, all for one'.[37]

Notes

1 I discuss some of the themes of this chapter further in my 'Politics of the Body and Eugenic Discourse in Early Republican Turkey', *Body and Society*, 11:3, 2005, 61–77.

2 For eugenics in the ancient world, see A. G. Roper 'Ancient eugenics', *Mankind Quarterly*, 32, 1992, 383.

3 F. Galton, *The Hereditary Genius*, Gloucester: Peter Smith, 1972 (originally published 1869).

4 See W. H. Schneider's *Quality and Quantity: The Quest for Biological Regeneration in Twentieth-Century France*, Cambridge: Cambridge University Press, 1990; D. J. Kevles, *In the Name of Eugenics: Genetics and the Uses of Human Heredity*, New York: Knopf, 1985; and S. Kühl, *The Nazi Connection: Eugenics, American Racism, and German National Socialism*, New York: Oxford University Press, 1994.

5 N. L. Stepan, *The Hour of Eugenics: Race, Gender, and Nation in Latin America*, Ithaca and London: Cornell University Press, 1991, p. 32.

6 For Latin America see Stepan, *The Hour of Eugenics* and A. M. Stern, 'Responsible Mothers and Normal Children; Eugenics, Nationalism and Welfare in Postrevolutionary Mexico, 1920–1940', *Journal of Historical Sociology*, 12:4, 1999, 369–97; for Romania see M. Bucur, *Eugenics and Modernization in Interwar Romania*, Pittsburgh: University of Pittsburgh Press, 2002.

7 For eugenics in Japan see J. Robertson, 'Japan's First Cyborg? Miss Nippon, Eugenics and Wartime Technologies of Beauty, Body and Blood', *Body and Society*, 7:1, 2001, 1–34.

8 See G. Broberg and N. Roll-Hansen, *Eugenics and the Welfare State: Sterilization Policy in Denmark, Sweden, Norway and Finland*, Michigan: Michigan State University Press, 1996 and Mark B. Adams (ed.), The *Wellborn Science: Eugenics in Germany, France, Brazil, and Russia*, New York and Oxford: Oxford University Press, 1990.

9 M. Foucault, *The History of Sexuality, Vol. 1: An Introduction*, trans. R. Hurley, London: Allen Lane, 1979.

10 N. Rose,'The Politics of Life Itself', *Theory, Culture and Society*, 18:6, 2001, 3.
11 'Fitter family' competitions began in Kansas in 1920. Families competed in small, medium and large categories and the judgement was based on family history, physical and psychological evaluations.
12 Z. Bauman, *Modernity and Holocaust*, Cambridge: Polity Press, 1989.
13 W. H. Schneider, 'Toward the Improvement of the Human Race: The History of Eugenics in France', *The Journal of Modern History*, 54:2, 1982, 268–91.
14 D. Kevles, 'Eugenics and Human Rights', *British Medical Journal*, 319, 1999, 435–8.
15 P. M. H. Mazumdar, *Eugenics, Human Genetics and Human Failings: The Eugenics Society, its Sources and its Critics in Britain*, New York and London: Routledge, 1992.
16 D. Stone, 'Race in British Eugenics', *European History Quarterly*, 31:3, 2001, 397–425.
17 H. P. David, J. Fleischhacker and C. Höhn, 'Abortion and Eugenics in Nazi Germany', *Population and Development Review*, 14:1, 1988, 81–112.
18 Ibid., 92.
19 W. H. Schneider, 'Towards the Improvement of the Human Race', 272.
20 Ibid., 286–91.
21 F. Dikötter, 'Race Culture: Recent Perspectives on the History of Eugenics', *American Historical Review*, 103:2, 1998, 467–78.
22 F. Darwin (ed.), *The Life and Letters of Charles Darwin*, New York: D. Appleton and Co., 1905, 2 vols., I, p. 286.
23 D. Kandiyoti, 'The End of the Empire: Islam, Nationalism and Women in Turkey,' in D. Kandiyoti (ed.), *Women, Islam and the State*, London: Macmillan, 1991, pp. 22–47.
24 See F. K. Gökay, 'Milli Nüfus Siyasetinde (Eugenique) Meselesinin Mahiyeti' (The Essence of Eugenics in National Population Politics), *Ülkü*, 3, 1934, 206–13 and B. Ö. Akalın, *Türk Çocuğunu Nasıl Yaşatmalı?* (How Should One Make the Turkish Child Live?) İstanbul: Ahmet İhsan, 1939.
25 C. Dole, 'In the Shadows of Medicine and Modernity: Medical Integration and Secular Histories of Religious Healing in Turkey', *Culture, Medicine and Psychiatry*, 28, 2004, 255–80.
26 Public Hygiene Law (*Umumi Hıfzıssıhha Kanunu*) *Resmi Gazete* (Official Gazette) 1489, 6 May 1930.
27 F. C. Shorter, 'Turkish Population in Great Depression', *New Perspectives on Turkey*, 23, 2000, 103–24.
28 The first national Child Protection Society was established in Istanbul in 1917. The emblem of the Society was a green crescent surrounded by a triangle of three words: health, morals and knowledge. The mission of the Society involved protecting children emotionally and physically, establishing institutes for correction of young delinquents and building playing grounds for physical activity. Between 1917–1920 the Child Protection Society opened branches in many cities. In 1921, the Republican regime opened its own Child Protection Society in Ankara by Atatürk's initiative, which reamined the central organisation after the dissolution of the Istanbul society.
29 Body Discipline Law (Beden Terbiyesi Kanunu) *TBMM Zabıt Ceridesi*, 2:29 June 1938, 487.
30 S. K. Tokgöz, *Öjenizm: Irk Islahı* (Eugenics: racial correction), Ankara: Sümer Basımevi, 1938.
31 S. B. Irmak, 'Milletlerin 'Tereddi' ve 'İstifa'sı' (Progress and Degeneration of Nations) *CHP Konferanslar Dizisi*, 12, 1940, 20–35.
32 Kemalism is an ideology that established the basic principles and values of the Turkish Republic. It is named after Mustafa Kemal – the military commander of the Independence War, the leader of the Republican People's Party and the first president of the Turkish Republic.

33 *Biyoloji ve İnsan Hayatı II* (Biology and the Human Life II), Istanbul: Devlet Matbaası, 1934, 321.
34 Z. R. Yalım, 'Firengi, Belsoğukluğu ve Alkolizmin Nesiller Üzerinde Yaptığı Tahribat' (The Damage of Syphilis, Gonorrhea and Alcoholism on Generations), *CHP Konferanslar Dizisi*, 12, 1940, 57–69.
35 Y. Arat, 'The Project of Modernity and Women in Turkey', in S. Bozdağan R. and Kasaba (eds) *Rethinking Modernity and Rational Identity in Turkey*, Seattle: University of Washington Press, 1997, pp. 95–112.
36 F. K. Gökay, *Kısırlaştırmanın Rolü* (The role of sterilization), İstanbul: Kader, 1938.
37 Gökay, 'Milli Nüfus Siyasetinde'.

8 'Human dregs at the bottom of our national vats'

The interwar debate on sterilization of the mentally deficient[1]

Sharon Morris[2]

The 1913 Mental Deficiency Act, which aimed to control the breeding of the mentally deficient by removing them from society, was very much a product of its time. Each generation believes that its achievements are greater – yet fears that its underclass is more depraved – than those preceding it, and this fear reached its zenith in the years leading up to the Great War. Eugenics was a dominant force of the early twentieth century but, as with any trend, subject to the specific concerns and beliefs of each community.[3] Britain at this time was the greatest nation in the world, having conquered much of it. While always a mongrel race, the United Kingdom had been gradually infiltrated as a result of her imperialism and, until the postcolonial years, had readily absorbed much of the influx. With the possible exceptions of the Jewish and Irish enclaves, England in particular was homogenized, and therefore discriminated more on the grounds of class and intellect than on other factors. Class and intellect were the result of breeding successfully, whereas degenerative aspects were the result of carelessness. The poor, the unemployed and the ignorant were scapegoats for the ills of English society. The Mental Deficiency Act was passed at the same time as the foundation of a range of corrective institutions and organizations which shared the intention of instilling discipline and citizenship in the individual. Borstals, homes for 'fallen girls', birth control clinics, the Boy Scout movement and other phenomena of the time were the direct manifestations of eugenics in England. Through the legal union and a permeable border with the Celtic nations, some of these ideas spread, some were assimilated with variations – for example, the Magdelen Houses in Scotland for the reform of prostitutes or the *Urdd* in Wales as a youth movement, albeit with the veneer of cultural heritage – and some were simply appended.

Apart from medical texts, the broader historiography of mental deficiency is largely confined to studies on eugenics or incidentally within studies of lunacy provision. Michel Foucault's seminal text *Madness and Civilisation*[4] has frequently been criticized for a perspective divorced from historical and political realities, yet in the 1970s and 1980s it provoked most of the debate contributing to the history of mental health reforms. Andrew Scull revised the association of reforms with liberal ideology, seeing the changing social structure as creating an unsupported lunatic population who were to be remodelled into more appropriate behaviour by the new elite of 'mad-doctors'.[5] Butler, however, offers the view that early reforms resulted from amateur pressure groups rather than professional interests, and highlights the paradox between growing state regulation and laissez-faire liberalism.[6] The late Roy Porter took a broad cultural perspective in his lively and thought-provoking studies,[7] while Kathleen Jones has written several chronological accounts, which are considered definitive.[8] The research of David Mellett explores the interpretation of reforms at regional level, focusing on mainly the London area,[9] the realization or failure of the Lunacy Commission's proposals at regional level, and the inevitable generation of bureaucracy as Poor Law and Lunacy Commissioners disputed classification. He too suggests a reluctance by workhouses to discharge mad inmates to asylums, particularly in the industrial north. This latter theme has been explored further in Peter Bartlett's recent book, in which he proposes that the workhouses continued to form a considerable part of the welfare provision for the insane poor after the 1845 County Asylums Act.[10] Mark Jackson's account of the Sandlebridge Institution in Cheshire serves as a helpful analysis of Edwardian provision and of the early career of Mary Dendy who was to become a Commissioner of the Board of Control.[11] Mathew Thomson's work depicts the Mental Deficiency Act as an administrative solution to the Poor Law and as a self-contained entity.[12] Pamela Dale's illuminating study of the Royal Western Counties Asylum reveals an eagerness by Devon and Cornwall to ascertain numbers of defectives yet a reluctance to admit any but the most trainable.[13] This chapter builds upon and chronologically extends the studies of late-Victorian/Edwardian mental health care at a time when Britain's supremacy was under threat both internally and externally. It is hoped that it will also demonstrate how the letter of the law is often open to interpretation in regions at a distance from central government.

Terminology is a sensitive issue in this field, but there is little doubt that a general distinction was made after the 1886 Idiots Act[14] between perinatal mental deficiency and later-onset mental illness. By the 1920s, the definition was extended further to include later-onset cerebral trauma resulting in mental deficiency. Many of the terms used at the time – ament, idiot, imbecile, cretin, moron, dullard, backward, defective – are no longer considered acceptable, but are necessarily echoed in this study in order to accurately reflect medical and cultural attitudes, and in some instances to clarify the legal status of the defective. Legal status was significant for the application of the Mental Deficiency Act and its precursors; as will be discussed, compulsory detention was applicable only to the lowest grades, and the corollary of this was that the Local Authorities therefore were duty-bound to provide care for only the lowest grades. As today, this left a majority of people with mental disabilities who were neither able to care adequately for themselves – thus remaining a burden on their families – nor entitled to support and accommodation by the state. Broadly speaking, the classifications were based on IQ levels, with the lowest grade being idiot at an IQ up to 25; an imbecile would achieve a score between 25 and 50 points, and a moron would straddle these two categories; feeble-minded was categorised as an IQ below 70. Cretinism involved a specific range of signs and was progressive unless its root causes were addressed but rarely reversible.

There is inevitably an overlap between provision for insanity and idiocy. The 1845 Asylums Act, resulting from the Report of the Metropolitan Lunacy Commissioners[15] and their supplementary Report on Wales,[16] may be seen as a prototype of the Mental Deficiency Act (as indeed the 1886 Idiots Act echoed the 1808 permissive legislation to establish lunatic asylums). It made mandatory the provision of an asylum for the pauper lunatics of every county and further defined and expanded the role of the existing Lunacy Commission, giving it responsibility for approval of design and situating of new asylums, and an obligation to visit and report annually. The 1845 Act differentiated, by omission, between lunatics and idiots: 'In a certain proportion of cases the Patient neither recovers nor dies ... A Patient in this state requires a place of refuge; but his disease, being beyond the reach of medical skill, it is quite evident that he should be removed from Asylums instituted for the cure of insanity'.[17] Unfortunately, they did not suggest to where these unsuitable chronic cases should be removed, although the initiative was taken with the voluntary establishment of a few idiot asylums in England, including the Starcross Asylum in the south-west, Sandlebridge in Cheshire, the Eastern Counties asylum, and the Earlswood, which served London.

The county lunatic asylums, built in response to a series of legislation from 1845,[18] had quickly been filled beyond capacity with enfeebled and chronic patients rather than the curable insane. Many of these had congenital mental disabilities and populated the 'dirty wards'. There was consequently a move to provide separate and perhaps more basic institutional facilities for this class of patient, with several institutions in England pre-empting the 1886 legislation. The burden of congenitally disabled patients was exacerbated by chronic physical conditions with neurological consequences – epilepsy, the general paralysis of the insane that was the result of tertiary stage syphilis, traumatic brain injury, and so on. However, the situation was confused again by the 1890 legislation, which, in failing to differentiate, gave carte blanche to local authorities to ignore the 1886 Idiots Act. The establishment of the county lunatic asylums therefore, while undoubtedly a civic achievement, did little to relieve the immediate or projected needs of pauper lunatics in the county; rather, they became more of an infirmary for the enfeebled than a treatment resource for the curable insane. In Wales and the peripheral English regions, the lunatic asylums and workhouses continued to be used for as long as possible as repositories for the mentally deficient by local authorities wary of the expense and doubtful of the need for separate provision.

The 1886 Idiots Act was not a mandate to the counties to address this pressing need, merely a suggestion that where a need was acknowledged it might be deemed appropriate to provide care apart from the asylum, gaol and workhouse. It was prompted by the Report of a Committee of the Charity Organisation Society in 1877.[19] The Committee, which included such medically eminent figures as John Langdon Down and William W. Ireland, discussed many aspects of the manifestations and management of mental disabilities over a series of 16 weekly meetings and visited various institutions. They resolved 'that the legislative provisions required for Idiots, Imbeciles, and Harmless Lunatics should be consolidated in a single Act distinct from those applicable to Dangerous Lunatics'.[20] Although somewhat equivocal in its conclusions beyond this recommendation, the Committee did commission an estimate of the numbers of idiots and imbeciles by region based on population. This resulted in a total of 17,749 for England and Wales.[21]

Given the desultory response to the permissive 1808 Asylums Act,[22] it is surprising that the appeal to the conscience of the authorities represented by the Idiots Act was thought to be of any value. Unheralded, ignored and destined to be repealed a quarter of a century later, it remains a perplexing example of Victorian legislation, both by its nature and uncharacteristic brevity. At a time when bureaucracy was intrinsic to statutory instruments, the vagaries of this brief permissive Act can be explained only by reason of well-intentioned naivety or connivance. It achieved nothing beyond confusion for those few institutions already providing care for the mentally deficient whose managers were unsure whether they still qualified under the new Act.[23] It has to be questioned why the management of mental deficiency was considered to be a great enough problem to require legislation, yet not so great that it be made mandatory. The fear of degeneracy and the need to improve society was a dominant theme in Europe at this time. It must be remembered that while England was the home of the forefathers of eugenics, the Darwins and their cousin Francis Galton (1822–1911), and Herbert Spencer,[24] there was ever a tendency to view the cultural movements of continental Europe with some reserve. The 1886 Idiots Act was, perhaps, a late example of paternalism but was at least benevolent in tone, as were the subsequent education acts applicable to the mentally unfit.[25] It is not easy, then, to adequately explain the apparent volte-face of the Mental Deficiency Act.[26] Something must have occurred between 1886 and 1913 to explain the chasm between the benevolence of the Idiots Act and the repressive tone and intent of its successor.

It is argued that the brief and surprising Idiots Act was designed to be unworkable and therefore prepared the way for mandatory segregation. Many of the early 'experts' in the field of mental deficiency, such as Ruth Darwin and Albert Tredgold, later emerged as eugenicists. The 1913 Act is typically viewed as the most overtly eugenic legislation of the period in Britain. Far from providing welfare as did the earlier lunacy and special education laws, its perceived intention was to remove from society the less able imbeciles and idiots and prevent them from breeding and polluting the nation's genetic pool. Perhaps, though, this view of the Act as coercive is taken only with the myopic hindsight of a post-fascism generation. Certainly Mathew Thomson argues against the view of the Act as eugenic in its intention, and suggests that 'rather than imposing our own judgements to portray mental deficiency policy as a sign of undemocratic tendencies in early twentieth century social policy ... we should view it in its own context'.[27] It is not disputed that the administration of the Act is worthy of analysis. However, this does not alter the fact that the legislation and its subsequent usage are indicative of the existing socio-cultural milieu, and it would be unwise to adopt a blinkered view; Thomson's insistence of 'its own context' must include acknowledgement of its influences. Analyses of the Act and the attitude of the Board of Control indicate a firm resolve to remove the mentally defective from society. Bolstered by the paternalism of the eighteenth and nineteenth centuries, there has long been an assumption that Britain chose not to embrace eugenics as passionately as Germany, Scandinavia and some American states. This assumption is refuted, concurring instead with Dan Stone's re-evaluation that class and race eugenics were so innate to British society that it was taken for granted, and that the prevailing view of British eugenics as only 'mildly threatening but basically embarrassing needs to be adjusted so that its full sinister implications can be seen'.[28] The culture and politics in Britain in the 1920s and 1930s were conducive to segregation and sterilization. However, economic conditions and the devolution of responsibility from state to local authority delayed concerted practical efforts until the Second World War, by which time eugenics had inherited a more sinister legacy.

The blueprint for the 1913 Act is to be found in the recommendations of a Commission nearly a decade earlier. The government had resisted calls for a further enumeration of idiots and imbeciles in the 1901 General Census. It was thought that 'some difficulty seem[ed] to have been felt on the last occasion in distinguishing between lunatics and imbeciles and they were therefore lumped together'.[29] The General Register Office concurred that 'the distinction, you will observe, was based solely on the statement of the occupier and not on any sort of *scientific definition*',[30] and the matter of a specific question on the 1901 Census was dropped. However, concern remained. The Commissioners in Lunacy were approached with a view to instructing asylums and other institutions to distinguish between lunatic and imbecile inmates in their returns. The Commissioners felt that such an instruction would 'be rather mischievous than useful' but revealed that there was to be an inquiry.[31] A Commission was ordered to discover the existing methods of dealing with defectives and the extent of the problem. It was impossible to do so for the entire British Isles, but 15 areas were chosen. They visited all public elementary schools, poor law institutions, charitable establishments, training houses, reformatories, common lodging houses, prisons, idiot asylums, hospitals and 'any other establishment likely to harbour the mentally abnormal'.[32] The 1904 Report of the Royal Commission for the Care and Control of the Feebleminded produced far higher numbers of 'aments' than the aforementioned Charity Organisation Committee. It suggested a total of 138,529 for England and Wales. This included the feebleminded, but even with these deducted the total for idiots and imbeciles was 33,750 or almost double that for 1877.[33]

Tredgold suggested that a higher incidence of the more severe degrees of mental deficiency was to be found in agricultural areas. There are a number of possible causes for this. Two forms of cretinism had been described by Edouard Seguin:

Endemic idiocy is interwoven with alpine or lowland cretinism ... Alpine cretinism is due to locality and to intermarriage, and it is never isolated: it affects the skin with a bistre or maroon colour. Its action does cease after having produced idiocy, for if its victim be put in a locality where cretinism will aggravate, idiocy will do the same; and if placed in circumstances of climate, of hygiene, of exercise, where cretinism may improve, idiocy will also improve ...The lowland cretinism of Belgium, of Virginia, etc., with its discrete goitre, its grey and dirty straw-coloured skin, bears the same relation to idiocy and imbecility as the more extensive alpine variety.[34]

The causative factor of thyroid deficiency, and high iodine and natural radioactivity levels are now understood, of course. Nevertheless, there are areas, Derbyshire for example, in which excessive incidence of hypothyroidism remains endemic. Rural isolation due to geographical features – mountains, lakes, inland seas, peninsulas – enforced intermarriage with a greater degree of consanguinity than elsewhere and exacerbated hereditary defects. Another factor may be the changing demographic patterns brought about by industrial development and their effects on traditional communities. The feebleminded that had been left behind in the rural counties were no longer seen as a communal responsibility. As the more able and ambitious moved away, the societal ties that had traditionally protected the more vulnerable unravelled. The more isolated communities found their genetic pool parched, again contributing to the increase of hereditary disorders. Regardless of the legal definition of mental deficiency, it was the social impact that gave impetus to the push to provide care. However, this same depopulation of the less industrialized regions made provision of an institution, as had been discovered with the (Lunatic) Asylums Act, too heavy a levy on the public purse to contemplate.

The recommendations of the 1904 Royal Committee stated:

That persons who cannot take a part in the struggle of life owing to mental defect ... should be afforded by the State such special protection as may be suited to their needs ... That the protection of the mentally defective, whatever form it takes, should be continued as long as is necessary for his good. This is desirable, not only in his interest, but also in the interest of the community. It follows that the State should have authority to segregate and detain mentally defective persons ... also that feeble-minded persons, moral imbeciles,[35] and such inebriates, epileptics, and blind or deaf and dumb persons, as are mentally defective, and of any age, may be admitted to suitable institutions in the same way.[36]

It seems impossible to dispute this evidence of eugenic intent, even as early as 1904 when the influence of Francis Galton on positive eugenics – encouraging the potential of the more adept, rather than limiting that of the less able – was still strong.

The 1913 Mental Deficiency Act imposed a statutory obligation on local authorities to ascertain the numbers of mentally deficient within their county, and to provide institutional care for those that required it within the definitions of the Act. In addition to those 'idiot asylums' already mentioned, some densely populated areas had established institutions in anticipation of the legislation or very promptly in response to the Act, such as the Bristol area with two colonies at Stoke Park and Brentry as well as a number of smaller institutions. Meeting the responsibilities of the later Mental Deficiency Act was therefore not such an overwhelming problem in urban parts of England. Despite the shared inconveniencies of war and Depression, there was a higher density of population, both exacerbating the need for provision and ensuring an achievable charge to the rates, and existing institutions for ascertained defectives. However, economy and welfare in both industrial and agricultural areas and more fundamental health issues were the priorities and far overrode any concerns about the numbers of idiots in each local authority, particularly when the financial pressures became insurmountable. The middle and late Victorian period had witnessed a growth in mandatory provision of a whole range of state institutions adding to the burden of local government. Lunatic asylums, police, prisons, elementary schools, libraries, county hospitals had all been added to the list of responsibilities of local authorities. The further provision of expensive accommodation for a stratum of society that would never repay the outlay or in any way contribute to their community was an institution too far for many rural local authorities. Unlike the bad and the mad, idiots and imbeciles were incurable. After all, they were not seen as being like other people and there was little room for common interest or empathy. Mental deficiency colonies were intended to remove this incompatible group from society. Some local authorities beyond the large towns and cities, however, balked at the extra expense, at the extra responsibilities and inevitably the extra time of committees to administer this restrictive legislation. The County Medical Officers in particular found the administration of the Act arduous, responsible as they were for so many other more pressing and obvious public health concerns. Aspects of the Mental Deficiency legislation seemed to replicate provision elsewhere; surely, between the poor law unions, lunatic asylums, schools and prisons the majority of mental defectives who were not being cared for by their families were already provided for elsewhere.

The legislation generally appealed to the bureaucratic pedantry of English officialdom. However, there are similarities in the experience of those councils on the periphery of England, as depicted for example in Steve Cherry's account of the Norfolk Lunatic Asylum.[37] Even had the will existed to comply with the legislation in the more rural and peripheral counties of England and Wales, the local authorities had already discovered with the provision of prisons and asylums that they could not justify the cost of such institutions to the ratepayers. It was not possible to enjoy the economy of scale envisaged by the central government. Colonies for 500 or more defectives were achieved without too much debate in urban parts of England, where a local authority might encompass several large towns and cities but elsewhere this was difficult to realise. It simply was not possible to provide a large colony singly, and if local

authorities combined, the geography and logistics of selecting a site were sufficient obstacles without the addition of politics and personality. In the more rural
areas, a feebleminded relative could be found simple work to do, and even in
more urban areas there might be repetitive work to do. Indeed, such free labour
was frequently necessary to farmers and small family businesses. Those whose
behaviour was too disruptive might end up in some other institution – the
asylum, the workhouse, the prison. Those who were severely disabled might not
survive to adulthood. Despite the great improvements in public health, there was
only so much that could be done for those vulnerable to injury, seizure and
infection, and it may be that even that much was spared when the result might be
release for both defective and family.

The Board of Control was established to administer the 1913 Mental Deficiency Act, amalgamating the Lunacy Commission, the Chancery Visitors and
the Masters in Lunacy. It may be argued that rarely was a government body
more aptly named. It had the power to insist upon ascertainment of need in the
local authorities and to dispute their accuracy. It had the authority to accept or
veto plans for institutional care, to assess the viability of such provision and
demand alterations, and could apply considerable pressure on local authorities to
provide joint institutional facilities. However, the Board's powers somehow
extended beyond its accepted remit of overseeing and enforcing the Mental
Deficiency Act; for example, its relationship with the Medical Research Council
[MRC] was tainted by the arrangement of allocating grants in exchange for its
Commissioners having places on the research committee.[38] The matter was
broached in December 1920, when the Ministry of Health suggested to the MRC
that 'arrangements are made whereby [the Board] would have a voice in
research expenditure in their line of country'.[39] The MRC quickly responded that
they 'would set up a special committee for research into mental diseases in con-
sultation with the Board of Control (or if preferred, by joint appointment)'.[40]
Taking full advantage of this offer, the Board responded:

> It would be a gratification to the Board if two of their Medical Commission-
> ers, Drs. Coupland and Bond, could be appointed to be members of that
> Committee. The Commissioners would be glad, if the Committee should
> think fit to consult them, to confer with the Council as to the selection of the
> other members of the Special Committee.[41]

Various institutions benefited from this special relationship, including £400 to
Cardiff Asylum for the establishment of a Chemical Laboratory and an unspecified sum to Rainhill (Lancashire) Asylum for research into the 'value of cerebro-
spinal fluid examination in Asylum practice'.[42] However, this convenient
arrangement was evanescent and altered when the grant-making decisions were
transferred by the Ministry of Health to the MRC independently of the Board of
Control.

Once the legislation was fully implemented after the First World War, the
Board of Control was keen to ensure that it was followed to the letter, and

engaged in debates with those authorities that suggested that its meaning was ambiguous. In 1914, the Board expressed concern that Section 30 of the Mental Deficiency Act was open to abuse. In an attempt to define where the Act stood in relation to the earlier Lunacy legislation, it stated:

> Provided that ... nothing in this Act shall affect the powers and duties of local authorities under the Lunacy Acts, 1890 to 1911, with respect to any defectives who may be dealt with under those Acts, nor shall local authorities under this Act have any duties or powers with respect to defectives who for the time being are, or who might be, provided for by such authorities as aforesaid.[43]

The Board suggested that there was a danger that defectives who were also lunatic would 'fall between two stools and be neglected alike by the authorities bound to enforce Lunacy Acts and the authorities bound to enforce the Mental Deficiency Act'.[44] The legislation might be seen to apply only to the feeble-minded and moral imbeciles. In retrospect it may have been better, and financially more viable, to have focused on these classes. Administratively, Section 3(iii), to reclassify and remove to more appropriate institutions those defectives already in institutions for other state dependents, became a liability. Lunatic asylums joined with Poor Law Institutions in chivvying the harassed mental deficiency committees to remove lunatic defectives and pauper defectives to institutions that did not yet exist. Increasingly the immediate aim seemed to be to provide institutions for those already institutionalized, at the neglect of those remaining in the community.

On occasions, the precision of the Board created problems. In 1916, the case of Edith Rose Foster revealed that some of the assumptions of the Act were illusory. Section 13 stated that where a defective was sent under Order to an institution, the authority issuing the Order might 'make an order requiring the defective, or any person liable to maintain him, to contribute such sum towards the expenses of his maintenance'.[45] Foster was living at home with her father in Taunton but, when the NSPCC received reports of neglect, she was removed to the workhouse and thence to Chasefield Laundry Home in Fishponds, Bristol. Her father was then ordered to contribute to the cost of her maintenance in the institution, but refused to do so, and was taken to court by Somersetshire County Council. The Board of Control were informed that 'an application for an Order under Section 13 of the Act requiring George Henry Foster, the father of the defective, to contribute towards the cost of her maintenance in an institution was refused after a hearing by the Judicial Authority apparently on the ground that as the defective was over the age of twenty-one her parent was not "liable to maintain her"'.[46] This caused considerable concern as this test case proved that Section 13 would be limited 'to such an extent that only, it is thought, in a comparatively small proportion of the cases which arise can a contribution order be made'.[47] Nor would this be confined to the 1913 Act; Lamotte, the Attorney-General, realized that the 1908 Children's Act had a section almost identically worded, and failure to resolve the Foster case might jeopardise orders amounting to £20,000 *per annum*.[48] The Treasury Solicitor funded an appeal by Somersetshire, but it was rejected. At the appeal, Foster was defended by Leslie Scott KC, the Chairman of the Central Association for the Care of the Mentally Deficient, an extremely active organization with branches throughout England.[49] Scott expressed the view that there was indeed no obligation under Common Law on a father to support his children once they had attained their majority, and that a person over the age of 18 not maintained by someone, or able to maintain himself, would become a charge of the parish or local authority. The Treasury Solicitor was forced to concede that 'once a defective is of age no-one is liable to maintain him otherwise than in consequence of the Poor Law'.[50]

Institutional care was required only for certain categories of idiots and imbeciles, and there was concern that the more mentally and physically able, particularly the 'moral imbeciles' were not subject to segregation under the Act and would breed more mental defectives. Articles were produced by The Eugenics Society and the Medico-Legal Society and were refuted or supported by a variety of 'experts'. Draft Sterilization Bills were produced, questions were asked in the Commons, and delegates from local authorities visited both the Board of Control and the Home Office. Segregation, even where provided, was not the solution. The issue seemed to be encapsulated in the rhetorical enquiry of Lord Riddell: 'Can the community afford to spend so much on a section of the population obviously of the worst type? Are you going to penalise the fit for the unfit?'[51]

Riddell presented his paper to the Medico-Legal Society on 25 April 1929 at the height of the sterilization debate. He outlined a number of case studies, commencing with the following:

Case No. 1. – Father: Welsh collier. Mother: feeble-minded
(1) Daughter, born 1895, feeble-minded. In institution for three and a quarter years. Died therein of influenza and pneumonia.
(2) Son, born 1899, feeble-minded. In certified institution for four years. Died therein of bronchial pneumonia.
(3) Son, born 1897, imbecile. Under care in institution for mental defectives since August 1915.
(4) Son, born December 1900, imbecile. Under care in institution for mental defectives since March 1918.
(5) Son, born August 1904, imbecile. Under care in institution for mental defectives since September 1920.
(6) Daughter, born October 1908, feebleminded. Under care in institution for mental defectives since March 1928.[52]

Riddell's argument was two-fold: the fecundity of the unfit and the cost to the British public. Having outlined five further cases, he suggested that, had the original six defective parents been segregated early in life, they would not have bred another 29 defectives requiring institutionalization. Despite the instruction and birth control that was influencing the health of the nation, 'mentally defective parents must create centres of degeneracy and disease which welfare work can never reach'.[53] Riddell went on to describe another case reported by the South Wales Commissioner, Dr. Lewis, of a feebleminded woman living in squalor with her verminous low-grade imbecile sister and five illegitimate children, three of whom were also feebleminded.[54] Riddell suggested that 'the sexual instinct is very powerful amongst mental deficients, who will go to any lengths to give expression to it, just in the same way as they will go to any lengths to get food and drink . . . Unless we are careful, we shall be eaten out of house and home by lunatics and mental deficients'.[55]

Lord Riddell's impassioned speech was compelling and struck a chord in his, admittedly sympathetic, audience. This same audience, of eminent lawyers and physicians, were representative of the intellectual elite of the time. However, the broader question of a degenerative society had emerged some half a century earlier. Britain had escaped the revolutions of Europe of the nineteenth century, enjoying the spoils of her own industrial and territorial successes, but some feared that the cost to society was too high. Improved public health and medicine reduced mass morbidity rates from poverty and contamination. The Malthusian scythe was blunted, resulting in the survival of the less fit. New evils of insidious mental and moral disorders emerged to couple with urbanization and a less God-fearing society. There seemed to be an inescapable correlation between progression and degeneration.[56]

Contemporary fiction serves as a barometer for the ideas of the period. Robert Louis Stevenson's *Dr Jekyll and Mr Hyde* (1886) clearly reflects Darwinian notions of the beast within. Bram Stoker's *Dracula* (1887) explores degeneracy, pathology, mesmerism and psychoanalysis and refers to thyroid deficiency goitre. It is interesting to note that the Dr Seward of Stoker's tale had a real-life counterpart; he was the medical superintendent of Colney Hatch Lunatic Asylum. Oscar Wilde's *The Picture of Dorian Gray* (1890) has parallels with Francis Galton's efforts at composite photography, illustrating how deviant traits would leave physiognomic signs. Perhaps the clearest expression of the fear of the growth of two subspecies of human life is to be found in H. G. Wells' *The Time Machine* (1894). In the future, two races evolve – the frail but beautiful Eloi and the baser but cunning Morlocks – echoing Henry Maudsley's caveat on the dangers of positive eugenics without simultaneous culling or curbing of the unfit. Britain may have lacked experts in the field of degeneration theory such as Alphonse Bertillon[57] and Cesare Lombroso,[58] but Dr Henry Maudsley added a professional respectability to the British fear of degeneracy. Maudsley was the medical superintendent of Manchester Lunatic Asylum and then moved to the South London institution that still bears his name. His work on *Body and Mind* (1870) was a persuasive and highly influential appeal for use of the physiological approach in the analysis of mental function and gave impetus to the reductionist model that eventually came to dominate psychiatry in the first half of the twentieth century. Nevertheless, for all its prescience, it still ratified the notion that Man was a superior life form and that any individuals who detracted from that superiority, particularly with regard to intelligence, were not human but a subspecies. With this notion, the parameters of care and duty to the mentally defective were confined to consideration of the greater good. With such guidance from the alienist experts it is little wonder that eugenics policies found support amongst the politicians and public.

Many of these Victorian gothic works found a wider audience and visual realization in the 1920s and 1930s through film adaptations. *Dracula*, directed by Tod Browning and starring Bela Lugosi, was released in 1931, having previously been filmed silently as *Nosferatu* in Germany.[59] Adaptations of *Dr Jekyll and Mr Hyde* appeared in 1921 and 1931,[60] and *Frankenstein*, famously starring Boris Karloff as the Monster, appeared in 1931.[61] The most sensationalist film of the period, subsequently banned in Britain for 30 years, was Tod Browning's *Freaks*, which 'starred' a cast of American side-show oddities, including three microcephalic[62] women, who take apt revenge on the trapeze-artist whose morals are more monstrous than their deformities. Browning justifies his subject in the movie's textual prologue:

> The revulsion with which we view the malformed and the mutilated is the result of long conditioning ... Never again will such a story be filmed, as modern science and teratology is rapidly eliminating such blunders of nature from the world. With humility for the many injustices done to such people (they have no power to control their lot) we present the most startling horror story of the ABNORMAL and THE UNWANTED.[63]

Britain lacked an enduring or defined social theory of degeneration, and early eugenic efforts were always aimed at improvement and encouragement rather than restriction. However, as early as 1906 there were voices seeking a disturbingly clinical approach:

> Long lulled in *laissez-faire*, the British Public is now awakening to the consciousness that its constitution is not just what it ought to be, and that something must be done ... Pick-me-ups will no longer avail; a systematic course of treatment is required.[64]

Galton's eugenics had been a positive aesthetic and intellectual movement, but by the 1920s it was undoubtedly a darker, more brutal drive for the suppression of the dysgenic elements of society. No longer was it a matter of education and reform. Segregation under the Mental Deficiency Act was a toothless saw, ineffective for pruning the wilder offshoots. It controlled only those whose very disability already limited their potential to breed. Moral imbeciles were seen as the greatest threat, particularly the female feebleminded. Tredgold explored the correlation between venereal disease and the failure to control such girls,[65] concerned at the risk posed to men taking advantage of the promiscuity of moral imbeciles who would actively seek 'chance solicitations'[66] leading to dangerous sexual liaisons. As a consequence of the First World War, there was an increased incidence of girls formerly confined to the home now employed in domestic service and other 'single routine occupations'.[67] This meant that the defective girls' greater liberty plus their 'erotic tendencies' put them at risk of being preyed upon by young men on leave from the military. Tredgold asserted that 'it is not punishment but protection which should be meted out to them',[68] but it is unclear from the text whether he referred to the female imbeciles or the soldiers. Male moral imbeciles were, it seemed, fewer in number and less dangerous, if only on the assumption that it was the man who initiated intimate contact and a feebleminded man was unlikely to do so with success.

Demands became more overt. Despite the caution of churchmen that some experts were 'far too ready to impose what they call Restrictive Eugenics on certain classes',[69] the general mood was becoming less tolerant, less disposed to improvement and training and more towards imposing restrictions. An education conference in 1922 opened with the recommendation that mentally defective children be removed from elementary schools – 'it is unfair to the teacher, to the child itself, and to the children with whom it has to associate'[70] – and gained support for the expulsion of 'a drag and an incubus'.[71] In the same month, a Labour Party Public Health Advisory Committee deplored the proposals of the Education Authorities in London to close Special Schools. It resolved that attempts to educate mentally defective children in mainstream schools 'are a waste of educational effort and cause serious interference with the progress of normal children'. In more general terms, the report observed that 'in areas where the existing powers of the Mental Deficiency Act are not being adequately used, it is possible that the numbers of defective persons are increasing'.[72] Other authors were adamant that nature had gone awry – ' "Civilisation" has done away with traditional culling of the unfit'.[73] The inevitable consequence of continuing with a liberal society was self-destruction. In a move away from earlier theories that hereditary afflictions were self-limiting and would die out within several generations the same authors stated bluntly that 'if their number increases to more than a minute percentage of the whole, they not only impose an intolerable burden on the saner and sound elements of the society, but endanger the survival of the whole'.[74]

The possibility of an increase in numbers was emerging as a political issue. A further Royal Commission on the feebleminded was mooted, but parliamentary time was running out. Neville Chamberlain, the Minister for Health, was approached on the matter by several prominent eugenicists. However, while he admitted to Lady Asquith that he did not dissent from the view that a further enquiry was desirable, it was 'too late in the life of the present parliament'.[75] The change to a Labour government in 1929 meant that no Commission on sterilization was ordered. Nevertheless, the question was considered, even if no conclusion was reached. The House of Commons Question and Answers sessions in 1928 featured two queries from MPs – Robert Thomas of Anglesey and Erskine of St. Georges – in the space of three months. The question of sterilization was raised again in 1930 but the Minister of Health deferred any inquiry.[76]

In this political climate Leonard Darwin – President of the Eugenics Society and grandson of evolutionist Charles – drafted his Sterilization Bill. He explained to his niece, Ruth Darwin, 'It will come up for the first time for discussion on Wednesday February 9th and it is quite on the cards that they will turn it down altogether. Part III I know will be opposed although it is my opinion it is only in some such way that racial decay can be prevented'.[77] Part III was concerned with pauperism and crime. Darwin sought a restricted welfare system for itinerant paupers, alleging that they frequently claimed public assistance of any sort. He proposed that a man who had claimed public assistance frequently would be denied further outdoor relief, unless he was married with no more than two children or 'it is reasonably believed that he is incapable of further procreation, whether as a result of sterilization or otherwise'.[78] The drafting of the Bill was the subject of debate amongst the members of the Eugenics Society. Darwin himself was not against the marriage of two defectives – 'if there is no chance of fertility, marriage in such cases may be highly advantageous, especially if both parties are somewhat below normal'.[79] Darwin's concerns seemed to focus on imbeciles from poor backgrounds who imposed a burden on society. This may be simply for reasons of economy, or possibly stemming from an innate belief that it is precisely these classes who bred more dependency through poor habit and intellect. Realistically, those from financially independent families did not tend to impose a burden on the state and would have private care where appropriate.

Darwin discussed the wording of the Bill with Sir Frederick Willis, Chairman of the Board of Control, and met privately with him. He also provided notes which explained that his object was to 'make illegal all the objectionable uses of sterilization in order that its use, whenever legal, might be freely recommended' – but Willis pencilled in 'but it is not now legal to sterilize anyone merely in order to prevent procreation'.[80] Willis even drafted a Sterilization Bill for the Society, although he cautioned Darwin that 'should you care to use this draft, I should prefer it that it should not be known that I have had anything to do with it; it does not, *necessarily*, represent my views'.[81] Willis's draft was a shorter and more precise document, with Darwin's grandiloquence and Part III omitted. Darwin accepted the revision, but the Bill did not proceed. In 1929, Darwin wrote to Sir Hubert Bond at the Board of Control seeking an authoritative overview of law and practice concerning the mentally defective. The Eugenics Society were concerned with 'the defective individual and the family often sorely handicapped by the irresponsible conduct of a member who cannot be certified and yet causes a devastating amount of loss and worry'.[82] He was referred to the Board's lawyer, W. H. Gattie, but did not pursue the matter further.

Bernard Mallet succeeded Darwin as the President of the Eugenics Society. He drafted a further Bill, a more concise version of Willis's, and sent it to Brock, chairman of the Board of Control with the comments:

The sub-committee feels that clause one is the most comprehensive and also the most debatable clause. It has been inserted provisionally because the sub committee has been influenced by the findings of the Mental Deficiency Committee that the group of high-grade defectives who are most likely to be dealt with by guardianship and supervision and to whom clause two will therefore be most applicable, spring from the so-called 'social problem' group. This group is estimated as comprising a tenth of the total population of the country, and from it are recruited the bulk of low grade persons in the community whose excessive fertility is highly dysgenic.[83]

This unsolicited approach was dismissed with a rebuke by Brock that Mallett should not expect him to 'succumb to the temptation of expressing any opinion'.[84] Undaunted, a month later Mallett invited Brock to attend the Eugenics Society summer dinner with 'an open mind'. Surprisingly, Brock accepted quickly: 'I hope I am still sufficiently unbiased not to hold your Society responsible for the preposterous claims made by some of the advocates of sterilization. Even if I were not much interested in the question, I should be tempted to come to show my appreciation of your novel and merciful method of propaganda'.[85] Unfortunately there is no record of how Brock reacted to the after-dinner speech.

The remaining years of the 1930s saw the question of sterilization placed firmly on the political backburner as other domestic and foreign pressures increased. There was a deputation to the Ministry of Health by a group of county councillors in 1932,[86] which led to the establishment of the Brock Committee in June 1930 to consider the value of sterilization of the mentally deficient. The Committee's Report in 1933 showed there to be 33,000 people in England and Wales with mental deficiency, with one-third of these segregated in institutions:

> It is with the rest, who are living in the community, that the problem of sterilization arises ... Compulsory sterilization would not be justified, because it was not possible to prove beyond reasonable doubt that the children of particular individuals suffering from mental defect or disorder would also suffer from them.[87]

The Committee agreed that in principle those with a mental defect or disorder or a 'graver physical disability' should have the *right* to request sterilization but only with the recommendation of two doctors, the patient's consent and written approval from the Minister of Health.

Following this, the question of sterilization of the mentally deficient faded away. In the end, need was a matter of perception and perspective. Families of defectives may not have adopted the politically correct attitude of 'specialness' that would characterize more 'positive' approaches to mental deficiency in the late twentieth century, but nonetheless were reluctant to consign their relatives to often remote institutions, especially when they might have to contribute to their upkeep. The various councils and other agencies, such as the poor law unions and the health and education boards could not work together effectively, either to provide a systematic service that did not leave some defectives vulnerable, or to avoid replicating aspects of the care. This remains pertinent today; a person with a learning disability is passed from school to social service to hospital to daycare provision with little effort to marry provision into a holistic package, and it is suspected that the resurrection of the local health boards and the trend of local authorities to move from service providers to commissioning agents will result in no better provision.

Eugenics are still seen as a peculiarity of the time, emerging as the movement did from a particular socio-cultural milieu of growing urbanization, rural depopulation, improved public health and fear of degeneration, and inevitably associated by the public with the more heinous activities of the Nazi reign in Germany. Yet eugenics are still practised in Britain, if covertly, through genetic counselling, ante- and post-natal screening, and the relentless repair of those who are born less than 'perfect'. Perhaps the Mental Deficiency Act was a specific product of its time and doomed to fail. Perhaps it did not matter how ardent its supporters, damning its detractors or apathetic its administrators were; the Act was, after all, sandwiched between two global wars and made impracticable by the economic climate. Ultimately, need, provision and response to the Mental Deficiency Act by local authorities were not proscribed by statistics or legislation, but by perception.

Notes

1 National Archives [hereafter NA], MH58/103 *Sterilisation of the Unfit*: paper read by Lord Riddell before the Medico-Legal Society, 25 April 1929, p. 24.
2 This chapter is drawn from research funded by an Arts and Humanities Research Council Competition A award and supervised by the School of History and Welsh History, University of Wales Bangor: S. A. Churchman-Conway [i.e. Sharon Morris], 'Acts of Idiocy – Need, Perception and Responses to the Mental Deficiency Act 1913 by Local Authorities in Wales 1880–1940' (2003).
3 National varieties of eugenic policies are discussed in Chapter 7 of this volume.
4 Michel Foucault, *Madness and Civilization: a History of Insanity in the Age of Reason*, New York: Vintage Books, 1973.
5 Andrew Scull, *The Most Solitary of Afflictions: Madness and Society in Britain 1700–1900*, New Haven: Yale University Press, 1993; idem, *Masters of Bedlam: the Transformation of the Mad-Doctoring Trade*, Princeton: Princeton University Press, 1996.
6 Tom Butler, *Mental Health, Social Policy and the Law*, London: Macmillan, 1985.
7 For instance, Roy Porter, *Mind-Forg'd Manacles: A History of Madness in England from the Restoration to the Regency*, London: Athlone Press, 1987.
8 Kathleen Jones, *Asylums and After: A Revised History of the Mental Health Services from the Early Eighteenth Century to the 1990s*, London: Athlone Press, 1993. This work revises and condenses her earlier volumes into one text.
9 D. J. Mellett, *The Prerogative of Asylumdom: Social, Cultural and Administrative Aspects of the Institutional Treatment of the Insane in Nineteenth-Century Britain*, London and New York: Routledge, 1999.
10 Peter Bartlett, *Poor Law of Lunacy: the Administration of Pauper Lunatics in Mid-Nineteenth-Century England*, Leicester: Leicester University Press, 1999.
11 Mark Jackson, *The Borderland of Imbecility: Medicine, Society, and the Fabrication of the Feebleminded in late Victorian and Edwardian England*, New York: Manchester University Press, 2000.

12 Mathew Thomson, *The Problem of Mental Deficiency: Eugenics, Democracy, and Social Policy in Britain* c.*1870–1959* Oxford: Oxford University Press, 1998.

13 Pamela Dale, 'Implementing the 1913 Mental Deficiency Act: Competing Promises and Resource Constraint Evident in the South-West of England before 1948', *Social History of Medicine*, 16:3, 2003, 403–18.

14 49 & 50 Vict., June 25, 1886.

15 *Report of the Metropolitan Commissioners in Lunacy to the Lord Chancellor concerning the construction and condition of asylums and recommendations* (1844).

16 *Supplemental Report of the Metropolitan Commissioners in Lunacy to the Lord Chancellor concerning the general condition of the insane in Wales* (1844).

17 *Report of the Metropolitan Commissioners in Lunacy*, p. 80.

18 5 & 6 Vict. Lunatic Asylums Act 1842, 8 & 9 Vict. Lunatics (Care and Treatment) Act and Regulation of Asylums Act 1845; 16 & 17 Vict. Lunatic Asylums Act 1853 and amendments of 1862, 1865 and 1889; 16 & 17 Vict. Lunacy Regulation Act 1853 and amendments of 1855, 1862, and 1882; 53 & 54 Vict. Lunacy Act 1890.

19 *Education and Care of Idiots, Imbeciles, and Harmless Lunatics: Report of a Special Committee of the Charity Organisation Society*, London: Longman, Green and Co, 1877.

20 Ibid., p. 38.

21 Ibid., p. 39. Numbers for 'harmless lunatics' deducted.

22 45 & 46 George III.

23 NA, MH51/783. Licences were again automatically renewed in 1913 for institutions already registered under the Idiots Act [NA, MH51/415].

24 Herbert Spencer (1820–1903) applied the evolutionary theories of Darwin to social development, and used the phrase 'the survival of the fittest' to describe how society grows through the competition of the social jungle.

25 62 & 63 Vict. Elementary Education (Defectives and Epileptic Children) Act 1899; 3 Edw. VII Elementary Education Amendment Act 1903.

26 3 & 4 George V, 15th August 1913.

27 Thomson, *Problem of Mental Deficiency*, p. 304.

28 Dan Stone, 'Race in British Eugenics', *European History Quarterly*, 31:3, 2001, 397–426.

29 NA, RG19/7 Census returns; R.B. Provis of the Local Government Board to John T. Hibbert.

30 NA, RG19/7; Reginald MacLeod to Provis.

31 NA, RG19/7 18 March 1901.

32 A. E. Tredgold, *Mental Deficiency (Amentia)*, First Edition; London: Bailli_re, Tindall and Cox, 1908, p. 5.

33 Ibid., extrapolated total.

34 Edouard Seguin, *Idiocy: and its Treatment by the Physiological Method*, New York: William Wood & Co., 1866, pp. 45–6.

35 Moral imbecile was a term used to describe those whose mental deficiency or illness reduced their inhibitions with resultant socially irresponsible, lewd or promiscuous behaviour.

36 Tredgold, *Mental Deficiency*, pp. 373–5.

37 Steve Cherry, *Mental Health Care in Modern England* c.*1810–1998*, Woodbridge: Boydell Press, 2003.

38 NA, FD1/1392. Noted on document to be 'not on public record'.

39 NA, FD1/1392, Arthur W. Robinson to W. Morley Fletcher, 10 December 1920.

40 NA, FD1/1392, L. G. Brock to Board of Control, 1 January 1921.

41 NA, FD1/ 1392, W. P. Byrne to the MRC, 15 January 1921.

42 NA, FD1/1392, correspondence between Board of Control and the MRC; 31 March 1921, and 19 April 1921 respectively.

43 Mental Deficiency Act 1913 s. 30(iii).

44 NA, LCO2/389, correspondence from Board of Control to the Lord Chancellor, 23 January 1914.
45 Mental Deficiency Act 1913, s13(1).
46 NA, TS27/45, Treasury Solicitor to Board of Control 14 June 1916.
47 NA, TS27/45.
48 NA, TS27/45, correspondence between Lamotte and W. P. Byrne, Board of Control, 12 September 1916.
49 NA, NATS1/727. Leslie Scott, the Chairman of the CAMD, was also Conservative Member of Parliament for Liverpool Exchange 1910–29 with a particular interest in the conservation of rural England.
50 Ibid.
51 MH58/103, 'Sterilisation of the Unfit', paper read by Lord Riddell to the Medico-Legal Society, 25 April 1925.
52 Ibid.
53 Ibid., pp. 4–6.
54 Ibid., pp. 7–8.
55 Ibid. pp. 13–14.
56 For further discussion on this idea, see Daniel Pick's *Faces of Degeneration: A European Disorder 1848–1918*, Cambridge: Cambridge University Press, 1993 edn., in particular Part III, or Dorothy Porter's '"Enemies of the race:" Biologism, Environmentalism, and Public Health in Edwardian England', *Victorian Studies*, 34:2, Winter 1991, 159–78.
57 Alphonse Bertillon (1853–1914), bureaucrat credited with devising fingerprint analysis.
58 Cesare Lombroso (1835–1909), Italian physicist and criminal anthropologist, author of *L'Uomo Delinquente* (The Criminal Man), 1876, and *Le Crime, Causes et Remèdes* (Crime, Its Causes and Remedies). 1899. Lombroso is discussed in more detail in Chapter 3 of this volume.
59 Prana (1921), directed by F. W. Murnau, starring Max Schreck.
60 Paramount Artcraft (1921), directed by John B. Robertson and starring John Barrymore; (1931), directed by Rouben Marmoulian and starring Frederic March.
61 Universal (1931), directed by John Whale.
62 Microcephaly [Greek, 'small-head'] was a congenital deformity with inevitable mental deficiency.
63 Metro-Goldwyn-Mayer, 1932.
64 Sir James Crichton-Browne; foreword in James Cantlie, *Physical Efficiency: A Review of the Deleterious Effects of Town Life upon the Population of Britain, With Suggestions for their Arrest*, London: G. P. Putnam's Sons, 1906, pp. xix–xx.
65 A. E. Tredgold, *Mental Deficiency in Relation to Venereal Disease*, London: National Council for Combating Venereal Diseases, 1918.
66 Ibid., p. 5.
67 Ibid., p. 3
68 Ibid., p. 9.
69 Rev. Thomas J. Gerrard, *The Church and Eugenics*, Third Edition, Oxford: Catholic Social Guild, 1921, p. 7.
70 Lieutenant-Colonel Alderman W. E. Raley JP, Barnsley Education Council, Caxton Hall, Westminster, 27 July 1922; in *Report of a Conference on Mental* Deficiency (London: Central Association for Mental Welfare, 1922).
71 H. A. L. Fisher in ibid.
72 NA, MH58/103 Ministry of Health: Sterilization of Mental Defectives. Report in *The Causes and Prevention of Mental Deficiency*, Labour Party Research and Information Department.
73 Ferdinand Canning and Scott Schiller, *Eugenics and Politics*, London: Constable & Co., 1926, p. 7.
74 Ibid, p. 88.

75 NA, MH58/103, 19 April 1929.
76 NA, MH58/103. Raised by Mander, Labour MP Wolverhampton on 26 May 1930.
77 NA, MH51/547, Ministry of Health: Sterilization papers, Darwin to Miss Darwin, 28 January 1927.
78 Loc. cit.
79 Loc. cit., Darwin to Sir Frederick Willis, 25 April 1927.
80 NA, MH 51/547 Sterilization Bill Notes.
81 Loc. cit., Willis to Darwin, 8 July 1927.
82 NA, MH51/547.
83 NA, MH51/547, Mallett to Brock, 12 April 1930.
84 Loc. Cit., Brock to Mallett, 14 April 1930.
85 Loc. Cit., Brock to Mallet, 13 May 1930.
86 NA, MH51/547. Led by Cemlyn-Jones, MP for Anglesey, who urged that the numbers of mental defects in his area has increased by 100 per cent in the past two decades.
87 HMSO, Sessional Papers, Departmental Committee 1933–1934. Cmd 4485, xv, 611. (authors: Brock, Adams, Crawley, Miss R. Darwin, Fisher, Lewis, Tredgold, Trotter).

9   'That bastard's following me!'

Mentally ill Australian veterans struggling to maintain control

Kristy Muir

Maintaining control of the body has been an instrumental part of Australia's military history. Military personnel were instilled with aggression and were taught to repress most other emotions in training. This behaviour was further encouraged in war and it was reinforced once veterans returned home by notions of masculinity. Most veterans continued to exercise control over their feelings and some continued to solve their problems with violence and aggression. For veterans who returned from war suffering from psychological disorders, controlling the body is of immense importance. These veterans attempt to control their bodies both physically and psychologically to shield their private problems from the public sphere. Social isolation is one method some veterans use to control their emotions and subsequent behaviours. Others use drugs, especially alcohol and nicotine, to chemically alter their mental states. Despite some veterans' efforts to control their bodies, negative emotions such as anxiety, nervousness, paranoia, moodiness and anger dominate their behaviours. As such, some mentally ill veterans experience profound difficulty in their working, social and home lives.

This chapter uses clinical evidence and the testimonies of 26 Australian Second World War and Indonesian Confrontation veterans and their family members to demonstrate that some veterans from very different conflicts are left with very similar postwar problems and these veterans often use comparable strategies to deal with and attempt to control these problems.[1] These veterans' oral histories are a reflection of how they feel and how they perceive their situation. Perceptions are important because perceptions shape emotions and behaviours, and thus indirectly govern bodily control.

The Second World War and Indonesian Confrontation

The Second World War and Indonesian Confrontation were significantly different conflicts. Almost one million Australians were mobilized during the Second World War (1939–1945), 396,661 men and women served overseas, and approximately 45,000 personnel lost their lives.[2] Comparatively, 3,500 Australians served in the Indonesian Confrontation (1963–1966) and 23 were killed (seven of which were battle related).[3] While the Second World War mobilized the nation and was renowned for its carnage, the Indonesian Confrontation was a conflict largely shrouded in silence.[4] Most of the Second World War service personnel were volunteers in the Second Australian Infantry Force, the Royal Australian Air Force and the Royal Australian Navy (RAN), while regulars predominantly fought in the Indonesian Confrontation.

While the nature of the Second World War and the Indonesian Confrontation was vastly different, service personnel from both conflicts were on active service in stressful situations; both carried weapons and were fighting an enemy equally willing to shoot. For the personnel who served, the threat of death in both situations was very real. And for both Second World War and Indonesian Confrontation veterans military training involved the strict control of emotion and behaviour.

Military training and emotons

Learning the discipline of bodily control has played an instrumental role in military history. Military training was based on notions of masculinity, which were equated with mental toughness, violence and aggression.[5] Men were taught to avoid thinking, feeling or talking about 'emotional or physical discomfort'[6] to ensure they remained emotionally numb while on active service.[7] Emotional control was considered critical because soldiers on active service could not be distracted by emotions like fear, grief, guilt or sadness.[8]

Instilling militaristic traits in service personnel was fairly straightforward. Many recruits joined the services at an age when they were still developing their personal identities and hence could be easily moulded by the military.[9] Those who had already formed an identity, Hawkes claimed, were stripped of their character 'by techniques of bastardisation' so they could be given new traits appropriate to war.[10] Eisenhart, in his article entitled 'You Can't Hack it Little Girl', described the process as 'dehumanization'.[11]

Some of the Indonesian Confrontation veterans who were interviewed reported experiencing this type of military training. An ex-member of the RAN and an ex-infantry soldier recalled that their training incorporated a system of 'bastardization'. The infantry veteran explained:

> You are treated extremely badly. You are made to feel like nothing. There is constant abuse. The idea is to weed out the people who can't handle it – the sooks, the babies, the mummy's boys. It was a system of bastardisation to make you tough and to weed out the people that they didn't consider to be tough.

Emotional numbing was just as important for those who served in earlier conflicts. A Second World War veteran noted the avoidance of emotions in his training: 'There were no emotions or feelings or anything involved'.

Battle conditions reinforced emotional numbness. William Clarke, a British soldier in the First World War reported becoming 'hardened in the trenches':

Seeing so many corpses became just another sight. Often when you moved in the trenches you trod and slipped on rotting flesh. Your feelings only came to the fore when it was a special mate who had been killed or wounded and then it would quickly go away.[12]

In the Vietnam War service personnel were still repressing their emotions. As one veteran explained, 'one of the mechanisms that helped you survive in Vietnam, was the ability to shut off feelings. If you couldn't shut off feelings, you ended up a raving lunatic'.[13]

Like emotional repression, aggression played a major part in military training. The military's aim, as Spragg outlined, was 'to provide a force which will direct its aggression in the most effective and sustained way against the nominated enemy'.[14] Aggression was 'drilled' into an Indonesian Confrontation veteran when he was trained as a Navy gunner, and an army veteran recalled becoming imbued with aggression during his training:

> They teach you to be aggressive ... They teach you how to fight with a knife or a bayonet and they want you to be tough, so you are tough. You carry huge weights, you pound along roads and uphill and down dale ... They [only] tap you on the wrist if you get into fights. They don't really take a bad view of it, although it's contrary to military code ... So when you get to the Battalion you just merge in.

Therefore military training and war conditions left service personnel with the ability to shut off certain emotions while at the same time react aggressively. These learnt behaviours may have proved appropriate during active service, but difficulties arose when they were carried over into postwar life. Control proved especially problematic for veterans who returned with mental health problems.

Military traits and mental illness

Those suffering from Post-Traumatic Stress Disorder (PTSD) are clinically known to place great emphasis on maintaining control because if the symptoms of this disorder cannot be avoided, then veterans experience thoughts and behaviours that are outside of their control. Most PTSD symptoms, as set out in the *Diagnostic and Statistics Manual of Mental Disorders IV*, are related to veterans not being able to control their thoughts.[15]

The exact number of Australian veterans with mental health problems is unknown because there have been no comprehensive studies.[16] Research that has been conducted, however, suggests mental illness is widespread in this community. In 1999 the National Centre for War-Related PTSD in Australia estimated between 12 and 15 per cent of veterans on active service and in peacekeeping roles will develop PTSD and an additional 12 to 15 per cent will develop some of the disorder's symptoms.[17] These figures do not include veterans suffering from other mental illnesses. If Australia's Department of Veterans' Affairs (DVA) treatment population is indicative of the broader veteran community, more than one in four people suffer from mental health problems as a result of war-related service or living with a family member who served.[18]

Although the precise number of veterans who returned with a mental illness is unknown, psychological problems plagued some veterans, and continue to haunt others; and these illnesses, coupled with military training and war experiences, have left a legacy of veterans attempting to physically and psychologically control their bodies. The strategies some veterans use to exercise control can be categorized into three broad areas: chemically altering the mind; physical isolation; and avoidance – as Second World War and Indonesian Confrontation veterans demonstrate.

Inducing a chemical change

Second World War and Indonesian Confrontation interviewees used prescribed medications and chemically altering drugs, such as alcohol and cigarettes in an effort to maintain control. The differences in the types of medication veterans took was reflective of their generation and the medical response of the time. The majority of Second World War veterans (both those interviewed and the late veteran husbands of the widows interviewed) were heavily reliant on Valium throughout their postwar lives. Valium was their wonder drug. Some veterans took it once a day; others used it as a sleeping aid. One of the wives of a Second World War veteran was even offered Valium by her general practitioner to help her 'stay with [her husband]'. The Indonesian Confrontation veterans were on medication usually prescribed by a psychiatrist. Prescription drugs, however, only played one role in the effort some veterans undertook to induce a chemical change.

Alcohol and cigarettes were the most common chemically altering substances used by the veterans interviewed. Smoking and drinking were encouraged by the military and the habit stayed with a number of veterans.[19]

Nicotine dependence is known to be high among war veterans, especially those with a mental illness. The DVA noted the high incidence of nicotine use reported by veterans' families. This is further corroborated by worldwide evidence of smoking and smoking related illnesses in people with mental health problems.[20]

Veterans from both conflicts smoked during their active service as a means of controlling stress and smoking continued to be used as a means of stress relief in their postwar lives. One Second World War veteran was 'damned glad to grab a cigarette when things were getting a bit rough'. His smoking habit continued to such an extent in his postwar life that he developed severe emphysema.

The widow of another Second World War veteran discussed her late husband's dependence on his pipe. Although he did not smoke before he left for active service, when he returned he only ever put down the pipe he was eating or drinking:

[He] couldn't put the pipe down and hold his hands still. One hand was always on it. Even if he was reading a book, there was one on the book, one the pipe. He'd put the book down to turn the page, and hold the pipe. He wouldn't put down the pipe and turn the page, he couldn't; he just couldn't.

Cigarettes were also popular among the Indonesian Confrontation veterans. All but two of them became nicotine dependant after they joined the services. One veteran reported smoking 60 cigarettes (almost two and a half packets) a day for 11 years after he left the army. Another veteran smoked 50 a day for over 30 years after he returned.

War experiences and alcohol and substance abuse have been linked by a number of clinicians.[21] While the level of alcohol consumption may be influenced by the trauma experienced, veterans as a whole consume more alcohol than their civilian counterparts. Grayson *et al.* maintained that this was a result of the military lifestyle. In 1996 approximately 25.2 per cent of civilians consumed alcohol regularly, compared to 39.2 per cent of Vietnam war veterans and 37.9 per cent of enlisted servicemen. Another study reported the alcohol consumption of the latter two groups to be even higher, 50.6 per cent and 41.8 per cent respectively.[22]

It is difficult to ascertain levels of alcohol intake among interviewees because the accuracy of self-reporting regarding alcohol is questionable. What is evident is that some veterans used alcohol in an attempt to control emotions. Two of the Second World War veterans spoke about their heavy drinking during and after the war. One veteran explained how he learnt to drink alcohol in the army and after he returned home he continued to drink in an attempt to solve his 'war nervous neurosis'. He and his ex-servicemen mates 'thought the pub would fix their troubles'.

Four Indonesian Confrontation veterans admitted to heavy alcohol intake. Most of these veterans did not drink alcohol until they entered the military. As one ex-serviceman explained: 'It started with, "Have a can of beer, it's only ten cents" – I didn't drink. "Have a packet of cigarettes, they're only ten cents" – I didn't smoke'. After he came home he became an alcoholic and he smokes constantly.

Indonesian Confrontation veterans described their alcohol intake as a means of control. One veteran reported that he 'hit the grog' to avoid his depressive and angry moods, while another still binge drinks because alcohol helps 'things settle down'. A Navy veteran also testified that he had his first alcoholic drink while serving in the RAN. Alcohol soon became a method of 'getting away from the problems' and by the time he returned he 'became alcohol dependant' needing a 'few beers to get through the day' and a 'few' more to get to sleep. He still drinks and finds if he suffers from stress his alcohol consumption increases.

The women who were interviewed tended to protect their husbands from the stigma of alcoholism. Four wives reported their husbands drank excessive amounts of alcohol, yet they did not believe their husbands were alcohol dependant. One woman's husband went to the pub every night with his mates. And a late veteran's son recounted the arguments he and his siblings had with their mother over suggesting their father, who drank at lunchtime, early in the afternoon, after work at the pub and again when he came home, was an 'alcoholic'.

Thus veterans from both conflicts relied on medication, alcohol and cigarettes to help control their symptoms. These strategies were coupled with other controlrelated tactics, such as physical isolation.

Physical isolation

If veterans remove themselves from situations where they may potentially lose control, then the problem is theoretically solved. This isolation takes the form of geographical distance and personal withdrawal.

Evidence of mentally ill Australian veterans geographically isolating themselves is evident in the high proportion of veterans living in rural and remote areas. In 1997–1998 32 per cent of mentally ill veterans who were receiving treatment from the DVA lived in rural or remote locations.[23] Yet, according to the 1996 Australian census, only 14 per cent of the total population lived in these areas.[24] While male youth suicide rates are high and mental health services are virtually nil in rural and remote communities, the disproportionate number of veterans living in these areas reflect the fact that those with PTSD often choose to live away from crowded places.

This was certainly the case with some of the veterans interviewed. Two Second World War veterans and one Indonesian Confrontation veteran live in rural or isolated locations in Australia. The Indonesian Confrontation veteran further increases his isolation by not driving and discouraging visitors.

While the majority of veterans interviewed lived in metropolitan areas, most of them avoided social activity. The Second World War veterans who were interviewed did not openly discuss social withdrawal, but they indirectly spoke of it under the guise of apathy, disinterest and/or preoccupation. Most of them gave up sports and social activities they had enjoyed before they went to war. Others stated that they were 'too busy' building a home and an occupation for themselves to have time for a social life.

The widows of Second World War veterans were far more forthcoming in discussing the social isolation of their late veteran husbands. To varying extents, each of these women were isolated by their husbands' refusal to interact socially. Throughout her married life, one woman was known in her home town as a widow because she was almost always alone. Although her husband allowed her to participate in the community on some social levels, he hated her visiting friends or family and such occasions would result in drawn out arguments. This woman was not alone. Another widow conveyed the difficulties she faced in visiting family and friends. She was, for example, allocated a certain period of time to visit her mother in the nursing home, but visiting friends was prohibited and thus occurred in secret. The other women interviewed commonly reported their isolation, which was brought on by their mentally ill husbands' lack of social contact.

The Indonesian Confrontation veterans were all aware of their choice to isolate themselves. Most of these veterans admitted that the only social contact they have is with their immediate families. While one veteran extends this circle to his brother-in-law, he only socializes with this relative because he is a Vietnam veteran. Even spending time with immediate family proves difficult for one veteran. He rarely sees his four children and avoids all parties and celebrations because he does not feel he can control his drinking or aggression under these circumstances. In addition, he stopped driving because he cannot control his aggression in the car and at work he avoids confrontational situations because, as he explained, 'I overreact, I go into a complete panic attack and I go on the prod. And I will attack, there's no question of it'. Although one veteran conceded that his 'couch potato' behaviour isolates his wife, he refuses to go out for social occasions.

Avoidance by maintaining the silence

The methods veterans used to physically isolate themselves were coupled with another controlling method – silence. While most veterans continued to have social contact with their immediate families, very few shared their war experiences.

After the world wars people were warned not to discuss the war with veterans and veterans were encouraged to keep their stresses and emotions to themselves.[25] This, coupled with some veterans' feeling that civilians did not understand their experiences, the nature of PTSD, and Australia's masculine culture, where sharing feelings was frowned upon, caused great silence between many veterans and their families.

Some veterans interviewed admitted that they did not talk about their experiences with their families because they felt such communication would leave them vulnerable to losing control of their emotions. While one Second World War veteran has 'a chest full of medals', his family 'don't . . . even know what they're for' because he does not feel he can talk about his war experiences without crying. Similarly, an Indonesian Confrontation veteran is still haunted by an incident that occurred in Borneo where civilians were killed and injured, but he has shared 'nothing about it' with his wife because he fears he will break down if he tells her.

While the women interviewees were aware of the devastation war had reaped on their families' lives, they knew little about the service behind these problems and some were not even aware that their husbands had a diagnosed mental disorder. Although one interviewee had been married to her husband for 30 years and was aware that he had some severe problems after a day of marriage, she did not know that he was suffering from schizophrenia until she obtained his military case file four months after his death. Some of the women interviewed discovered the only way to find out what their husbands went through while serving was to 'overhear' when they spoke to other ex-servicemen.

While the silences may have helped some veterans to control their emotions in front of their families, they hindered communication and left some women feeling upset that after decades of marriage their husbands could not, or would not, talk to them about their experiences, feelings and/or mental illnesses.

Emotional turmoil

These veterans were not alone in attempting to maintain the emotional numbness learnt in the military. The Australian Vietnam Veterans' Counselling Service recognizes emotions as 'the current combat zone for many veterans' because although 'displaying emotion was considered a weakness' in the military, 'in the civilian world and in relationships emotions are desirable and essential'.[26] Hendid and Pollinger Haas consider the repression of emotions as one of the most significant causes of PTSD.[27]

The emotional difficulties some veterans experience surface in their relationships. One study completed in the United Kingdom revealed approximately half of all male veterans could not recall a close friend outside of work.[28] Relationship problems among Australian veterans are evident in their high divorce rates.

After the Second World War divorces were still socially taboo and legally difficult, yet divorce rates rose sharply in the immediate postwar years. In 1939 there were 3,137 divorces in Australia; by 1946 the number of divorces had risen to 7,235 and they rose again in 1947 to 8,803.[29] Divorce rates, however, were not equally divided among civilians and service personnel. Veterans were, and still are, more likely to be divorced than their civilian counterparts.[30]

While the majority of interviewees remained married (three were divorced and another separated), their relationships were plagued by social isolation and communication problems, among other difficulties. For the widows of Second World War veterans, divorce or separation was inconceivable because of financial and social constraints. Two widows revealed that they thought about leaving their husbands 'often', but traditional views and having 'nowhere to go' kept them in their marriages. One Indonesian Confrontation veteran was bewildered that his wife has never left him. He twice pondered, 'why she hasn't gone and told me to "go to hell," I don't know. If I'd have been her I'd have been gone so long ago'. After three divorces, another Indonesian Confrontation veteran has resolved that he is 'impossible to live with' and 'being alone is a better way than having to change, which I can't do'. Thus the consequences of emotional numbing and emotional turmoil were socially and domestically disabling. So how then did the veterans fare in maintaining control of their mental health problems?

Controlling the mind, or controlling minds?

Despite veterans' efforts to master control, their strategies largely failed to curb mental illness symptoms. In addition, the aggressive behaviour learnt in military training and reinforced during active service persisted once veterans returned home.

Aggression remained with some veterans because they were not taught how to deal with their 'anger, frustration, [or] rage'.[31] Some veterans' inability to control this learned aggression and violent behaviour is evident in Australia's postwar trends.[32] Homicide rates increased markedly after the First World War and did not begin to decrease until after 1920. This downward fall reversed again after the Second World War when homicide rates increased by a massive 32 per cent.[33] In both cases ex-servicemen were over represented as perpetrators.[34] Judith Allen's *Sex and Secrets* gives numerous examples of women suffering from sexual and physical abuse from their veteran husbands.[35]

While the veterans interviewed were not violent to the extent of committing homicides, they certainly had difficulty controlling their aggression. Three of the Second World War veterans admitted they had problems managing their anger after they returned home. While one veteran had been 'cold tempered' before the war, when he returned he found himself getting into fights. Another stated that he learned to be aggressive in the war and found this aggression difficult to suppress in his postwar life. He still cannot restrain his anger when he feels others are 'taking advantage', 'belittling' him, or if his wife does something 'the wrong way'. A Second World War veteran's son emphasized his father's volatile temper: 'By God he used to get cranky'. While this interviewee claimed his father was 'never violent', he admitted that he and his siblings were belted for punishment and the extent of his father's anger determined the level of pain: 'If he was really worked up over it, it could be quite bad ... Depending on what sort of day he had depended on how hard it was'.

Similarly, aggression and violence played a big part in the lives of six of the returned Indonesian Confrontation servicemen. Within 14 years one veteran had written off eight cars. He eventually gave up driving because he experienced blackouts and because his 'rage attacks' made him 'liable to drive the car straight into something'. The same aggression also resulted in his inability to solve problems with any method other than his fists. Two other Indonesian Confrontation veterans admitted they were still using physical fights to settle arguments almost 40 years after their return.

Although two Indonesian Confrontation veterans interviewed have learned to control their aggression, for many years they struggled to restrain themselves. One of these veterans physically removed himself from his home when he felt anger coming on to protect his family. He recalled living in military quarters after his return and hearing the yelling and screaming and seeing the black eyes and swollen lips of the servicemen's wives. He remarked that this was a regular occurrence with 'guys that had come back like myself'. The other veteran was 'angry all the time' for many years. Even simple tasks, like shopping, left him unable to control his anger:

> I could not go into a supermarket because of the noise, the kids, the trolleys. Some woman would ram you ... and I'd want to punch her. I'd get really hostile and probably say a few uncomplimentary things to the poor woman.

Like the inability to control aggression, the strategies veterans used to control their mental health problems proved largely unsuccessful. While interviewees used different terminology to describe their symptoms, neither of these veterans could control their problems and the social consequences of these symptoms were remarkably similar. The generational divide is most evident in the language veterans and their family members used to explain and understand mental illness symptoms. Terminology choices were influenced by changes in psychiatry and military psychology throughout history.[36] Veterans and their families were exposed to this changing terminology through popular culture, but also via the treatment they sought and received. Second World War veterans largely sought assistance from their general practitioners, while younger veterans (Indonesian Confrontation veterans included) are more likely to see mental health professionals.[37]

Second World War veterans described their inability to control their 'nerves' or other physical symptoms. After returning home from six years in the air force, one veteran began to suffer from terrible headaches and became very touchy, 'I could not even wear a wristwatch, tight clothes or a coarse knit sock. Many times I thought I was going around the bend and often lost two or more days a week off work'. Another veteran still suffers from constant headaches, ringing ears and twitching legs. And a widow reported that her late husband suffered from chest pains that were not caused by a physiological condition.

One widow of a Second World War veteran described the controlling nature of what she called her husband's 'nerves'. His 'nerves' were so unsettled that he could not sit still in a chair long enough to get through a meal; he paced around the house and broke teeth because he clenched so tightly on his pipe. Another widow also reported that her late husband's false teeth had to be replaced three times because they were worn down by his constant grinding.

None of the Indonesian Confrontation veterans referred to the term 'nerves', but they undoubtedly had similar feelings because 'anxiety' was commonly reported. In an anxiety rating scale test, one veteran scored a very high 33, with 36 being the highest level of anxiety on the scale.

Veterans from both conflicts also shared other incontrollable symptoms, such as 'mood swings'. For at least five years after returning home, one Second World War veteran broke down intermittently in uncontrollable tears. Likewise, an Indonesian Confrontation veteran divulged that he still cannot control himself from breaking down in tears at any moment. A widow of a Second World War veteran discussed her husband's drift into 'black moods'. Indonesian Confrontation veterans reflected on suffering from 'bad moods' for decades and getting into 'moods' they 'can't stand'.

While many of the veterans interviewed attempt to isolate themselves socially, there are occasions when they need to go out and some veterans have great difficulty coping in these situations. The general feeling, as one Second World War veteran explained, is 'expecting something might happen'. Two Indonesian Confrontation veterans revealed they suffer from panic attacks if they are left alone in their regional towns. Another Indonesian Confrontation veteran cannot go to a large supermarket, or anywhere people can get behind or around him. When he catches the train he sits on the long seats near the doors to ensure he can see everyone, places a tissue on the seat next to him so no one will sit down, and will only travel at five o'clock in the morning to ensure the train is relatively empty. Half of the veterans interviewed are so wary of other people that they refuse to sit anywhere but in the corner in public places to ensure they can see everyone around them. The majority remain alert and on guard in any social setting. An Indonesian Confrontation veteran described his paranoia:

> I've got a built in thing. Lets say there's a tree. I have a thing that I know there's a tree and until I see behind the tree there's someone there. I make sure no one's watching me. I'll leave my house and then back track to see if someone's there. I do behind the scenes surveillance. I won't do it for a week or so and then I'll do it three or four days in a row, 'That bastard's following me', but he's not really.

The impediments the interviewees face on a daily basis rule their lives. Every time they have to leave the house they are forced to face the symptoms that they cannot control in tangible ways.

The lack of control these veterans have over their thoughts is most evident in their inability to sleep soundly. Veterans from both conflicts are plagued by insomnia and nightmares. For years after he came home one Second World War veteran experienced nightly nightmares; they then subsided to two or three times a week; and only recently – over 50 years after he returned – his nightmares have decreased to a few times a month. He still 'hate[s] the thought of night coming on' because in addition to the nightmares he is an insomniac.

Equally, other veterans experience insomnia, nightmares and flashbacks. One Second World War veteran maintained that the war was easier to cope with than the nightmares because during the war he could rationalize that the occasion would be over soon, but with the nightmares 'you can't do that because your brain is orchestrating the darn thing'. This veteran still feels like he screams in his sleep from the nightmares, but his wife tells him he is just making strangling noises.

All of the Second World War veterans' wives reported that their husbands had sleeping problems – they too were insomniacs and suffered from nightmares. Even on Valium, one veteran only slept four hours a night and he kept his wife and usually his children up with him. Another woman revealed that her husband (Second World War veteran) could only sleep with the lights on and even then his sleep was very disturbed. He would often wake from his sleep screaming. Although they slept in twin beds, his wife was always cautious not to disturb him while he slept in case he attacked her.

All of the Indonesian Confrontation veteran interviewees sleep very poorly and all but[38] two still have service related nightmares. One veteran uses a 'few beers' and sleeping tablets to sleep, but he still suffers from nightmares and wakes after only a few hours. The service related nightmares only began in the

1990s for another veteran. The lack of emotional and behavioural control in some veterans is epitomized in two of the Indonesian Confrontation veterans who awoke attacking their partners. After he was newly married, one of these veterans awoke from a nightmare with his hands around his wife's throat.

The inability to control their anger, anxiety, moodiness, restlessness and other symptoms, led to multiple job changes for the majority of veterans. One Second World War veteran continuously moved on from job to job and town to town. As a result he lived in 35 different townships. And an Indonesian Confrontation veteran estimated having 40 jobs since he was discharged from the army.

The oral histories of Australian Second World War and Indonesian Confrontation veterans with mental health problems demonstrate that some veterans from vastly different conflicts have similar bodily controlling behaviours. The strategies they use to try to control their thoughts, emotions and behaviours and the symptoms they suffer from because they largely lack control are remarkably similar.

These Second World War veterans have been trying to control their problems for 60 years; and the Indonesian Confrontation veterans for 40. For decades veterans from both conflicts have used similar strategies in an attempt to stay in control – medication, alcohol and cigarettes, physical isolation and avoidance – and both have largely failed. While veterans could repress some emotions, they generally had no control over negative emotions like anger and negative behaviours like violence. They were also largely unsuccessful at controlling their nervous states, anxiety, paranoia or other symptoms. Consequently, war has left these veterans and their families with a legacy of social, domestic and employment related consequences.

Notes

1 These veterans were interviewed between November 1999 and February 2000. They remain nameless throughout the chapter to ensure their confidentiality is maintained.

2 M. McKernan, 'War', in W. Vamplew (ed.), *Australians: Historical Statistics*, NSW: Fairfax, Syme & Weldon Associates, 1987, p. 411.

3 Grey's figures have been used here. J. Grey, *A Military History of Australia*, Melbourne: Cambridge University Press, revised edition, 1999, p. 229. The number of Australians killed in the Indonesian Confrontation, however, differs between reports. The Australian War Memorial (AWM) also lists twenty three killed in the conflict on their website: www.awm.gov.au/atwar/confrontation.htm (accessed 15 October 2002). Yet, the AWM's other web pages and archival documents list fewer killed. The AWM237, Roll of Honour cards, supplementary sources, Casualties (Army), Korea – Malaya – Confrontation, expunged copy, compiled by CARO 1969, Item 746/2/1; AWM 151–152, Roll of Honour Cards, Indonesian Confrontation (Malay Peninsula, 1964–1966, Sabah/Sarawak, 1962–1966); and the AWM, Information Sheet 19, 'Australian War Casualties': www.awm.gov.au/research/infosheets/war_casualties (accessed 15 February 2002), cites 15 killed. The Roll of Honour Database posted on the AWM's website: www.awm.gov.au/database/roh.asp, listed 18 as having been killed in the Confrontation when the site was accessed on 17 February 2000 and 17 when the site was accessed on 15 October 2002. Like the number killed, the number of wounded in the Confrontation is also unclear. See Grey, *Military History of Australia*, p. 229 and McKernan, 'War', p. 414.

4 Among the general Australian public there is still little known about the conflict. Few histories have been written about Australia's involvement in the Indonesian Confrontation. P. Dennis and J. Grey, *Emergency and Confrontation*, North Sydney: Allen & Unwin in association with the AWM, 1996; D. Horner (ed.), *Duty First: The Royal Australian Regiment in War and Peace*, North Sydney: Allen & Unwin, 1990; and N. Smith, *Nothing Short of War with the Australian Army in Borneo 1962–1966*, Victoria: Mostly Unsung, 1999, wrote specifically on the Australian experience, but most of the other information available on the Confrontation is limited to a few pages in complete military histories or in relation to the United Kingdom. See, for example, P. Dickens, *SAS: The Jungle Frontier: 22 Special Air Service Regiment in the Borneo Campaign, 1963–66*, London: Arms and Armour Press, 1983; R. Jackson, *The Malayan Emergency: The Commonwealth Wars 1948–1966*, London: Routledge, 1991; H. James and D. Sheil-Small, *The Undeclared War: The Story of the Indonesian Confrontation 1962–66*, London: Leo Cooper, 1971.

5 W. Eisenhart, 'You Can't Hack It Little Girl: A Discussion of the Covert Psychological Agenda of Modern Combat Training', *Journal of Social Issues*, 31:4, 1975, 16.

6 B. Arndt, 'Why Masculinity is a Health Hazard and What we Can Do About It', National Men's Health Conference 10–11 August 1995, Canberra: Commonwealth Department of Human Services and Health, 1995, p. 88.

7 T. Lloyd, 'Risking their Health – Young Men and Masculinity', National Men's Health Conference 10–11 August 1995, Canberra: Commonwealth Department of Human Services and Health, 1995, p. 33.

8 Ibid.

9 R. Hawkes, 'Readjustment Issues of the Returned Vietnam Veteran', *Australian Social Work*, 40:3, September 1987, 13.

10 Ibid.

11 Eisenhart, 'You Can't Hack It Little Girl', 15. See also Dave Grossman, *On Killing: The Psychological Cost of Learning to Kill in War and Society*, Boston: Little, Brown and Co., 1995, p. 323.

12 J. Bourke, *Dismembering the Male: Men's Bodies, Britain and the Great War*, London: Reaktion Books, 1996, p. 77.

13 Hawkes, 'Readjustment Issues', 13.

14 G. S. Spragg, 'Psychiatry in the Military Forces', *The Medical Journal of Australia*, I, 8 April 1972, 746.

15 American Psychiatric Association, *Diagnostic and Statistical Manual of Mental Disorders IV*, Washington: American Psychiatric Association, 1994, pp. 428–9.

16 Commonwealth DVA, *Mental Health Disorders in the Veteran Community and their Impact on DVA's Programs: An Analysis of Available Data*, Canberra: DVA, 2000, p. 64.

17 National Centre for War-Related Post-traumatic Stress Disorder (NCPTSD), *Post-traumatic Stress Disorder (PTSD and War-Related Stress: Information for Veterans and their Families)*, Victoria: NCPTSD, 1999, p. 4.

18 The treatment population consists of ex-service personnel and their dependants who have a gold or white card, which entitles veterans and their families to medical and pharmaceutical concessions. To obtain these cards veterans must have a mental or physical disability accepted as war-related. Commonwealth DVA, *Mental Health Disorders*, p. 4.

19 Cigarettes and alcohol were issued to Australian service personnel in both the Second World War and the Indonesian Confrontation.

20 Commonwealth DVA, *Issues and Options for a Mental Health Policy: Towards a 'Whole Person' approach to veteran mental health care*, Canberra: DVA, July 2000, p. 30. A study of the smoking habits of American Vietnam veterans revealed that veterans with PTSD were not more likely to smoke than veterans without PTSD, but those with PTSD were heavier smokers. J. Beckham, A. Kirby, M. Feldman, M.

Hertzberg, S. Moore, A. Crawford, J. Davidson and J. Fairbank, 'Prevalence and Correlates of Heavy Smoking in Vietnam Veterans with Chronic Post-Traumatic Stress Disorder', *Addictive Behaviors*, 22:5, September–October 1997, 637–47.

21 See for example H. Hendid and A. Pollinger Haas, *Wounds of War: the Psychological Aftermath of Combat in Vietnam*, New York: Basic Books, 1984, p. 89; A. Magarey, J. Tiddy, and P. Wilson, 'The Diets of Elderly Men and the use of Dietary Supplements: Australian Non-Veterans Compared with War Veterans', *Australian Journal of Nutrition and Dietetics*, 50:1, 1993, 25; and W. Ward, 'Psychiatric morbidity in Australian Veterans of the United Nations Peacekeeping Force in Somalia', *Australian and New Zealand Journal of Psychiatry*, 31, 1997, 184.

22 D. Grayson, R. Marshall, M. Dobson, B. O'Toole, R. Schureck, M. French, B. Pulvertaft and L. Meldrum, 'Australian Vietnam Veterans: Factors Contributing to Psychosocial Problems', *Australian and New Zealand Journal of Clinical Psychology*, 43:6, November 1987, 609–11.

23 Commonwealth DVA, *Mental Health Disorders*, p. 13.

24 See graph 5.19 in Australian Bureau of Statistics, 'Population: Population Distribution'. Online. Available at: www.abs.gov/ausstats (accessed 2 August 2001).

25 V. Hogancamp and C. Figley, 'War: Bringing the Battle Home', in C. R. Figley and H. I. McCubbin (eds), *Stress and the Family, Vol II: Coping with Catastrophe*, New York: Brunner/Mazel, 1983, p. 159.

26 Vietnam Veterans' Counselling Service, 'Combat Experiences and its Effects'. Online. Available at: www.dva.gov.au/health/vvcs/combat.htm (accessed 23 August 1999).

27 H. Hendid and A. Pollinger Haas, *Wounds of War*, p. 7.

28 Hawkes, 'Readjustment Issues', 13.

29 P. McDonald, L. Ruzicka and P. Pyne, 'Marriage, Fertility and Mortality', in Vamplew (ed.), *Australians: Historical Statistics*, p. 47.

30 S. Garton, 'War and Masculinity in Twentieth Century Australia', *Journal of Australian Studies*, 56, March 1998, 92.

31 Vietnam Veterans' Counselling Service, 'Combat Experiences'.

32 'Source book of Australian Criminal and Social Statistics, 1804–1988', in National Committee on Violence, *Violence: Directions for Australia*, Canberra: Australian Institute of Criminology, Canberra, 1990, p. 17.

33 D. Archer and R. Gartner, 'Violent Acts and Violent Times: A Comparative Approach to Postwar Homicide Rates', *American Sociological Review*, 41, December 1976, 958.

34 J. Allen, *Sex and Secrets: Crimes Involving Australian Women Since 1880*, Melbourne: Oxford University Press, 1990, p. 132.

35 Ibid., p. 132.

36 For a comprehensive discussion of this see B. Shephard, *A War of Nerves: Soldiers and Psychiatrists 1914–1994*, London: Jonathon Cape, 2000.

37 Commonwealth DVA, *Mental Health Disorders*, p. 52.

10 Afterword – regulated bodies

Disability studies and the controlling professions

Sharon Snyder and David Mitchell

Archaeology of abnormals

At the beginning of a lecture on 15 January 1975, Michel Foucault responded to a criticism of an audience member that his research failed to arrive at the experience of *persons* deemed abnormal. At the time, Foucault responded in the following manner:

> At the end of last week's lecture, someone asked me if really I was not mistaken and had given a lecture on expert medico-legal opinion rather than the promised lecture on abnormal individuals. These are not at all the same things, but you will see that starting from the problem of expert medico-legal opinion I will come to the problem of abnormal individuals'.[1]

This explanation condenses Foucault's most commonly employed methodology: namely the promise to move from an analysis of institutional discourse to the site of silenced populations. As he famously explains in *Madness and Civilization*, professions of the body have become monologues about the persons they impact; therefore 'I will not write the history of that language, but rather the archeology of that silence'.[2]

In Foucault's own corpus, the topic of abnormals first emerges as the social management of bodies that defy the determinism of a disease course or the temporal nature of infection. One thinks of the abandoned leprosaria that preface his reflections on confinement or the environment of the clinic teeming with infectious agents. Within his histories of quarantine and public health as a policing agent, state-sponsored quests commence anew for the discovery of alternatively disruptive derelict bodies – those in need of institutional control. His accounts of efforts to re-populate once thriving and now emptied institutional structures has encouraged several generations of readers to explore the interconnections of social institutions with power/knowledge, discourse, subjectivity, and the body. Yet while Foucault's research often heads toward analyses of more explicitly 'social' categories, as in his work on sexuality or criminality, disability studies has resolutely kept its analytical focus on those bodies categorically claimed as impaired by medical, rehabilitation, and legal jurisdictions.

Parallel to Foucault's research and in affiliation with nascent disability rights ideas, disability studies emerges as the necessity of finding a better way to understand medical and confinement policy. Erving Goffman's work on asylums and nursing homes, for example, traces out the history of incarceration and the perspectives of confined persons. Irving Zola, founder of the *Newsletter in Disability Studies and Chronic Disease* (1981) as well as the Society for Disability Studies, dedicated a series of editorial columns to explications of Goffman's *Asylums*, and also *Stigma*, as 'classics' in disability studies. At the advent of disability studies' scholarship in the US at the beginning of the 1980s, Zola claims Goffman's analyses of regulatory institutions as essential reading, while calling for scholarship that will not leave the fate of their constituencies to the hidden operations of medical establishments. Zola often described his own emergence into disability studies as a matter of dissent from methods in medical sociology that created a distance from disabled persons while re-enshrining a medical point-of-view.

We mention these founding works of Goffman and Zola, because while the volume before you incurs numerous debts to Foucault for its commitments to analysing the systems of control and management that oversee disability, it also could benefit from the insights of disability studies: namely, the contribution of the perspective of disability as an enunciated subject position to the intersection of social, legal, scientific and medical designations of human 'abnormality'. Like Foucault, the field often begins with an articulation of the professions of control that oversee disabled people while ultimately arriving at the perspective of those who find themselves as the objects of such institutions. Consequently, one of the major contributions of disability studies is its commitment to the 'identity-claim' that disability perspectives enunciate positions not otherwise recuperable within diagnostic and normalizing discourses.

This, of course, is not an insignificant venture. On the one hand we have Foucault's anatomy of institutional regimes and their myriad mechanisms of normalization. And on the other, we find the efforts of disability studies scholars to evoke a meaningful agency at work in populations oppressed by social regulation and medical practices. While Foucault himself was unwilling to play the game of an alternative positivism, thus undercutting the potential of the utility of his work for 'emancipatory discourse', he nonetheless identifies regimes that can be followed into the fashioning of subjectivities formulated as positions of resistance, co-optation, subjection, and performance. Foucault theorized the systemic production of individuals through categories of aberration and pathology, whereas disability studies scholars seek out disability as enunciated through experiences in more banal cultural locations such as in clinics, in laboratory science, in the special school classroom, and in other locations that regulate the segregation of non-normals. In other words, whereas Foucault's work premises the transition from a disciplinary society to a society of control, disability studies sits squarely in a developed analysis of the latter with its more intricate mechanisms for controlling bodies. Consequently, disability studies analyses trace out perspectives and subject formations wrestling with the constraints of exclusively medico-juridical assignments, while also tossing in a healthful suspicion of the forms of control that have been exercised under the benign rubric of *care*. The research currently focuses on critiques of modern management systems, regimes of classification, and the investments of control professions in defining and certifying prospects for people with disabilities.

Foucault's research is concerned with the history of institutions, but it is also a history of disability. Insomuch as he addresses the formation of disciplinary and methodological modes of knowledge production, his work sets down a pathway for disability studies in its challenge to professions that authorize their own views in the name of persons with disabilities. One finds, in disability studies, the kind of insider qualitative research and reporting that resembles, most of all, the internships Foucault undertook early in his career at the Salpetriere. In many cases disability studies showcases research produced by disabled researchers themselves: those who were once subject to and are now interlocutors of the structures they analyze. Those who, like Foucault's own personal critiques of institutionalization and proliferating sexual pathology, pursue forms of insider qualitative research. These analyses do not necessarily foreground first-person experience as such; instead they allow individual identifications with subject populations to inform and deepen the scholarly enterprise.

Perhaps most importantly for disability studies, Foucault's analyses made health legible as power and domination of bodies. His research also made medicine comprehensible as clinical and technical production of power relations across bodies. Health became less a description of a state of being and more a category of social exclusion, a barometer of deviance, and an imposition of ideas about contamination upon different bodies. Informed by a unique combination of Foucauldian and disability studies methodologies, this volume presents a collection of critical perspectives on what we often think of as the most benign incarnations of contemporary institutions such as community care, orthopaedic surgery, special education classrooms, and assistive technology delivery systems. In doing so, disability studies questions the very legibility of disabled subjects within discourses established to make disability coherent and available for liberal intervention schemes.

As a parallel to Foucault's own discomfort, liberal intervention schemes and would-be rescuers pose serious troubles for disability studies. The implications of such efforts have to do with the problem of always taking a managerial view of disability: the medical, clinical, diagnostic, therapeutic, and social work evaluations necessary for special dispensations that merely enable equality of participation. Among these ever expanding domains of surveillance, some have argued that we must essentially extend the authority of medical gazing to any gatekeeper in modernity – from the motor vehicle department teller to the movie theatre usher. For example, in disability studies programmes, issues of authority and the gaze come up in mixed student groups of therapists, disabled students, and disabled therapy students where complaints are made about the extension of diagnostic strategies into classroom dynamics. Rather than objectification as a product of pornographic spectacle, disability objectifications are understood as ritual mandates of disclosure when qualifying for services, treatment, or even social participation. All bodies may be subject to a clinical gaze, but some bodies are made to endure forms of repetitious subjection.

For example, disability services offices in academia serve as the mechanism by which accommodations, such as extended test-taking, are authorized. Yet when students with learning disabilities do well on tests following the provision of accommodation, an extra re-authorization inquiry may be initiated. For many disability studies scholars and activists, demands for continual re-certification of one's body deficiencies in exchange for differential treatment represents a clinching of the noose, rather than an exalted moment of inclusion. In a perfectly Foucauldian twist, restrictive operations now function without the need of walls or physical coercion; instead, we now find disabled bodies subject to roving and arbitrarily applied surveillance mechanisms. Such developments hail the need to recognize our own era of de-institutionalization – one that requires extrication from what Foucault called the 'government' of abnormals.[3]

Finally, Foucault's research ultimately *did* bring him to exemplary 'abnormal' subjects, as in the case of the writings of Herculin Barbin. The publication of Barbin's memoir seeks to flesh out knowledge about resistance and survival tactics for those who occupy pathologized bodies. Also, it is well known that Judith Butler, brilliant explicator of Foucault, hinges her own discussions of performance and agency on Foucault's histories of sexuality. Butler's work also brings readers to the gates of silencing. For example, on a rare personal note, in the 1999 preface to *Gender Trouble*, Butler tells readers of an institutionalized uncle in Kansas whose incarceration haunted her childhood: 'I grew up understanding something of the violence of gender norms: an uncle incarcerated for his anatomically anomalous body deprived of family and friends, living out his days in an 'institute' in the Kansas prairies'.[4] And thus we eventually find ourselves among those who resist institutional labels and seek out transgressive alternatives. The rather restrictive opportunities to find some room for manoeuvre in clinics, in facilities, in households, and across professional discourses that confine, erase, and ultimately mystify the lives of disabled persons.

From Foucault to disability studies

Disability studies, then, might be thought of as the effort to operationalize some manoeuvrability for bodies deemed excessive, insufficient, or inappropriate on the basis of their impairments (actual or perceived). In doing so, the field functions as the theoretical arm of international disability rights movements. As an interdisciplinary field of study and scholarship, disability studies analyses the meanings attributed to human corporeal, sensory, and cognitive differences. Participants examine the role that disability serves in expressive traditions, scientific research, and social science applications. They study the status of disabled persons, often by attending to exclusionary scholarly models and professional structures. Interestingly, a key aspect of disability studies has involved focusing upon the privilege that accrues to non-disabled persons within built environments. Implicitly, then, researchers question the ethics of inbuilt social exclusions by tracing out their origins. As a result, they track down many historical pathways concerning practices and attitudes toward disabled persons.

In seeking to understand the variety of interpretations that make disability an evident facet of human diversity, the field includes many methodologies such as: quantitative studies, qualitative interpretation, critical analysis, and historical work. Nonetheless, because disability studies marks a departure from fields of knowledge and professional training that may have sustained exclusionary practices and mandated social shame, participants in disability studies primarily engage in efforts to re-evaluate the implications of traditional approaches to disability. New scholarship proposes research topics that allow disability perspectives to emerge with the result that experiences which infuse life with a disability are valued for insights that can be culled for strategies to assist new generations. The study of disability perspectives bring to the forefront of cultural commentary a body of insight previously marginalized within many universities during an era of scholarship in which eugenics ideas prevailed.

It should be emphasized that disability studies initiatives, research projects, and curricula have been developed worldwide, but here we will limit our discussion to the US, and, to an extent, Canada, the United Kingdom, and Australia, with formations primarily in global urban centres and wealthy nation states. Disability studies takes place when groups of committed advocates, activists, and scholars pursue work locally in order to make the persistence of disability exclusions across a variety of regional and global contexts better understood, documented, and interpreted. Only very recently, during the last decade of the twentieth century, did disability studies begin to be more generally recognized as an area of academic inquiry, while the moniker, 'disability studies', came into usage during the 1980s. The new term sought to differentiate its concern with the well-being of disabled persons from what one scholar has termed the 'disability business'. The disability business was perceived as a megalithic operation of management interests and government surveys that were frequently answerable to the goals of non-disabled persons at the expense of their disabled clients, family members, or neighbours.

At present, disability studies consists of a nascent, yet rapidly expanding scholarship that draws researchers from across a diversity of academic fields. Most universities have been inaccessible to disabled persons; as a consequence, scholars in disability studies observe the ways in which curricular ideas also suffer from this central exclusion, taking as a given that disability experiences offer a substantial vantage upon human existence. Because aspects of fields of study may reiterate the perpetuation of 'able-ist' bias, disability studies often involve a rejection of habits, methods, and undertakings of universities in the past in their assumptions about bodies and capacities. Thus, disability studies also entails studying the myriad ways that traditional fields have been willing to study their topic from a distance without embracing the ideas of disabled persons concerning their own predicament. The distinction entails making claims for critical insights to be gained by partaking of disability-based experiences, knowledge, and life predicaments.

Disability studies scholars distinguish their undertaking as 'new' in order to mark a distance from the viewpoint of modern eugenics that sought to 'improve human stock'. At the beginning of the twentieth century such an enterprise targeted the eradication of disabilities from human populations. Not only are many events and public spaces of modern life organized by policies that effectively segregate persons with disabilities from a civic mainstream, but traditional responses to disabled persons, termed the 'study of disability' as opposed to 'disability studies', also see disabled persons as clients, informants, or research objects to be treated, managed, regulated, controlled, and investigated. So not only must social barriers to the inclusion of disabled persons be broken down, as disability rights proclaims, but the sources for misperceptions about disability experiences need to be redressed. These objectives require studies of discourse, and of the etiologies and histories of the definitions of pathology and aberration, in addition to study of the histories of the development of environments and communication modes that privilege some players and exclude others.

Universities, many such as renowned Stanford University, whose first president David Starr Jordan promoted eugenics ideas about the obvious inferiority of disabled persons' lives and bodies, may not be perceived as immediately welcoming of disability perspectives. Recently, for example, Princeton University garnered international press coverage for hiring eugenics theorist Peter Singer in the prestigious Ira W. DeCamp Professorship of Bioethics. Singer argues that not only should parents decide whether severely disabled infants should be killed at birth, but also that adult disabled persons have little evaluative criteria to contribute to a discussion over the value of a life lived by a disabled infant.[5] Able-ist biases in top-flight universities, from their physical plant specifications to their presumptions about body qualifications, make them chilly places for disabled persons. Many note how ideas for gas chambers, first developed as a means to ease the difficulty for health practitioners in administering lethal injections, were developed within academic settings and with demonstration project methodologies. When Harriet McBryde Johnson, a disability rights lawyer and noted disability rights commentator, visits Princeton for a series of forums with Peter Singer, she reflects upon the ethical problem such a visit provokes. On the way out, she thinks about her 'brothers and sisters', the 14 arrested protestors for Not Dead Yet, who 'were here before me and behaved far more appropriately than I am doing'. Johnson's statement recalls that of Virginia Woolf, who, when invited to speak at an Oxford college, still could not access the Bodleian Library to review a manuscript on the basis of her gender. 'And I thought how it was better to be locked out than to be locked in', Woolf comments with a similar ambivalence, even as she has been invited to guest lecture on campus.[6]

Just as they were previously closed to the participation of women or discriminated against members of racial or ethnic groups, universities have not immediately embraced the influx of 'out' disabled persons into their hallowed halls. As a result, many well-worn ideas and representational practices await critical re-examination with the supposition that patterns of interpretation likely uphold unrecognized investments concerning the inferiority of disabled persons. Research conducted to endorse ideas about eugenic segregation, the sterilization of those assessed as 'feebleminded' or hereditarily deficient, or prevention of disabled persons on the premise of the social burden they present, simply support oppressive disability ideologies of a previous, yet not quite antiquated, era. Old-school disability research may verify reasons that disabled persons should be excluded from public forums and civic roles. Furthermore, many technologies have been developed as means for containing unruly bodies and punishing the disruptions associated with bodies that 'deviate' from the normal.

A key issue for disability studies, then, has been to determine the extent to which newer professionals who work within these frameworks can update disciplinary practices in order to make their research feasible for progressive disability goals. Similar questions had been asked about psychiatry, for example, after Holocaust genocide and medical experimentation implicated practitioners who had been schooled in the field and proceeded to generate from it violent medical interventions on disabled children and adults. Were premises in the field corrupting or did these perverse practices simply represent a complete aberration from mandated formats of investigation and hence only reflect violent impulses in the practitioners themselves? A similar revolutionary questioning guides disability studies as it surveys the current state of the university and interrogates fields such as behavioral and abnormal psychology for their routine support of evaluation practices designed to condemn disabled persons for their differences.

Scholarship in disability studies affords a unique and divergent vantage point from the paradigms that sustain traditional study, management, and interventions. For example, disability studies research would interview clients not in order to decide who would make the best fit for counselling or special education services, but in order to find the unique worldview that disabled persons have imbibed as a result of their marginalized social predicament. Those who endure demeaning cultural practices can often best assess the sources and mechanisms of their operation.

Following the advent of disability studies in the 1980s, many academic approaches toward disability were routinely put to the side as simply too 'medical' in nature. What the first generation of scholars meant by this criticism of a 'medical model' was that the research upheld an exclusively interventionist and individualized approach to disabled bodies. All insufficiency appeared localized within the dysfunctional body itself. A medical model approach proceeds on the assumption that the only valuable knowledge concerning disabilities would need to be directed toward curing, concealing, or fixing bodies so that individuals could be made to 'pass' as normal. For a first generation of disability studies scholars, cure approaches reinforced social ideas that impaired bodies should be rejected. At the very least, these scholars focus upon social barriers that disabled persons face and leave aside fields that pay attention to the repair of impaired bodies.

Importantly, the limitations of a medical model that early disability studies references may itself have little relation to actual practitioners of medicine. Instead, concepts of a 'medical model' refer to the social premise, frequently held outside of medicine, that disability requires referral to the purview of medical practitioners. Several disability studies scholars have shown how factions of physicians in the American Medical Association initially resisted the idea that insurance decisions should be assigned to clinical assessments. Nonetheless, legislatures in Germany and the US, for instance, decided that physicians would function as the gatekeepers for disability verification. They thus inaugurated a class of medical authorizers to diagnose and certify the validity of all disability claims. This professional gatekeeping, the practice of which often divides disabled people from the services they need, has become one of the formal obstacles addressed by disability studies today – particularly in countries that lack universal health care systems such as the US.

This system of evaluation requires disabled persons to endlessly submit to professional gazing in order to qualify for social supports. But the enforcers of this policy, that is now a habit of thought in many Western countries, may trickle down to the shoe store clerk who will not sell a shoe to a person with lower limb muscle spasticity prior to obtaining a doctor's note. In an increasingly bureaucratized social state, the medical model has left disabled persons frequently vulnerable to the whims of general practitioners in spite of the fact that such professionals may have little knowledge about the condition in question. Consequently, one often finds practitioners invested with the power to assess patients for the purpose of qualifying for benefits, supports and general consumer services such as airline travel or equipment.

In contrast, a rights era of disability studies endorses a cross-disability and non-specialized approach to meaningful inclusion for disabled persons. Subsequently, as this analysis observes, disability studies will ask for the modification of practices that are premised on privileging some bodies and excluding others.

Prior to the rights-based disability platform of the 1960s, a focus on disability in society entailed advocating for charitable contribution and safekeeping for persons with particular kinds – even 'brand names' – of disabilities. For instance, mid-nineteenth century institutions governed their populations so that they housed only the least severe cases. This assured patient success and further supported ideas behind the rejuvenating mission of cures in benevolent nature. A return to the community for each institutionalized individual formed a key objective. More difficult disabilities were left to the family where they sometimes received local support in the form of outdoor relief or made up a large percentage of those housed in indoor relief efforts such as almshouses. A widely accepted international theory of disability at this time established by the French educator, Eduoard Seguin, argued that those diagnosed as idiots suffered from a weak will. Training schools sought to correct this insufficiency – or at least ameliorate it – by subjecting disabled individuals within their charge to extensive rituals of personal hygiene tasks of rote repetition. Patients found themselves locked into an inflexible regimen of care and engaging in tasks that demanded concentration for extended periods of time. In cultivating such habits training institutions aimed to improve a 'defective' internal landscape by targeting the external body as a site of personal management.[7]

From the 1920s onward, rehabilitation era disability professionals emphasized the acquisition of personal adjustments and skills that could enable a disabled person to survive in a society that was not built to accommodate them. In the US, France, and Germany, for example, special schools that aimed to 'salvage' human beings by educating the physically weak emerged in urban centres. These schools for 'crippled children' pre-date legislation for disabled children that provides rights for a free and appropriate formal education. For example, according to the Department of Education US public schools educated only one in five children with disabilities prior to 1970.[8] Even after the passage of the Education for All Handicapped Children Act [EAHCA] in 1975, one-third of disabled children still did not have access to a formal, integrated education.[9] Federal mandates in the United States continue to update this effort at social inclusion and the necessity of public education for schoolchildren with differing bodies, minds, and emotional habits alongside all others in a 'least restrictive' environment.

In the 1920s, evolving from hospital schools, and offering an alternative to segregated warehousing, special schools for children with physical disabilities offered a curriculum that included rehabilitation services; in-house dentistry; occupational, physical, and speech therapies; Franklin Delano Roosevelt (FDR) era swimming pools; and a variety of wheeled transport and home-styled modification devices – all within the confines of a one-stop educational facility. Special schools explained their mission as a matter of 'salvaging' the educable from the disability mix that had simply been consigned to training schools and workshop labour under the expansive eugenics-era category of 'feebleminded'.

In this mould, special schools accompany the expansion and professional credentialing enterprise of other helping industries, in addition to nursing. Participants at schools for handicapped children also underwent continual assessments in specialized quadrants of the schools – for example, physical, emotional, dental, personal hygiene, and small and large motor control. But like rehabilitation medicine itself, special schools also sought distance from medical environments and fix-it approaches to disability. They too critiqued a 'medical' approach in favour of education and rehabilitation. It is important to differentiate the agonistic distancing of professional service industries from medical approaches and the medical model critiques of disability studies. Unlike professionals who advocate for rehabilitation as a solution to a problem presented by disabled persons, disability studies represents the social and material predicament of disabled persons as a matter of inclusion, recognition and social change. Furthermore, disability attends to the environmental resistance to inclusion – attitudes and the enforcement of normative expectations upon bodies – as opposed to individual adjustments.

Disability studies, uniquely, must put the status and experience of disabled persons prior to its own success as a professional operation. Thus, whereas rehabilitation and a rehabilitation movement could oppose disability rights in favour of principles of intervention, service, and care, disability studies aims to place the perspectives of the objects of scrutiny and remediation front and centre to its concerns. One is reminded that even in the closing of the most inhumane institutions, a variety of interests will come forth to oppose such efforts: care-worker unions will protest out of a desire to keep their jobs in a specialized field; family members will often ally themselves with care-workers and claim that the work of keeping a disabled person at home lacks sufficient social supports to be feasible; local businesses catering to institutional living complain that their economic livelihood will be undermined; nearby neighborhoods will resist under the argument that 'freeing the inmates' poses threats to everyone's wellbeing. Yet, disabled persons themselves, on the verge of emancipation, offer up ambivalent and less certain opinions. Few yearn to keep institutions open in that they represent sites of state-sponsored incarceration, but neither does it seem appropriate to look forward to a life where one may be viewed as a persistent burden, economic drain, and social misfit. Scholars in disability studies seek to expand upon the limited choices offered to disabled persons to live meaningful lives by redressing the social constraints that continue to underwrite such hostile public beliefs. Rather than individual insufficiency, disability studies aims its critique at the material social conditions – such as poverty, unemployment and disability insurance restrictions on wage earning – that produce abject dependency.

Historically, populations of dependents have found themselves concentrated in poor houses, workshops, and almshouses with others who cannot effectively sell their labour in a competitive market rife with prejudice toward functional and aesthetic differences. One function of this lumping together of the unemployable was the development of large bin categories of disabilities; such classification strategies emerged in the mid-twentieth century – an era dominated by rehabilitation and charity model approaches. Bin categories include 'muscular dystrophy', a label that represents more than 37 manifestly different etiologies of neuromuscular disorders, or 'cerebral palsy', a general term for hugely divergent muscular rigidities. Etiological clusters, like such as paralyzed veterans or people with epilepsy, receive attention and management from agencies designed to attend to their lesser social opportunities. Thus, children with vision impairments might be sent to a blind school to acquire different skills such as Braille along with white cane techniques or canine companion assistance. Deaf children might be channelled to a deaf school where they acquire sign language or vocalization skills in the press to access regular educational curriculum. Multiply disabled children, those who were projected to be low-achieving by means of newly minted evaluation tools such as intelligence tests, and ranging from those termed 'retarded' to those negotiating cultural barriers or non-standard literacy, underwent institutional referral and placement throughout the twentieth century. A substantial number of infants and children with all kinds of disabilities continue to be abandoned and placed as 'wards of the state'. Individuals located within such sweeping categorizations represent not only disabled people, but rather the fallout from modern standardization practices that prove inflexible and unduly narrow when it comes to the rote expectations of all bodies within capitalism.[10]

While pointing out the permeability of these categories of human differences, disability studies reassesses the historical solutions that have been arrived at in terms of placement, tracking, and a deterministic foreclosure on social possibilities. Yet the advent of the field has also been theorized as developing from experiences that issue from clustering together kinds of bodies that share designations of deviance. Collectivities can better foment collective action for improved social situations. Strongholds for initiatives in disability rights have come from collectivities of individuals who may have endured segregation at one time and now resist oppressive protocols. In other words, disability studies is also linked in history to the predominance of kinds of disabled living and the social opportunities afforded to highly particular groups. These include veterans groups, who sometimes claimed exclusive rights to remediation services but also precipitated the development of technologies such as power wheelchairs and curb cuts that benefited others. Not only did a post-polio President, Franklin Delano Roosevelt, seek to include disabled citizens as beneficiaries of services for disabled veterans, but in the late 1940s, disabled Canadian veteran John Counsell formed the Canadian Paraplegic Association, an advocacy group that demanded the supply of accessible cars outfitted with hand controls to all who could use them. Furthermore, in the 1960s 'person first' advocates sought to upgrade social awareness by interrogating the linguistic implications of referring to persons with disabilities as handicapped, crippled or disabled. In Britain during the early 1970s, the Union of the Physically Impaired Against Segregation (UPIAS) was formed as a coalition among those who had fought to escape confinement in nursing homes. The members of this organization may have been the first to formulate what would come to be recognized as the 'social model of disability': one that viewed impediments as the product of social rather individual liabilities. UPIAS put forth mandates about the social nature of disability experience that merits repeating:

> In the view of disability studies scholars, it is society that disables physically impaired people. Disability is something imposed on top of our impairments, by the way we are unnecessarily isolated and excluded from full participation in society. Disabled people are therefore an oppressed group in society. It follows from this analysis that having low incomes, for example, is only one aspect of our oppression. It is a consequence of our isolation and segregation, in every area of life, such as education, work, mobility, and housing, etc.[11]

Notes

1 Michel Foucault, *Abnormal: Lectures at the Collège de France, 1974–1975*, trans. Graham Burchell, New York: Picador, 2003, p. 31.
2 Michel Foucault, *Madness and Civilisation: A History of Insanity in the Age of Reason*, [1965], trans. Richard Howard, New York: Vintage, 1988, p. ix.

3 Michel Foucault, *Abnormal*, p. 48.
4 Judith Butler, *Gender Trouble: Feminism and the Subversion of Identity* [1990], New York and London: Routledge, 1999, p. xix.
5 Peter Singer, *Practical Ethics*, New York: Cambridge University Press, 1993, pp. 185–6 and ch. 7 *passim.*; Wesley Smith, 'Pushing Infanticide: From Holland to New Jersey', *National Review Online*, 25 March 2005. Online. Available at: www.nation-alreview.com/smithw/smith200503220759.asp (accessed 25 October 2005); Not Dead Yet, Fact Sheet on Singer's Ethical Theories with Respect to Killing People with Disabilities. Online. Available at: www.notdeadyet.org/docs/anotatedsinger.html (accessed 25 October 2005).
6 Harriet McBryde Johnson, 'Unspeakable Conversations', *New York Times* Magazine, 16 February 2003; Virginia Woolf, *A Room of One's Own* [1928], New York: Harcourt, Brace, Jovanovich, 2004, p. 24.
7 Sharon Snyder and David Mitchell, *Cultural Locations of Disability*, Chicago: University of Chicago Press, 2005.
8 US Department of Education, 'Twenty-five Years of Progress in Educating Children with Disabilities through IDEA'. Online. Available at: www.ed.gov/policy/speced/leg/idea/history.html (accessed 4 November 2005).
9 Ruth O'Brien, *Crippled Justice: The History of Modern Disability Policy in the Workplace*, Chicago: University of Chicago Press, 2001.
10 Colin Barnes, *Disabled People in Britain and Discrimination: A Case for Anti-Discrimination Legislation*, London: Hurst and Co., 1991, pp. 12–13; Ravi Malhotra, 'The Politics of the Disability Rights Movements', *New Politics*, 8.3 Whole number 31 [Summer 2001]. Online. Available at: www.wpunj.edu/~newpol/issue31/malhot31.htm (accessed 25 October 2005); Snyder and Mitchell, *Cultural Locations*.
11 Union of the Physically Impaired Against Segregation (UPIAS), UPIAS Policy Document 1975/5. Online. Available at: www.leeds.ac.uk/disability-studies/archiveuk/UPIAS/UPIAS.pdf (accessed 17 October 2005).

Further reading

Albrecht, Gary, *The Disability Business: Rehabilitation in America*, Thousand Oaks: Sage Publications, 1992.
—— (ed.), *The Handbook of Disability Studies*, Thousand Oaks, CA: Sage Publications, 2001.
Armstrong, Felicity and Barton, Len (eds), *Disability, Human Rights, and Education: Cross-Cultural Perspectives*, Sheffield: Open University Press, 2000.
Barnartt, Sharon, *Disability Protests: Contentious Politics, 1970–1999*, Washington, DC: Gallaudet University Press, 2001.
Barnes, Colin, *Disabled People in Britain and Discrimination*: *A Case for Anti-Discrimination Legislation*, London: Hurst & Co, 1991.
Barnes, Colin, Oliver, Mike and Barton, Len (eds) *Disability Studies Today*, Cambridge: Polity Press, 2002.
Barnes, Colin and Mercer, Geoff (eds), *Disability (Key Concepts),* Cambridge: Polity Press, 2003.
Brueggemann, Brenda Jo, *Lend Me Your Ear: Rhetorical Constructions of Deafness*, Washington, DC: Gallaudet University Press, 1999.
Charlton, James, *Nothing about Us without Us: Disability Oppression and Empowerment*, Berkeley: University of California Press, 2000.
Corker, Mairian, *Deaf and Disabled, or Deafness Disabled? Towards a Human Rights Perspective*, Sheffield: Open University Press, 1988.

—— *Deaf Transitions: Images and Origins of Deaf Families, Deaf Communities and Deaf Identities*, London: Jessica Kingsley, 1996.

Corker, Mairian and French, Sally, *Disability Discourse (Disability, Human Rights, and Society)*, Sheffield: Open University Press, 1998.

Davis, Lennard, (ed.) *The Disability Studies Reader*, New York: Routledge, 1997.

—— *Enforcing Normalcy: Disability, Deafness, and the Body*, New York: Verso, 1997.

Department of Education (US), 'Twenty-five Years of Progress in Educating Children with Disabilities through IDEA'. Online. Available at: www.ed.gov/policy/speced/leg/idea/history.html (accessed 4 November 2005)

Fine, Michelle and Adrienne Asch, *Women With Disabilities: Essays in Psychology, Culture, and Politics*, Philadelphia: Temple University Press, 1990.

Foucault, Michel, *Madness and Civilization: A History of Insanity in the Age of Reason*, [1965], trans. Richard Howard, New York: Vintage, 1988.

—— *Abnormal: Lectures at the Collège de France, 1974–1975*, trans. Graham Burchell, New York: Picador, 2003.

French, Sally, *On Equal Terms: Working with Disabled People*, Burlington: Butterworth-Heinemann, 1996.

Goffman, Erving, *Stigma: Notes Toward the Management of Spoiled Identity*, New York: Touchstone, 1986.

Hahn, Harlan, 'Towards a Politics of Disability: Definitions, Disciplines, and Policies', *Social Science Journal*, 87 (1985), 88–9.

Johnson, Harriet McBryde, 'Unspeakable Conversations', *New York Times Magazine*, 16 February 2003.

Linton, Simi, *Claiming Disability: Knowledge and Identity*, New York: New York University Press, 1998.

McRuer, Robert and Wilkerson, Abby L. (eds), *Desiring Disability: Queer Theory Meets Disability*, Durham: Duke University Press, 2003.

Malhotra, Ravi, 'The Politics of the Disability Rights Movements', *New Politics*, 8.3 Whole number 31 [Summer 2001]. Online. Available at: www.wpunj.edu/~newpol/issue31/malhot31.htm (accessed 25 October 2005).

Marks, Deborah, *Disability: Controversial Debates and Perspectives*, New York: Routledge, 1999.

Mitchell, David and Sharon Snyder (eds.), *The Body and Physical Difference: Discourses of Disability*, Ann Arbor: University of Michigan Press, 1997.

—— *Narrative Prosthesis: Disability and the Dependencies of Discourse*, Ann Arbor: University of Michigan Press, 2000.

Morris, Jenny, *Pride Against Prejudice: Transforming Attitudes Towards Disability*, Philadelphia: New Society, 1993.

—— *Encounters with Strangers: Feminism and Disability*, London: Women's Press Limited, 1999.

Not Dead Yet, Fact Sheet on Singer's Ethical Theories with Respect to Killing People with Disabilities. Online. Available at: www.notdeadyet.org/docs/anotatedsinger.html (accessed 25 October 2005).

O'Brien, Ruth, *Crippled Justice: The History of Modern Disability Policy in the Workplace*, Chicago: University of Chicago Press 2001.

Oliver, Michael, *Understanding Disability: From Theory to Practice*, New York: St. Martin's Press, 1996.

—— *The Politics of Disablement*, New York: St. Martin's Press, 1997.

Price, Janet and Shildrick, Margrit (eds), *Feminist Theory and the Body: A Reader*, New York: Routledge 1999.

Priestly, Mark, *Disability and the Life Course: Global Perspectives*, Cambridge: Cambridge University Press, 2001.

Roman, Leslie and Eyre, Linda (eds), *Dangerous Territories: Struggles for Difference and Equality in Education*, New York: Routledge, 1997.

Saxton, Marsha and Howe, Florence (eds), *With Wings: An Anthology of Literature by and About Women with Disabilities*, New York: Feminist Press at the City University of New York, 1993.

Scotch, Richard, *From Good Will to Civil Rights: Transforming Federal Disability Policy*, Philadelphia: Temple University Press, 2001.

Self Preservation: The Art of Riva Lehrer. Dir. by Sharon Snyder. 36 mins. Brace Yourselves Productions, 2004.

Shakespeare, Tom (ed.), *The Disability Reader: Social Science Perspectives*, London: Cassell, 1988.

Shapiro, Joseph P., *No Pity: People with Disabilities Forging a New Civil Rights Movement*, New York: Three Rivers, 1994.

Shaw, Barrett (ed.), *The Ragged Edge: The Disability Experience from the Pages of the First Fifteen Years of The Disability Rag*, Louisville: Advocado Press, 1994.

Shildrick, Margrit, *Leaky Bodies and Boundaries: Feminism, Postmodernism, and (Bio)Ethics*, New York: Routledge 1997.

—— *Embodying the Monster: Encounters with the Vulnerable Self*, Thousand Oaks: Sage, 2002.

Shildrick, Margrit and Price, Janet, *Vital Signs*, Edinburgh: Edinburgh University Press, 1998.

Singer, Peter, *Practical Ethics*, New York: Cambridge University Press, 1993.

Smith, Wesley, 'Pushing Infanticide: From Holland to New Jersey', *National Review Online*, 25 March 2005. Online. Available at: www.nationalreview.com/smithw/smith200503220759.asp (accessed 25 October 2005).

Snyder, Sharon and Mitchell, David, *Cultural Locations of Disability*, Chicago: University of Chicago Press, 2005.

Snyder, Sharon, Brueggemann, Brenda and Garland–Thomson, Rosemarie (eds), *Disability Studies: Enabling the Humanities*, New York: Modern Language Association MLA Press, 2002.

Stiker, Henry-Jacques, *A History of Disability*, Ann Arbor: University of Michigan Press, 1997.

Stone, Deborah, *The Disabled State*, Philadelphia: Temple University Press, 1986.

Swain, John, French, Sally and Cameron, Colin (eds) *Controversial Issues in a Disabling Society*, Sheffield: Open University Press, 2003.

Garland-Thomson, Rosemarie, *Extraordinary Bodies*, New York: Columbia University Press, 1996.

Waldschmidt, Anne, *Das Subjekt in der Humangenetik: Expertendiskurse zu Programmtik und Konzeption der Genetishcen Beratung, 1945–1990*, Munster: Westfälische Dampfboot, 1996.

—— *Selbstbestimmung als Konstruktion: Alltagstheorien behinderter Frauen und Männer*, Opladen: Leske & Budrich 1999.

Woolf, Virginia, *A Room of One's Own* [1928] New York: Harcourt, Brace, Jovanovich, 2004.

Vital Signs: Crip Culture Talks Back. Dir. by Sharon Snyder. 48 mins. Brace Yourselves Productions, 1996.

Ware, Linda, *Ideology and the Politics of (In)Exclusion*, New York: Peter Lang, 2004.

Wendell, Susan, *The Rejected Body: Feminist Philosophical Reflections on Disability*, New York and London: Routledge, 1996.

Union of the Physically Impaired Against Segregation (UPIAS), UPIAS Policy Document 1974/1975, Online. Available at: www.leeds.ac.uk/disability-studies/archiveuk/UPIAS/UPIAS.pdf, (accessed 19 October 2005).

Index